MINISTERIAL AND COMMON PRIESTHOOD
IN THE EUCHARISTIC CELEBRATION

MINISTERIAL

AND

COMMON PRIESTHOOD

IN THE

EUCHARISTIC CELEBRATION

E IGITVR CLEMENTISSIME
PATER PER JESVM CHRIST
FILIVM TVVM DOMINVM
NOSTRVMSVPPLICES ROG
AMS AC PETIMS VTI ACC
EPTA HABEAS ET BENEDIC

THE PROCEEDINGS OF THE FOURTH INTERNATIONAL COLLOQUIUM

OF

HISTORICAL, CANONICAL, AND THEOLOGICAL STUDIES

OF THE

ROMAN LITURGY

CIEL UK

THE SAINT AUSTIN PRESS
296 Brockley Road
London
SE4 2RA
Tel. +44 (0) 181 692 6009
Fax + 44 (0) 181 469 3609

and

CIEL UK
PO Box 587A
Kingston & Surbiton KT5 8YD
Tel: +44 (0) 181 300 1459
Fax: +44 (0) 181 715 2316

A catalogue record for this book is available from the British Library.

Set in 8 and 10 point TimesLiturgia by William Pitfield-Perry

Printed in Great Britain by BPC Wheatons, Exeter.

ISBN 1-901157-86-5

CONTENTS

PREFACE

His Eminence, Darío, Cardinal Castrillon

Cardinal Castrillon is the Prefect of the Congregation for the Clergy

A PROPER understanding of the distinction and mutual relationship between ministerial priesthood and 'common' priesthood lies at the heart of the Church's vitality. So even if from 1975 the Church was coming out of a crisis and vocations were numerous (60,142 major seminarians in 1975, 106,345 in 1995), here and there there were practices, often inspired by good will, which, unfortunately led to a diminishment of the appreciation of the priest on the part of the laity. It was only when the the ministerial priesthood was correctly understood and exercised authentically that the proper encouragement of the common priesthood could be guaranteed!

One might consider that the lack of priests is not the real problem (955 catholics per priest in Switzerland, 10,941 per priest in Haiti, according to the statistics in the 1996 *Annuario*), but rather that the laity ought to be making better use of their priests. Or perhaps to better understand them. The gift of priesthood ought then be able to relate to their daily lives.

In this sense, one can prove that the countries in which one most positively perceives the mystery of the priesthood nowadays, where it is lived, where every layman knows that he is a christian because there is a priest who is his shepherd, whose presence he desires, and where this all leads to a great abundance of solid vocations; these are the countries where the changes in the rites have taken place peacefully, arranged calmly, with a sense of the sacred and respect for peoples' sensibilities, with a sense of deep continuity and without ever provoking dissension.

So, ministerial priesthood and common priesthood both contribute to the building up of the body of Christ which is the Church: 'though they differ essentially and not just in degree, the common priesthood of the faithful and the ministerial...priesthood are none the less ordered to one another; each in its own way shares in the one priesthood of Christ. The priest, minister of Christ, thanks to the sacred power that he has, instructs and governs the priestly people; in the person of Christ he makes the sacrifice of the eucharist and offers it to God in the name of all the people; the faithful, by virtue of their royal priesthood take part in the offering of the Eucharist and exercise that priesthood by the witness of a holy life, of self-denial and active charity. *Lumen Gentium 10.*

I thank C.I.E.L. for having chosen this theme of priesthood, and for the love of the Church which this enterprise manifests. May the Lord bless you.

Darío Card. Castrillón H.

Prefect of the Congregation of the Clergy.

From the Vatican, 26th February 1999

FOREWORD

T HE purpose of this foreword is twofold: to trace briefly the history of the International Centre for Liturgical Studies so far, and to give a more detailed account of the recent fourth Colloquium, of which *Ministerial and Common Priesthood in Eucharistic Liturgy* constitutes the proceedings.

The *Centre International d'Etudes Liturgiques* (French acronym C.I.E.L.) sprung from modest beginnings. A group of French university students, finding themselves ill equipped to defend their liturgical preference for *La Messe de Toujours,* resolved to set up a world wide school of studies. The aim was to build a tribune of informed defence for the traditional Mass. In 1994 C.I.E.L. was founded in Paris under the patronage of Cardinals Silvio Oddi and Alfons Stickler.

In October 1995 the inaugural Colloquium for theological and historical research of the Roman Catholic liturgy took place at the sanctuary of Notre Dame du Laus in the French Alps. The language of the Colloquium was French and the proceedings of the first Colloquium *La Liturgie Trésor de l'Eglise* have only ever been published in French.

The following year the second annual Colloquium was also held in Gap, by which time CIEL UK had been formed, and the Proceedings *The Veneration and Administration of the Eucharist* were later published in English and also in German.

CIEL UK was officially launched on March 1st 1997 with Solemn High Mass at St James' Spanish Place, London, attended by an estimated congregation of a thousand. It became a registered charity in September 1997.

In October 1997 the third Colloquium was held in Poissy. A third of the participants came from the United Kingdom, America and Canada, thus spreading the Colloquium's range of influence to the English speaking world.

In March 1988 the Proceedings of *Altar and Sacrifice,* published in French, English and German, were officially launched in Rome. Presentations of the book in three languages were also made to the Cardinal Prefects of various Vatican congregations, all of whom responded with warmth and interest.

On 2nd May 1998 Pontifical High Mass was celebrated at St James' Spanish Place by Rt Rev Dom Gerard Calvet, Abbot and Founder of La Madeleine monastery at Le Barroux. This was followed by the first CIEL UK conference at the Wigmore Hall chaired by the Hon. Lord Gill. The speakers were M. Loïc Mérian, Mgr Schmitz and Fr Aidan Nichols OP.

Ministerial and Common Priesthood in Eucharistic Celebration was the theme of the fourth Colloquium of C.I.E.L., which took place from the 6th to 9th October 1998.

For the second year running delegates from all over the world converged on the quiet Foyer de Charité, La Part-Dieu, at Poissy, to be welcomed by a community more accustomed to accommodating silent retreats than the animated discussions which took place between talks and at meal times.

Delegates arrived from various parts of France, Italy, Austria, Germany, Canada, Switzerland, UK, Poland, Belgium and the U.S.A. This time a third of the participants came from the UK alone, which according to the young President, M. Mérian, 'shows the vitality of Catholicism in that land of martyrs'

Once more altars were erected in the long tribune overlooking the dimly lit Grande Chapelle for the continuous private Masses of the priests, which sanctify each day before it dawns.

On Wednesday 7th the conference started as ever with the singing of the *Veni Creator* and an introduction by the President. M Loïc Mérian explained the attitude of the Colloquium towards the position of the lay faithful, stressing that it was not aiming to claim any kind of priestly equality, but to clarify the fundamental differences between states of life, which are themselves a rich source of grace.

Following so closely on the recent Vatican instruction of 1997 from the Congregation for the Clergy, signed by the heads of no fewer than eight Vatican Congregations (which is possibly unprecedented) and approved by the Holy Father 13th August 1997 the theme this year was highly topical. Lay participation has been the catch phrase of the post war liturgical movement, and used to justify a variety of liturgical practices.

Thirteen papers were given over the three day period. In addition, two speakers who were unable to deliver their talks sent in their written contributions. We are pleased to be able to publish here Dr Waldstein's philosophical paper on 'Liturgy and Personality in the thought of Dietrich von Hildebrand', and the historical contribution of Dom Alban Nunn which traces practices in the early Church and precedes that of Dr. Gribbin concerning the role of the faithful in liturgical celebration through the ages.

Three main conditions soon emerged for true participation in the sacred mysteries:

Firstly, that irrespective of state of life participation is solely dependent upon grace. Fathers Gallet, Deneke, and Contat developed the point that every Christian must avail himself of the graces proper to his state of life. Frs Edwards, Barreiro and Nay developed the concept that participation can only take on a human dimension after the individual's immersion in that union between the Divine and the human which takes place within the sacred mysteries. Fr Edwards showed how an overemphasis on activity can destroy participation.

Secondly, profound understanding is needed of the objectivity of the sacred rites. Fathers Finnegan, de Butler, and Drs Gribbin and Pérès showed that much trouble had been taken in the past through the historical development of the liturgy to safeguard this objectivity through the means of sacred language, chant, gestures and symbolism. Fr Finnegan reminded delegates that the last supper and the worship of the early Church was conducted in sacred languages and not in the vernacular. Dr Gribbin gave us a fascinating account of the English laity of the Middle Ages who, contrary to common assumption, were intense, devout and knowledgeable. As the only U.K. lay contributor, we will surely hear more from this inspiring young academic.

The third condition for true participation is a sense of communion with the whole Church under the Vicar of Christ, without which a Christian's participation, however devout, must be defective. This ecclesial sense was developed by Fr Quoëx, and the role of preaching during the liturgy expounded by Mgr Brandmüller

To attempt to condense such concepts is to risk diminishing their meaning and depth, but they are clearly explained by Mgr Rudolph Michæl Schmitz in his conclusion. Mgr Schmitz, the academic and spiritual adviser to C.I.E.L., as in previous years introduced each speaker and simultaneously translated the debates which followed. It is through his influence that a C.I.E.L. Colloquium strangely reconciles the atmosphere of an academic forum with that of a spiritual retreat. Since the conference, Mgr Schmitz has been appointed Domestic Chaplain to His Holiness.

The talks each day were followed by Solemn High Mass according to the 1962 liturgical books. Mgr Wach, Superior of the Institute of Christ the King in Florence, celebrated the first Mass and in his homily preached on the public nature of the liturgy and its effect on society. The Rt Rev Mgr Laise Bishop of San Luis, Argentina, celebrant on the second day, preached on the need for a truly sacred liturgy to combat the effects of modern ideologies. For the first time it fell to the British priests this year to celebrate *la Messe de Clôture*. Dom Andrew Southwell OSB. was the celebrant and Fr Seán Finnegan preached on the sacrificial and eschatological nature of eucharistic liturgy.

One of the most exhilarating aspects of a Colloquium is the universal character of the Catholic Church, which this dynamic gathering demonstrates. In an era of stagnation and decline this is perhaps a timely reminder of Christ's promise that the gates of Hell will never prevail against his Church.

OPENING REMARKS

Loïc Mérian

M. Loïc Mérian, aged 32, is a former pupil of the Ecole Nationale Supérieur des Télécommunications. *Following a career as an engineer, he has taken up university studies in history. In 1995, after several years as Director of the movement* Jeune Chrétienté, *M Mérian became President of the* Centre d'Etudes Liturgiques *(C.I.E.L.), which is responsible for the organization and presentation of the various colloquia.*

THE theme of our fourth colloquium is *Ministerial and Common Priesthood in Eucharistic Celebration.* We live in a de-Christianized age in which the Church itself sees its influence declining, replaced or rivalled by ideologies, new religions, new philosophies. Whereas we could be witnessing the birth of a new vigour, born of the adversity of a dramatic situation, instead we find complete and utter confusion. This confusion affects, of course, the priesthood and the liturgy which are at the heart of Church life. This is only to be expected, seeing as the Eucharistic celebration is the principal event in which every member of the Catholic Church should participate regularly. As proof of the confusion which reigns, we could of course quote the Instruction on certain questions concerning the collaboration of the lay faithful in the ministry of priests, published in August 1997 and signed, exceptionally, by six prefects of congregations. [1]

After a clear theological summary, [2] the Instruction lists all the ecclesiastical situations in which the common and ministerial priesthood are confused, mixed up, misunderstood, giving rise to grave theological errors. Then, in a number of articles it gives examples of the common errors in this domain. [3] The solemnity and seriousness of this document underlines the urgency of the clarification needed amongst the faithful and the clergy.

It is to this task that the many speakers at this fourth colloquium will devote themselves over the next three days. Clerics or laymen, each in their own field and with their respective competencies, will demonstrate the fundamental difference which exists between the two kinds of priesthood and how this difference is embodied and developed in the liturgical rites, in keeping with a homogeneous tradition. History, theology, and the study of rites show, uncontroversially, the veritable riches which constitute this ontological difference.

It is not unusual to see lay people demanding more rights, more powers, on the pretext that any distinction between them and the celebrant is degrading. Unfortunately, too many pastors give in to these demands in liturgical celebrations where it is 'the assembly which celebrates' and where the celebrant acts simply as chairman of the proceedings. This demand for equality of priesthood is not part of our purpose. As lay faithful, we wish to participate in the liturgy in our proper place. What we really want, however, is for the priest to dispense to us all the treasures of grace which only he can communicate by the sacraments, and especially the Eucharist which gives us Christ himself, sacrificed for each one of us.

It could, of course, be said that the papers which will be given here, and which we hope will be nothing more than the faithful expression of the faith of the Church, can inspire all forms of the Roman rite, from the most classical to the most current. Theoretically this is true. It is also clear, however, that, through the precision of the rite, that the faith is embodied and unfolds with clarity and radiance in the celebration of the Eucharist according to the classical or traditional missal. The unique character of the priest's ministerial priesthood, the spiritual participation of the faithful who unite themselves to the sacrifice, the role of the celebrant *in persona Christi,* his consecrated state: all these elements are clearly expressed, emphasized, detailed and set out for all to see in the rites and rubrics of the traditional missal, currently officially authorized in the *editio typica* of 1962. Of course, other forms of the rite also contain these elements, depending on the quality of the celebration or the celebrant, and the choices of the community - but not, however, with the same force, or so precisely.

It is not the aim of C.I.E.L. to promote divine worship in any one particular form. However, neither is the object of our studies some archæological vestige, but the very life of the Church as expressed through the public act of worship which it offers to God. Let us pray that the work which will be presented over the next three days will nourish the faith of the laity and clergy alike, so that their complementary priesthoods provide them with that which all human societies give their peaceful and law-abiding members: the common good and, in these particular circumstances, eternal salvation through the grace of the sacraments.

Over the past months, as it develops, C.I.E.L. has already received some encouraging signs. The Proceedings are circulated in almost fifteen countries and we do not have the time or the resources to follow up all the contacts which our work generates. Several hundred bishops receive the Proceedings in their own language and in the vast majority of cases the reception is positive. However the most important encouragement has come from Rome where, last March, we officially presented the international publication of the Proceedings to numerous authorities. The warm letters from Cardinals Medina and Meyer, respectively current and former Prefect for the Congregation for Divine Worship, seem to invite us to continue our work so that the Roman liturgy be better known and better loved. This is what we shall do.

NOTES:

1. The Pro-Prefect of the Congregation for the Clergy, the President of the Pontifical Council for the Laity, the Prefect of the Congregation for the Doctrine of the Faith, the Pro- Prefect of the Congregation for Divine Worship and the Discipline of the Sacraments, the Prefect of the Congregation for Bishops, the Prefect of the Congregation for the Evangelization of Peoples, the Prefect of the Congregation for Institutes of Consecrated Life and Societies of Apostolic Life, the President of the Pontifical Council for the Interpretation of Legislative Texts.

2. The Instruction already quoted: 'The ministerial priesthood is rooted in the Apostolic Succession, and vested with potestas sacra consisting of the faculty and the responsibility of acting in the person of Christ the Head and the Shepherd.' 'It is a priesthood which renders its sacred ministers servants of Christ and of the Church by means of authoritative proclamation of the Word of God, the administration of the sacraments and the pastoral direction of the faithful... and is completely at the service of the Church'. Priests have been given 'a particular gift so that they can help the People of God to exercise faithfully and fully the common priesthood.'

'The common priesthood of the faithful is exercised by the unfolding of baptismal grace - a life of faith, hope and charity, a life according to the Spirit'.

3. For example:

Article 1:

Concerning the terminology of the functions the laity may carry out by deputation of the clergy (bishop, or at times the priest); the use of terms such as ' pastor', 'chaplain', 'co-ordinator', 'moderator' ' is reserved absolutely for the clergy in order to avoid confusion of roles.

Article 2:

concerning the Ministry of the Word; pastoral preaching and catechetics are 'the duty of the bishops and of his collaborators...priests and deacons'. The lay faithful may collaborate, after instruction, 'if in certain circumstances it is necessary..., if in particular cases it would be useful...'. Canon 766 makes clear the exceptional nature of such cases. This provision which is not a right, must not 'be regarded as an ordinary occurrence nor as an authentic promotion of the laity' and care must be taken to instruct 'on the role and figure of the priest'.

Article 3:

concerning the Homily - during Holy Mass - this is 'strictly reserved for sacred ministers'.

Article 4:

concerning the Parish Priest and the Parish, the role of the non-ordained faithful is not 'directing, co-ordinating, moderating or governing the parish'—even if they have arrangements for Sunday assemblies without priests. It is a question of participating ob sacerdotum penuriam'; and for example, reaching the age of 75 by the parish priest 'does not of itself (ipso iure) terminate his pastoral office', especially if he does not have a successor.

Article 5:

concerning the Structures of Collaboration in the Church. ' With regard to the Council of Priests (Presbyteral Council) ...membership in it is reserved to priests alone'. The Pastoral Council and the Parochial Finance Council only give 'consultative advice'. 'It is for the parish priest to preside at parish councils' and thus it cannot meet without him, even in parishes 'entrusted' to the laity under arrangements for Sunday assemblies without priests. The advice of study groups or of groups of experts cannot overturn decisions of presbyteral and parish councils. Thus something which follows from this, but which should be pointed out is that 'Diocesan councils may properly and validly express their consent to an act of the bishop only in those cases in which the law expressly requires such consent'.

Article 6:

concerning Liturgical Celebrations. 'In Eucharistic celebrations deacons and non-ordained members of the faithful may not pronounce prayers - especially the Eucharistic Prayer...'. 'Neither may deacons or non-ordained members of the faithful use gestures or actions which are proper to the priest celebrant'. 'In the same way, the use of sacred vestments which are reserved to priests or deacons (stoles, chasubles...)...is clearly unlawful'. The impression must not be given that the non-ordained member of the faithful is presiding at the ceremony; on the contrary 'Every effort must be made to avoid even the appearance of confusion'.

Article 7:

concerning Sunday Celebrations in the Absence of a Priest. It is necessary that non-ordained members of the faithful who lead Sunday celebrations should have a mandate from the Bishop which specifies 'the term of applicability, the place and conditions in which it is operative'. As such celebrations are temporary solutions 'the text used at them must be approved by the competent ecclesiastical authority'; 'the use of the Eucharistic Prayers, even in narrative form, at such celebrations is forbidden'.

Article 8:

concerning Holy Communion; non-ordained members of the faithful may distribute Holy Communion in cases of true necessity, such as 'an insufficient number of ordained ministers' or 'there are particularly large numbers of the faithful who wish to receive Holy Communion'. They 'may be deputed by the diocesan bishop, using the appropriate form of blessing for these situations to act as extraordinary ministers'. 'In exceptional cases or in unforeseen circumstances, the priest may authorize such *ad actum*'. The faithful entrusted with this task must be instructed concerning the doctrine and 'the discipline on admission to Holy Communion'. In addition 'certain practices are forbidden—extraordinary ministers receiving Holy Communion apart from the other faithful as though concelebrants;— association with the renewal of promises made by priests at the Chrism Mass.'

Article 9:

The Apostolate to the Sick; the Instruction stresses that 'In this area, the non-ordained faithful can often provide valuable collaboration '—one only has to think of the work of charitable organizations. 'The non-ordained faithful particularly assist the sick...by encouraging them to receive the Sacraments of Penance and the Anointing of the Sick'—that of Baptism should the occasion arise—always ensuring that 'the priest is the only valid minister' of the sacraments.

Article 10:

concerning Assistance at Marriages; assistance cannot be delegated to the non-ordained faithful 'except in special circumstances and where there is a grave shortage of sacred ministers', only after the bishop has conceded this delegation and he has obtained 'a favourable *votum* from the Conference of Bishops and the necessary permission of the Holy See'. 'In such cases, the canonical norms concerning the validity of delegation, the suitability, capacity and aptitude of the non-ordained faithful must be observed'. In circumstances where there are no ordained ministers - and one thinks particularly of certain Churches in the East and in Asia - the priest can concede this deputation.

Article 11:

concerning Baptism: the co-operation of the faithful is very praiseworthy in circumstances 'of persecution [in the Church} or in missionary territories'; however this must not be extended in our countries to suit personal convenience , such as the priest living a long way away or 'his non-availability on the day on which the parents wish the Baptism to take place'.

Article 12:

concerning the Celebration at Funerals: the Instruction reminds us that 'this can be one of the most opportune pastoral moments in which the ordained minister can meet with the non-practising members of the faithful'. When there is a true absence of sacred ministers the non-ordained faithful may lead these obsequies but they must be 'well prepared both doctrinally and liturgically'.

Article 13:

Finally some practical information on the selection and adequate formation of lay faithful who are to be entrusted with such duties. Thus it is necessary 'to select lay faithful of sound doctrine and exemplary moral life', and not to retain those who do not conform to the moral teaching of the Church.

THE PRIEST: A MAN SET APART FOR THE SACRED OR A MAN FOR THE PEOPLE?

Jean-Louis Gallet sv

Fr Gallet was born in 1958. He became a religious of the Society of St Vincent de Paul in 1980 and was ordained priest in 1986. Currently, Fr Gallet is Superior of Notre Dame de Lys in Paris and teaches at the seminary of his congregation at Mûres-Erigné.

THERE are many elements in the crisis which is affecting the priesthood today. I have been asked to consider one of them in this doctrinal talk: *The priest: a man set apart for the sacred, or a man for the people?* The question is usually put antithetically, by those who have been alerted to it, studied it or attempted to resolve it. An antithesis because one cannot be both at the same time. The 'man set apart for the sacred' cannot also be 'a man for the people', and vice versa.

Putting the question in this way is to enter into a dialectical situation, thesis opposed to antithesis, a trap into which those who put the question antithetically want us to fall. The trap can be avoided by denying from the outset that such an antithesis exists.

What underlies the proposition: a man set apart for the sacred/a man for the people? It is that there are two great separate and distinct domains: the domain of the sacred and the domain of the profane. Priests, so the argument goes, belong to the domain of the sacred and so cannot understand the lives of ordinary men and women. They form a caste or clique with its own vocabulary and vision of the world. The rites and rituals they perform look like a kind of magic to ordinary people, carried out with artificial gestures and in a dead language. In addition, their distinctive dress cuts them off from the rest of humanity making them, together with everything else we have mentioned, distinct and remote. They ought to get more involved in the struggles of ordinary people and spend less time with their useless rituals. Let them come down to our level, into the arena rather than being up in the clouds, being spiritual.

These are the complaints made, amongst others, by those who champion a radical secularization programme. They argue that the situation they describe has been fabricated by churchmen who have tried—not without some success—to propagate their ideas amongst the faithful, thus troubling those who are weak-minded or ill informed, who remember the music without bothering to go and see if the words are in the Gospel.

This mentality, even if it is disappearing, is still strong in certain places where special attention has been given to cultivating it. That is why it is necessary, in a talk on the priesthood, to look at this question and see how we are to reply to those who advocate it or who simply, in all sincerity, believe it to be the truth.

A BRIEF HISTORICAL SKETCH.

One would have to be a specialist, or have to have at one's disposal the right documents and plenty of time to see if practice has led to a change in theology or the other way round... Nonetheless it is a point which could certainly be illuminating...

Very often there is an interaction between theory and practice. Either theory influences practice, as its cause, its source, its justification, in which case we must ask, how, by whom, where and why these changes came about? Or, practice having changed over the course of time, one tries to justify the changes by appealing to theory. In that case we must ask why and how practice and behaviour have changed. It would seem, as I have said, that very often there is an interaction between theory and practice. No doubt we can find some examples in our own lives. Whatever the case we all know that it is not enough for a theory to be good for it to be translated into good practice, for there are many other factors which enter into consideration, nor is it right that a practice should never be questioned as to the theory behind it.

After this analysis let us look at the history of the question.

It would seem that it was from the United States that the wave of de-sacralization now rocking the barque first came some 30 years ago. Then, as now, American society had a power to fascinate, on account of its industrial strength and urban society, both of which have created grave moral problems. Secularization has been, above all, the acceptance of these factors as liberating for people and as an opportunity for the Church. Thence came the praise of industrial society, freeing from bondage to nature and climate and creating a climate of individualist liberty, and the free climate of urban anonymity where each person can lose himself.

Modern theology has interpreted this phenomenon and applied it to the Christian faith, and to the life of the Church. It has gone beyond secularization; it has ridiculed ontology, advocated the abandonment of religious language and become fearful of the sacred, preferring instead to become engaged in 'horizontal' realities, in political affairs. Also, it has encouraged a different 'lifestyle' for communities, especially religious communities, so as to modify their way of being present in the human city.

Ordinary Catholics, living in the real world, have had to translate, as well as they can, these theories coming from academia - the best of them and also the worst of them.

Europe has been hit by this wave from America, a wave which has hit the most traditional Catholic communities and Catholicism at its most sensitive point: its sacrality, its sacramentality, and its priesthood. It rapidly adopted the theories of recent philosophers and theologians such as Feuerbach and Bultmann. Some even proclaimed the death of God, and so forth. It would seem, according to some observers, like Fr Manaranche, that this movement existed for some time, then was overtaken by the charismatic movement and by a popular religion - a religion which the secularists thought had died.

Nonetheless there is one bastion against which the movement for secularization is firing its last shots. That area is the priesthood and sacrifice, both linked to the idea of consecration. So there are debates on such subjects as priesthood, sacrifice, character, ministry, liturgy, on everything which concerns the sacred, culture, and so on. And that is where the question which is the title of this lecture comes from.

The great theological debating point is the sacramental character of holy orders.

THE NOTION OF SACRAMENTAL CHARACTER

• *The doctrine of sacramental character in the scriptures*

St Paul alludes to it in three passages: 2Cor. 1:22, Eph. 1:13 and Eph 4:30 as also in the Apocrypha. The mark or seal indicates that the baptized person belongs to God, and will be a sign to distinguish him on the day of judgement, a sign which will open up for him the gates of Heaven. Therefore it is an invisible mark: the Fathers talk of a spiritual *sphragis* (seal) by which God recognises those who are his own.

• *The doctrine of sacramental character in the Fathers*

St Augustine began with his arguments against the Donatists about not repeating the baptism of heretics. There is, he says, in baptism a permanent element which he compares to the 'emperor's mark' received by soldiers, an indelible sign enabling them to be recognized. Elsewhere, in his *Contra Epistolam Parmeniani,* he establishes a parallel between baptism and priesthood, declaring that neither can be destroyed even in the case of wicked men and cannot be lost even by one who separates himself from the unity of the Catholic Church. Both are

> given to man by a kind of consecration, either in baptism or ordination,
> and that is why in the Catholic Church, neither can be repeated

Contra Ep. Parmeniani.

• *Sacramental character in the teaching of the Council of Trent*

The Council of Trent declares that:

> In three sacraments, baptism, confirmation and order, a character, that is a certain spiritual and indelible sign, is imprinted on the soul, whence it comes that these three sacraments cannot be repeated
>
> *Session VII concerning sacraments in general.*

This definition is important because it shows us that the sacramental character has an ontological reality. It is a sign imprinted on the soul making with it but one reality. This mark causes a real change in the man who receives it. In his very being there is created a capacity to exercise a particular function.

The permanence of this sign is not measured by the concrete aptitude to exercise that function. It remains for the subject's entire life on earth during which it cannot be repeated. As for eternity, nothing is explicitly taught. But in any case, tradition has never made a difference between the diverse characters when it comes to their definitive permanence and since the basic consecration of baptism continues in the life to come, even after the activities of life have ceased, it seems to follow that the even greater consecration of orders must also be destined to continue after the end of the Christian ministry here below.

For the priest to be, more especially than other Christians, the representative of God, possessing divine authority for his mission, he should have become God's possession at a deep level of his person, so that God may use him more efficiently as the minister of his divine activity.

• *The doctrine of sacramental character in more recent sources*

a) *Ad Catholici sacerdotii fastigium* (Pius XI, 20th December 1935)

'These powers conferred on the priest by this special sacrament are not temporary and transient but stable and permanent, since they have their origin in an indelible character imprinted on the soul, this character by which he has been made a priest for ever (Ps.109) like the one in whose priesthood he participates. This character a priest can never efface from his soul no matter into what dreadful depravities he may fall through the frailty of human nature.

b) *Mediator Dei* (Pius XII, 20th November 1947) On the Sacred Liturgy.

'This is why the visible and exterior priesthood of Jesus Christ is not conferred indiscriminately, but is conferred, rather, on certain chosen men and it constitutes one of the seven sacraments, order. This sacrament does not only give a particular grace proper to the priestly state and function but also confers an indelible 'character' which configures the sacred minister to Jesus Christ, Priest and renders him apt to exercise legitimately the acts of religion ordered to the sanctification of man and the glorification of God, according to the demands of the supernatural economy'.

As the waters of baptism distinguish all Christians and set them apart from those whom the holy water has not purified and are not members of Christ so in the same way the sacrament of orders sets priests apart from the rest of Christ's faithful who have not received this gift. For they alone replying to their vocation, by a kind of supernatural inspiration, have received the august ministry which has consecrated them to the service of the altar and made them divine instruments by which divine, supernatural life is communicated to the Body of Christ. But also, as we have said above, they alone have been marked with the indelible character which 'conforms' them to Christ the Priest. Their hands alone have been consecrated

> so that whatever they bless may be blessed and whatever they consecrate may be consecrated and sanctified in the name of the Lord Jesus Christ'
>
> *Roman Pontifical: Priestly Ordination, at the anointing of hands.*

To them, then, come all those who wish to live in Christ, for from them, they receive the remedy of Salvation thanks to which, healed and strengthened, they can escape that disaster whither vices lead. By them, finally their communal and family life will be blessed and consecrated and their last breath in this mortal life will become the entrance into everlasting blessedness.

c) Apostolic Exhortation: *Menti nostræ* to the clergy of the Catholic world on the sanctity of priestly life (Pius XII, 23rd September 1950)

'The priest is as it were 'another Christ' because he is marked with the indelible character which makes him a living image of the Saviour. The priest stands in the place of Christ, who says, 'As the Father sent me so I send you. And he who hears you hears me' (Luke 10;18).

Prepared by the call of God to this most holy ministry he is established for men for what pertains to the worship of God so that he might offer oblations and sacrifices for sins. To him therefore ought to go whosoever wants to live the life of the Divine Redeemer and obtain strength, solace and spiritual nourishment, and again, it is from him that anyone who wants to leave a sinful life for a fruitful life should seek the help he needs. Consequently, all priests can apply to themselves what St Paul says, 'we are co-workers with God' (1Cor. 3:9)'.

Let us pause now to see what those who oppose this theology have to say. We will come back to the present subject a little later when we look at the Decree of Vatican II *Presbyterorum ordinis* (7th December 1965).

CONTESTATION OF THE IDEA OF 'CHARACTER'

- *Different value according to the sacraments.*

According to certain theologians the character has a different value according to the sacrament that imprints it. In attributing to three sacraments the same indelible mark it has not been adequately appreciated that baptism and confirmation constitute 'Christian being' whereas the sacrament of order 'only adds a specialized function to the Christian's mission.' [1] The baptized person remains a Christian for all eternity whereas in the world to come when his specific function will no longer be necessary 'the minister will return to being a layman'. [2] Moreover, 'in the Church on earth no more than in the Church in Heaven, the ministry need not be something permanent'. [3]

- *The character pertains to Action not to Being*

What is more, we must admit, they say, a principle which goes against any right to permanence.

> The exercise of the ecclesiastical ministry has certain limits. These are the physical and moral limitations of the minister and the needs of the community. The community calls on the minister when it needs him, and if at the moment of that call he is not entirely apt and formed, it offers him the possibility of waiting for the day when he can comply fully with everything it demands of him. The community can also dismiss him. [4]

There is no necessity therefore, according to these authors, that a man should remain a priest all his life!

> If the Council of Trent affirms the existence of an indelible sign it is because the declarations of this Council are apologetic and refer to the practice then in existence. They are not strictly speaking theological pronouncements. The practice of not repeating ordination 'is certainly part of the Church's sacramental discipline, but it is not certain that the repetition of the sacrament is forbidden by the principles of theology'. Rather we should interpret this non-repetition as signifying a basic competence even if the ministry itself is no longer exercised: just as, for example an engineer is still an engineer even if he takes up a position in the diplomatic service. [5]

- *The character refers to a situation*

For other authors, like Fr Schoonenberg, the notion of character is linked to the idea of 'situation' and 'to be in a situation'. The character here 'causes no change in the ordinand's nature or being'. The sacrament of order simply puts its subject in a particular situation, a situation such that the ordination produces its effects and the ministry conferred by the ordination can be fulfilled. 'Being in a situation' carries with it the idea of a limit in the duration of the character.

Lastly, for Schillebeeckx, we need to demystify the notion of character. The Council of Trent and its interpretation are opposed simply to the Reformers of the epoch but they do not thereby sanction the teaching of the scholastics that the character is some ontological 'thing'. It has no value except for as long as one exercises the ministry and does not last for the whole life of the minister nor does it touch on everything he does. Finally, still according to Schillebeeckx, this demystification will help in ecumenical reconciliation for if one admits an aptitude to exercise the function of pastor in Christ's name then one is acknowledging the reality which underlies the idea of character.

CONSEQUENCES OF THESE POSITIONS

- *Part time Ministry and the Ordination of Lay People.*

One of the consequences of the theological ideas about character which we have been mentioning is the introduction of a part-time ministry, something which entails the ordination of lay people. This is seen as the ideal for the future by those who propose it. The part-time priesthood is a direct result of the absence of the priestly character. The Church can give so-and-so a task, or the subject of ordination can himself choose to limit the time he gives to the ministry or the area he ministers in or he can limit himself to the task to which he is best suited.

Bunnick thinks that no theological principle can be invoked in favour of a full-time ministry.

> The fact that many ministers spend most of their time specifically in the exercise of their ministry is not a theological necessity but only a question of organization, a practical question. [6]

And so we come to the second part of this section: the appointment of the greatest possible number of part-time ministers. For where the full-time ministers are not numerous enough to meet the needs of a community how can these needs be met other wise than by increasing the number of part-time ministers - that is by calling lay-people to these ministries?

> 'If the distinction between ordained and lay is diminished the unity of the People of God can only gain from it'.

Let us note in passing that it is not very clear if what is being proposed is the ordination of lay people or simply the choice of people to fulfil some role or other.

Lastly on this subject, the diminishing of the distinction between priest and people leads Bunnick to condemn the practice of concelebration which, in his eyes, is the manifestation of a clericocentric mentality and flatters the desire to assume a role. The full-time ministry has the drawback of making ministerial functions appear to be 'the supreme task in the Church'. Paradoxically the same author affirms that this type of ministry is more fitted to the service of the world, since the part-time minister is more involved in it. We will return to this point later, when we examine these positions critically.

Another paradox, even indeed a contradiction: the part-time minister enjoys an authority which comes from the exercise of his secular activity:

> his role as priest is shored up by his social standing and this social stand-
> ing can help him in his work as a minister of the Church.'

There, then are the first two solutions/consequences proposed by those who, as we have seen, deny the Catholic doctrine of character and so want to redefine the profile of the priest and his mission.

   •   *The abandonment of the ministry and the marriage of priests.*

The rejection of the expression 'priest for ever' together with the doctrine of the indelible nature of the priestly character make abandoning the ministry more acceptable. According to the theories we have just been looking at the ministry is simply a function and so the question of fidelity is just a simple question about a choice of functions. 'Is there no call from God?' , you might ask. Well, they reply, one calling can be succeeded by another.

> The decision to leave the ministry can then result from obeying a new
> invitation from God: to engage oneself wholly in the secular apostolate
> becomes 'the better part'. To speak in this context of 'degradation' is
> meaningless because however elevated the ecclesiastical ministry may
> be, it is not the 'best' task or mission in an absolute sense for every
> Christian.

We see here a reaction against the humiliating conditions of being 'reduced to the lay state', but even more importantly there is in this position a fundamental rejection of any notion of the superiority of the priestly ministry.

Amongst the causes which lead a man to leave the ministry these authors (Bunnick) place marriage.

> To fall in love, to get married is a new charism which takes the place of
> the charism of virginity. Marriage is also a way to God and nothing
> makes it inferior to the virgin state. Marriage is not a temptation which
> the celibate minister should strive to resist. It can be a new vocation.

Another widespread error is the appeal to conscience! ' He must act in accord-ance with the dictates of his own conscience'.

> Whatever the case, a man who leaves the ministry should not ask him-
> self if the ecclesial community and canon law morally condemn him.

As for the question of the relationship of fidelity to the priesthood and fidelity in marriage, no comparison is possible. The demands made by the ministry are not absolute for there is in marriage another kind of service of the Church and of the world. Also

the bond of matrimony is essentially different from the bond of order. A relationship of service binds the minister to the community. By contrast, matrimony creates a bond between individuals and thus creates an existential unity.

Let us note, finally, that according to this idea of priesthood the community can dismiss a priest - on account of his age, his lack of ability, sickness, social incompatibility and so on...

To finish, when a minister asks for leave for personal reasons

he should not be refused, because the personal development of an individual should take precedence over the functional needs of the community.

For the less liberal Schoonenberg, age and marriage do not justify abandoning the ministry. The only just motive for leaving the priesthood is 'not feeling at home in the Church or with the profession of faith'.

- *The suppression of a state of life.*

In the vision [of priesthood] that we have just described, a kind of life not much different from that of lay people, there are certain consequences which need to be underlined. First of all, there is much talk about a profession and about an engagement in politics or in trade unionism, as well about freedom to marry. The question of a 'state of life' is quickly settled if one thinks about it. 'No character' we have said. Consequently, minister and ministry are all about doing rather than being: a functionary does one thing today, something else tomorrow.

Priestly celibacy from the viewpoint of a state of life appears to be for the preservation of the sacerdotal caste. As for the group *Echanges et Dialogues* they ask that married priests should be allowed to exercise their priesthood. Others demand that married priests should be reintegrated into the Church because of the shortage of vocations. It is an idea which appears in a book published by *Editions du Cerf. Prêtres mariés mes frères* ('Married Priests my Brothers'). The author is himself a priest. He has just become the auxiliary Bishop of Paris.

• *The many consequences for priests who remain faithful but who are influenced by the present climate of thought.*

Here we will confine ourselves to mentioning only some of the many consequences which result from the above-mentioned positions and may even affect faithful priests who find themselves caught up in the machinery of their particular priestly milieu. Let us mention in passing

—the absence of any distinctive sign contrary to what the Church asked for at Vatican II (the religious state and its obligations).

—the introduction of this attitude into liturgical practice and the sacraments (sacraments which are no longer understood as mysteries in the Pauline sense, but as commitments!)

—there is confusion between *participatio actuosa* and in 'getting the faithful to do things'.

—more worryingly, some seem to think of the Church as a group founded by man, not as a gift from Christ and the Holy Spirit. This association gives out the roles, as we have said. It is a sort of 'co-op' where the priest is not necessary.

In this respect three hymns, amongst many others, seem to me to be significant:

1) 'To save the love of the Beloved from being forgotten
   -that is why we have come together';

2) 'Jesus Christ will never die again...
   if (like the bread) we share our lives';

3) *God is love* verse 2:
   'if we live at the heart of the world
   we will live in the heart of God'.

These three hymns demonstrate a theological inversion and a secularizing tendency. In the first it is not Christ who calls together and establishes the Church, it is the Church which comes together to remember him. In the second, we have this inversion: the members of the Church are said to 'share (like the bread) their life' whereas one should really say 'share their life like the bread'. Some people will say it is the same thing and we interpret the meaning unjustly, but, honestly, I do not think so. It is like 'justice' or 'solidarity' which we often hear mentioned in these songs but rarely if ever in a purely Biblical sense, free from political connotations. In *God is love* we again have an inversion. One should say 'if we live in the heart of God, then—as missionaries— we will live at the heart of the world etc...'.

In preaching too, we can see sometimes a change of emphasis. We hear, for example, that no one possesses the truth. No one person perhaps, but the Church?

Likewise, when speaking about Confirmation people talk about choosing Jesus Christ ... where is the gift, the gratuity? It is the opposite which is the case. And if I say I chose Jesus Christ rather than Jesus Christ has chosen me, then can I not make another choice tomorrow?

In our language too, we can mention a few things to avoid. For example 'We make the Church' and so forth.

When we are telling people who we are, is there not a difference between 'Church Youth Group' and 'Leisure Centre'? Certainly we should go along with official terminology for legal reasons - but let us, please, not be ashamed of our origins and our identity. We are not just teachers but priests and Christian educators.

Running through everything that we have been saying we find the theme of the separation of sacred and secular, the separation of God and the world. Why is this separation dangerous - particularly in the problems raised by certain types of language, and in the deliberate neglect of certain exterior signs?

Language first (which sung, is still language and indeed is often more memorable). Just as the piety of generations of Christians has been formed and forged by the prayers which express most clearly what it means to be a Christian—*lex orandi, lex credendi*—so also, hearing, indeed repeating and, as we have said, singing the new hymns of the kind we have been discussing, leads to people's mentalities being changed by new ideas, and not just mentalities but behaviour as well. This is the reason why careful attention should be paid to what resources are used in the present day liturgy.

The basic error which underlies all these positions is this: as everything is called to become holy or consecrated, it is easily said that there is no difference between the sacred and the profane. Furthermore this is expressed, not by consecrating what is profane, but—dare I say it—by profaning what is consecrated, by introducing profane matters into the area of the consecrated, without transforming them but retaining their secular significance.

All this may seem like a digression. But it is not. These things touch so closely the life of the priest, the minister of sacred things, himself consecrated, that they are relevant to our subject.

Now that we have seen how the problem has been posed, and the theological crux of the problem, the theology of [priestly] character, and the ideas of those who oppose this theology (as well as the consequences of these ideas), let us attempt to resolve the problems with the help of what the Church teaches us: first in looking, briefly, at the Epistle to the Hebrews, then at some texts of Vatican II and some declarations of the Popes Paul VI and John Paul II.

THE REPLY TO THOSE WHO DENY THE TRADITIONAL TEACHING OF THE CHURCH
OR THE AUTHENTIC FACE OF THE PRIESTHOOD

- *In Scripture*

The Epistle to the Hebrews shows us the authentic face of the priesthood, and applies it to Jesus Christ who is the model and the source for all those whom He chooses to follow to become priests after him. In this Epistle the titles 'priest' and 'high priest' are applied to Christ. The Epistle emphasises the transcendence of his priesthood, defining it, to avoid confusion, as being 'of the order of Melchizedech', an order which is not limited by human genealogies. Jesus himself does not use these titles which belong to the Jewish priestly caste. He was not of a priestly family, as we can see easily from his genealogy. The tribe of Judah was not sacerdotal unlike that of Aaron, the tribe to which John the Baptist belonged, as we see in the Gospel according to St Luke. It is thus shown that the priesthood of the New Testament, whose great high priest Christ is, does not follow on from that of the Old Testament. It is neither an inherited privilege nor a caste, unlike the Levitical priesthood.

For us also it follows on that anything in the priest's life which favours a caste mentality is foreign to the will of God and that criticism of such a mentality is, in itself, in full conformity to the Gospel. Indeed it is by banishing the caste mentality of the Old Testament priesthood that the spirit of the new priesthood is fully expressed, a spirit which is filled with the greatest love of neighbour possible. In fact, it was the priests of the old dispensation who most readily opposed the new. Love is superior to every other obligation; but this fact was missed by the ministers of a ritualized priesthood only concerned with legal obligations.

Again separating himself off from the Levitical priesthood, Jesus insists in several places that holiness and the sacred, rather than being about places and objects—however worthy they might be—are really about the very person itself, himself in many cases. One instance of this is the passage about the destruction of the Temple by the Jews and its reconstruction in three days. This Temple is His Body (John 2:19).

The sacred is thus conceived of in a new way, less concerned with things, more with the person. It is humanity which is destined to be divinized and sacralization takes place through the human relation of one person to another through which the divine holiness is communicated. The divine energy operates in these relationships, beginning from Christ.

Another important point is that Jesus in the Gospel, and then, especially by those who are possessed, is declared to be 'Holy, the Holy One of God'. St Peter confesses him to be 'the Christ, the Messiah'. The account of the Annunciation also confirms that the one to be born will be holy. That is why we can conclude that this holiness is ontological. It touches his very being and is not merely functional. In other words, it is not a result of his mission, but of his divine origin. His actions are the manifestation of his divine holiness.

The redemptive sacrifice accomplishes in fullness this consecration and John 17:19 shows it to have been communicated to the Apostles 'And for their sake I consecrate myself, that they also may be consecrated in truth'. The Resurrection is the fulfilment of this sacrificial consecration.

Finally let us note, that this consecration requires of those who are consecrated a profession of faith, as was the case with St Peter.

But let us return to the Epistle to the Hebrews which shows us how we are to understand properly the new priesthood instituted by Christ and thus enables us to give a reply to the problem we have been studying.

Looking then at the Epistle to the Hebrews we find a spiritualization of the high priesthood in the case of Jesus: 'Every high priest is appointed to offer gifts and sacrifices' (Heb. 8:3). This Christ did once for all. The earthly liturgy is the image of a spiritual reality and so above the worship of the Old Testament. It is of a transcendent order; that of Melchizedech.

Moreover, the nature of Christ's priestly office is revealed to us by the title 'Mediator of the New Covenant'. Not only is he an intermediary (the literal meaning of the word) between God and man, he is also much more. As a central point He unites the two extremes, by offering his sacrifice and by the intercession which is its fruit.

Another title which fits our theme is 'great shepherd of the sheep, by the blood of the eternal covenant' (Heb. 13:20). The title 'Chief Shepherd', an equivalent of 'High Priest', shows us another aspect of Christ's priesthood. He is the leader of his flock. Christ's sacrifice is only relevant for the human community. When Christ enters the sanctuary, it is 'in the name of all humanity'. From then on the title of shepherd characterises both the sacrifice and human sanctification - for where but heaven is he leading his flock!

The characteristics of Christ's priesthood are thus the following :

 • He unites in himself the titles of Priest, king of peace (Melchizedech), reconciler and mediator and also shepherd (which includes the last two mentioned).

 • This priesthood has its origins in the transcendence of God the Father: *ex utero ante luciferum genui te.* [7]

 • It takes over the man entirely. Jesus abandons his family and his craft and there is in that a radical belonging to the Father with all his being, so that he can give himself entirely to the work entrusted to him. The sacrifice of the Cross shows how far this belonging to the Father goes. In this demand of the entire human being there is no question of leaving the ministry or changing vocation. The gift of self required by the priesthood is definitive, it is an existential priesthood which cannot be reduced to a profession.

• Christ is a servant. Since the ministry is a service it excludes all privilege, all rights to demand honour and to be esteemed by society. It places the priest on the lowest rung.

• *How does this apply to our problem?*

Well, the priestly character is a sign of consecration, but of consecration in the same way as Christ was consecrated for his priestly ministry in the world. The priest belongs to God in a special way, not only in the things pertaining to God but also in the way in which God bears himself and is borne, so to speak, towards humanity for its salvation. For Christ 'to be consecrated' and 'to be sent into the world' are two aspects of the Incarnation which are linked indissolubly. Thus priestly consecration must be understood and lived out according to the incarnation. The consecration of Christ in his humanity places divine holiness in the midst of the world and the consecration of the priest can have no other meaning than this.

• *Vatican II*

Vatican II—which underlines what we have just been saying—reacted against the idea of consecration as a separation from the world. True consecration, while implying a certain distinctiveness from the world certainly implies an engagement in it. Engagement not in any temporal sense, political, syndical or similar, but in the sense of a spiritual ministry at the heart of the world. This appears especially in the decree on the priesthood *Presbyterorum Ordinis*, which quotes the definition of the priest given in the Epistle to the Hebrews, thus showing the two sides of priestly consecration: 'The priest is taken from amongst men and appointed for men' (Heb. 5:1). 'By their vocation and ordination the priests of the New Testament are, in a certain fashion, placed apart in the body of God's People. This is not to be separated from his people—nor indeed from anyone at all. It is to be wholly consecrated to the work to which the Lord has called them (Acts 13:12). They could not be ministers of Christ, were they not witnesses to and dispensers of another life, different from this earthly one. But also they could not be able to serve their fellow men if they remained aloof from their everyday life' [8]

As one can see, this teaching is very balanced and both aspects of the priestly vocation are closely linked together: consecration and separateness which enables priests to be the ministers of Christ and devoted to the service of their fellow men. As *Presbyterorum Ordinis* §17 puts it, quoting the Gospel itself, the priest is in the world, but not of the world.

In paragraphs 3 and 12, it recalls the duty of a holy life for the priest.

They must strive to live out more and more a holiness which will make of them instruments always better adapted to the service of all God's people' [9]

This is made more necessary still by the fact that the consecration given by the priestly character configures the human being to Christ, imprinting on their souls his likeness. This likeness is essentially, as we have seen in the Epistle to the Hebrews, the image of the Good Shepherd which implies for the priest the power of fulfilling a pastoral role in the name of Christ.

The function of the priest, united to the bishop, is to participate in the authority of Christ who himself builds up, sanctifies and governs his Body [10]

It is an ontological demand, founded on the nature of priesthood. The character engenders in the priest's soul a likeness which must be lived and recognized, the portrait of the shepherd-servant. This implies again that he who gave his life for the sheep, the Good Shepherd Jesus Christ demands of his servant in the pastoral ministry the gift of their whole existence. Like the Apostles in the Gospel who left all to take up a full-time ministry, they have the model of Jesus Christ himself.

Now, to close, some quotations from the teaching of Popes Paul VI and John Paul II.

- *Paul VI. Message to Priests - 20th June 1968*

Man of God, Man of the Community

We can thus highlight certain features which distinguish the Catholic Priesthood. First, the sacred dimension. The priest is a man of God, the minister of the Lord. He can perform acts which surpass the natural order, because he acts *in persona Christi.* There passes though him a power from above, a power of which he is at times the humble yet glorious, efficacious instrument; he is the vehicle of the Holy Ghost. A singular relationship, a delegation, a divine trust pass between him and the divine world.

Nonetheless this gift is not received by the priest for himself, but for others. The sacred dimension of the priesthood is entirely ordained to the apostolic dimension, that is, mission and priestly ministry.

We know well that the priest is not a man who lives for himself but for others. He is a man of the community. This aspect of the priesthood is the one best understood today. There are some who find there an answer to the aggressive questions about the survival of priesthood in the modern world. The service the priest gives to society, especially to the ecclesial society, fully justifies his continuing existence. The world needs him. The Church needs him.

In saying this a whole series of needs come into mind. Who does not need the preaching of the Gospel? Who does not need faith? Who does not need grace? Who does not need someone who devotes himself to him with a disinterested love? And what limits can we place on pastoral charity? Is it not there where the desire for this love is least that it is most needed? The missions, the young, schools, hospitals, and in our days with an ever more pressing urgency the workers form a continual appeal to the heart of the priest. And so how can we doubt that the priest has a place, a role, a mission in today's world? What we should be saying is, how can we respond to all the needs there are for the priest, how can our personal sacrifice correspond to the increase of our pastoral duties and apostolic activities?

Perhaps as never before, today the Church is conscious of being the indispensable means of salvation, for never before has the dynamism of her dispensation been so great as now. And yet we dream of a world without the Church and of a Church without ministers, ministers prepared, trained and consecrated! The priest is in himself, the sign of Christ's love for the world, the witness to a total engagement by which the Church seeks to make real his love, the love which led him to the Cross.

• *John Paul II*

2nd July 1980 at Rio de Janeiro.

Different Homilies on the Priesthood

Message for Holy Thursday 1989 to priests

(we may mention also the book *Avec vous je suis prêtre* (With you I am a priest) - a short collection of our Holy Father Pope John Paul's reflections on the priesthood during his apostolic travels)

Who are you, priest? What is your mission?

Who am I? What do people expect of me? What is my identity? This is the sort of question which the priest asks himself in these days when he is not sheltered from the blows of the crisis of transformation which is shaking the world.

As for you, my very dear sons, you no doubt feel no need to ask these questions. The light which fills you, fills you with an almost tangible certainty as to who you are and to what you have been called. But it may happen tomorrow that you will meet brothers in the priesthood who, filled with uncertainty, ask themselves questions about their identity and it may indeed happen that once your first fervour dims, you yourselves will ask the same questions, and that is why I want to share with you a few reflections on the true face of the priest, to sustain your priestly fidelity.

Certainly it is not in the human sciences nor in the socio-religious statistics that we will find our reply, but much rather in Christ, in the Faith. We will ask the Divine Master and seek humbly from him the answer to who we are, how he would think we should be, and what is our true identity before him.

• *The Sacerdotal Order*

Having developed three affirmations - the priest is called, the priest is consecrated, the priest is sent - then having spoken of the relation which exists between priesthood and people, the Pope insists on the necessity of the priest being more than ever a sign and an instrument of the invisible world.

Prudent but confident you will live amongst men to share their sorrows and their hopes, to fortify them in their efforts for freedom and justice. Do not therefore become enslaved by the world nor by its prince, the evil one. Do not conform to the opinions and the tastes of the world. As St Paul says: *Nolite conformari huic sæculo* (Rom. 12:1-2). Rather insert yourselves, with your aspirations into God's will.

The power of a sign does not lie in its conformity but in its difference. Light differs from darkness so as to be able to enlighten the way of him who walks in obscurity. Salt is different from food, to give it taste. Fire differs from cold to warm those who are numbed with frost. Christ calls us to be the light and the salt of the earth. In a divided and confused world, as ours today, the power of a sign lies precisely in being distinct. The sign ought to stand out more clearly because apostolic activity demands that we should be more fully inserted into the world.

When we lose sight of these bright horizons, the figure of the priest is darkened, his identity enters into a crisis, his duties become unreasonable and contradictory, his very purpose in being a priest is weakened.

This fundamental purpose cannot be found while the priest is just 'a man for others'. For is this not what anyone who desires to follow the Divine Master should be?

The priest is assuredly 'a man for others' but it is because he is a man set apart in a special way to be a 'man for God'. The service of God is the foundation on which should be built an authentic service of men, which consists in freeing them from the slavery of sin and leading them back to the necessary service of God. For God desires that the human race should become a people who adore him 'in spirit and in truth (John

4:23) [11]

CONCLUSION

In conclusion, I hope to have shown that nothing justifies the criticism and problems that are forced on us as something coming from the grassroots. As so often in the Church it is a matter of disputes by certain theologians and thinkers, who, not devoid of talent, have a certain audience and influence, and who would, like everyone, to follow their ideas. Fortunately it is the Holy Spirit who guides the Church, and will lead it in the right direction in spite of the sometimes violent contrary winds that attack the barque of Peter.

So, is the priest the man of the sacred or the man for others? I will leave the conclusion to the Holy Father, John Paul II, who spoke to the Vincentians gathered on St. Peter's Square for the 250th anniversary of the canonization of St. Vincent de Paul:

> There were two loves in his life: God and the poor. In this the great historian of Christian life, Henri Brémond, is right when he says,
>
> 'it was not love for men that led him to holiness, but rather holiness made him truly and effectively charitable. It was not the poor who gave him to God, but rather God who gave him to the poor. Whoever sees him more as a philanthropist than as a mystic, who does not see him foremost as a mystic, shows himself a Vincent de Paul who never existed'.

Let us ask God to be 'priests after his heart', entirely directed towards men, our brothers, for our lives will be sanctuaries of the presence of God.... or, as the motto of our founder, Father Jean-Leon le Prevost (1803-1874) puts it: 'Let us form Jesus Christ in ourselves, in order to show him to others in our works'.

NOTES:

1. *Priests:* Fr Bunnick

2. *ibid.*

3. *ibid.*

4. *ibid.*

5. *ibid.*

6. Bunnick: *op.cit.*

7. From the womb before the dawn I begot you Ps 109

8. *Presbyterorum Ordinis* §3.

9. *ibid.* §12

10 *ibid* §2c

11 Extracts from a homily preached on 2nd July 1980 at an ordination in Rio de Janeiro.

THE UNDERSTANDING OF PARTICIPATION IN SACRED RITES IN THE EARLY CHRISTIAN CHURCH

Dom Alban Nunn

Dom Alban Nunn, born in 1961, studied music at the University of Melbourne, theology at the University of Flandres, and archæology at the University of Oxford. A monk at Ealing Abbey, where he is Magister Choralis *(Choir Master), he continues his studies of 18th century sacred polyphony.*

Abstract: This paper examines the primary evidence for an understanding of participation in sacred rites in the early Church commencing with the scriptural evidence and concluding with the Rule of Saint Benedict. This evidence points to a very early implied tradition of *participatio actuosa* allowing an emphasis on internal disposition of the participant consistent with the continuing Catholic tradition.

INTRODUCTION

- *Rationale*

THE purpose of this paper is to glimpse behind the terminology describing participation in the early Church. It does not intend to provide a catalogue of liturgical actions attributed to early Christians but rather to reveal through some of the language surrounding these accounts in what sense early Christians really understood these actions to be participation. This paper is work *a propos* of a history of *participatio actuosa*. It does not, therefore, claim to be an exhaustive treatment of the subject but rather an overview pointing towards a reassessment of the literalistic and generalized interpretation of texts documenting the early liturgical practices of Christianity.

- *The problem of evidence and its interpretation*

An initial disclaimer must be made to cover the problem of our current understanding of languages used in the period. Two problems must be recognized. (i) our understanding of some words, especially technical language, is imperfect. Frequently we are aware that a term exists that is significant in our discussions. The Latin *jubilus* is frequently referred to in patristic literature and from the context it seems clear that it refers to some form of utterance associated with ecclesiastical singing. Its exact definition continues to be debated and we should be careful not to read later understandings of *jubilus* back into an earlier context without caution. (ii) secondly, the texts that we are dealing with often have a long history of transmission—primary 'Western' texts have been transmitted through Eastern channels and some Greek texts of the earliest sub-apostolic evidence are only available through Latin transmission. The degree to which terminology has taken on later understandings in its translations is often obscure, but the existence of this problem must suggest a degree of caution to any conclusion drawn purely from textural analysis without the safeguard of established tradition.

• Gospels or Epistles first?

The hierarchy attributed by academia, generally outside Catholic tradition, to early Church documents is problematic. The placing of the Gospels after the Epistles presumes a late date of origin for the Gospels in their current form. Recent interpretative methods have allowed for early traditions in the Gospel so that material of 'liturgical' significance, such as the hymn sung before the disciples immediately before the Passion (Mt. 26:30 = Mk. 14:26), is currently being reassessed as a tradition belonging to the actual time of Jesus rather than a later embroidered memory of the event.

• Musical references as a control test

Many of the references that will be cited in this paper deal with musical matters. Whilst not a formal musicological study—this is impossible because of the almost total lack of primary evidence—it is impossible to avoid musical considerations. These references are the most fruitful body of material in dealing with attitudes to participation as we have here an element of Christian worship which seems to have vexed the early Church. Considerable time is spent by patristic authors on the type of music sung and indeed the question of who sings in Christian worship is essential in determining what was considered valid participation within the liturgical context. The early appearance of lectors and the slightly later appearance of cantors as a defined class in the Christian community is one of the strongest pieces of evidence confirming that valid participation was understood as listening as well as singing.

• Perimeters—Western, not Eastern

Finally in this paper I have dealt primarily with Western texts in preference to the early Eastern texts. This bias is intentionally to provide material that belongs directly to the early 'pure' Roman tradition before the cross-fertilization between East and West that resulted ultimately in the classical form of the Western Mediæval Rite. It should also be noted that each century, if not each document, that we refer to is worthy of a study in its own right. We are thus providing a general overview in essence a background for comparison with the material that Joseph Gribbin will present.

THE FIRST CENTURY

The Reverend Robert Skeris has eloquently described the essential connection between Christian liturgy and the sacrifice of the cross:

> The sacrificial death of Jesus Christ the High Priest on Calvary is and will remain the basis for the active participation of the faithful in the liturgy. Membership in the Church, which is brought about by valid baptism, makes one a part of the Mystical Body of Christ, the Priest, to whose priesthood one is interiorly conformed through the baptismal character. [1]

It must be admitted that the writings of the first century do not provide a comprehensive picture of contemporary worship and liturgy but rather offer us fragments that may be interpreted in the light of the Jewish and Hellenic background of the early believers or in the light of later developments. It is a matter at this stage of not only observing described actions but also understanding the language used to describe them. Almost without exception biblical references implying some sort of participation in a corporate act reflects strong theological language carrying far much more in its meaning than pure description.

- *The Epistles*

Throughout the Epistles participation is expressed most frequently in the terms of κοινωνία. It is this word, which the Vulgate renders on one occasion as *participatio,* that is used in that purple passage in 1 Corinthians 10:16, which seems to be the origins of much of early Christian traditions about the participation of the believer:

> *calicem benedictionis cui benedicimus nonne communicatio sanguinis Christi est et panis quem frangimus nonne participatio corporis Domini est?* [2]

Here we have the richest statement of the earliest belief of Christians: that is, that participation in the sacred mystery of the Mass is not merely a formal function of duty but rather a mystical participation in the very essence of Christian salvation. Throughout the Vulgate New Testament κοινωνία is translated with distinctions that seem clear to the translators of the time but which are not always picked up by modern translations. For example κοινωνία appearing twice in 1 Corinthians 10:16 is rendered by the Revised Standard Version on both occasions as 'participation' in the Body of Christ in the first clause, and in the second clause in the Blood of Christ. The Vulgate translators seem to have understood a distinction between the two translating the first use as *communicatio* and the second as *participatio*. Three possibilities come to mind at this point, which I will place as questions: (i) Is this purely an element of literary style - that is in avoiding the repetition of *participatio* or *communicatio* the phrase would be better literature? (ii) Is there a real difference between the chosen translations that reflected a theological distinction that is obscure to us but would have been clear to the original audience? (iii) Is this a deliberate uniting of language in that two terms in use in the Latin speaking community were shown as being the same? The most common rendering of κοινωνία in the Vulgate New Testament is as *communicatio* followed closely by *societas* or its cognates. The rendering of κοινωνία as *participatio* seems to be peculiar to the Corinthian correspondence appearing again at 1 Corinthians10:18 where similar sacrificial imagery is in play:

> *videte Israhel secundum carnem nonne qui edunt hostias participes sunt altaris.* [3]

The Vulgate use of *participatio* and its cognates is frequently in association with the imagery of sacrifice (1Cor. 9:13, 10:17,18,21; Heb 2:14 cf. 1Esd 5:40). Whilst it is not possible to make an absolute conclusion concerning the use in the Corinthian correspondence it would seem likely that at least, in part, the Vulgate was keen to emphasise an association already present in a Latin speaking mind: that *participatio*, the sacrificial concept, and *communicatio*, the social aspect of the common life that the Greek speakers expressed as κοινωνία, were inextricably bound together. Moving this parallel across to our specific topic we suggest that this is strong supportive evidence for both active (*communicatio*-communal) and passive (*participatio*-sacrificial and internal) understandings in the early Christian community of participation in worship.

• *The Gospels and Acts of the Apostles.*

The 'historical' books of the New Testament do not provide detailed information about the nature of early Christian worship save that it provides sufficient contemporary proof of the early Christians operating liturgically, at least, at first, within the ambit of Temple and early Synagogue. Considerable time has been spent on trying to gauge how much the Christians of the Gospels conformed to contemporary Jewish practice in worship, but no definite conclusions can be drawn. A common opinion is voiced, that a definite break with Jewish practice is underlying some of the attitudes towards the Jewish people found in the Gospels and the *Acts of the Apostles,* particularly in matters of initiation and ritual purity. The connection between early Church and Synagogue has been the matter of important studies: though these have concentrated on concrete elements rather than less tangible attitudes.

The imagery surrounding formal acts of worship in the Gospels and *Acts* does not seem to deviate from descriptions available of the Second Temple. As to worship in 'domestic' situations such as in the cases of the institution of the Mass or of Paul and Silas praying in prison, remains close to Rabbinic expectations. It would seem reasonable to suggest that, whilst a fundamental change did occur with the death and resurrection of Jesus, attitudes to worship in the early Church accepted the conventions of the Temple where the singing of psalms on behalf of the assembly by professional singers formed part of the *cultus*—on high days at least—and the concept of such acts performed on behalf of the community remained in place until the destruction of the Temple in AD 70, and in the popular mind well beyond this. With the ending of the Temple *cultus* the sacrificial element of Jewish religion was renewed in the concept of 'sacrifice of praise' reflected in Hebrews 13:15. Contemporary Judaism already identified by its variety of sects, largely delineated by their attitude to the Temple *cultus,* was thrown into confusion by the destruction of the *cultus.* The earliest followers of Jesus, representing this variety, were possibly united in worship for the first time as Christians.

In summarizing the New Testament we need to underline this problem. As the early Church grew by conversion and developed its methods of expounding the sacred revelation entrusted to it, particularly to those outside the Jewish heritage, the culture of its converts, and with it their languages attitudes and philosophies, became tools to express the Christian truth. Within the Gospels, this leads to the possibility of a variety of attitudes. Within the Epistles, especially the Pauline corpus we can detect the first expression of the important connection between internal and external disposition in worship.

THE SECOND CENTURY

The second and third centuries are, in a sense, for our topic, an introduction to the fourth century. Many of the tendencies in liturgical practice and attitudes seem apparent within the sub-apostolic literature, often amplifying scripture, but it is not until the fourth century and the Council of Laodicea that the question of liturgical functions are codified. Here again we must acknowledge a problem of interpretation as the function of the laity becomes confused with various theories about a 'development' of specific ministries within the early Christian Church. Amongst these ministries that of the cantor warrants special attention. The questions that this poses say much about attitudes towards participation. If the work of cantors is accepted as an integral and distinct part of worship, then we may accept that an attitude existed which allowed for participation at a passive level in the verbal elements of the liturgy. The writer of the *Epistle to the Antiochenes* greets, amongst others, the cantors of the Church there. [4] Whilst contemporary discussions of the passage [5] are quick to dismiss the letter itself as belonging to some centuries later, an important fact is overlooked. If the writer of this letter was not Ignatius himself it certainly was written by somebody who considered cantors to have an ancient function in the Church.

It is evident, by the terminology used, that the cantors derived their name from one of their specific responsibilities; that is, the execution of the psalter. Closely associated with any more specific identification of the cantor is the problem of the use of psalmody. The catalogue of possibilities is enormous and has been repeated many times. I do not propose to repeat such a catalogue here, save to comment that responsorial psalmody in the modern sense seems to have little foundation in arguments drawn from the literature of these early centuries. What seems certain, however, is that the execution of the psalter contained solo singing or recitation by those able or selected to do so. That a particular task existed in the execution of psalmody is clear from the *Odes of Solomon* (late first - early second century) where we read:

> As the task of the husbandman is the plough, and the task of the helms-man the steering of the ship, so also is my task the psalm of the Lord in his hymns; my craft and my occupation are in his hymns because his love has nourished my heart, and even unto my lips he poured out his fruits.

We have two important clues in developing a picture of attitudes towards participation. Firstly, an office existed that derived its name from a particular element in the early liturgy, that is psalmody, and, secondly, that early in the period these officers were able to describe this function not only as a service or something that they did with the whole assembly, but rather a profession that could be compared with others. Whilst not referring specifically to psalmody, Justin Martyr provides a picture of the appropriate milieu in which such a profession could exist, where the varying abilities of the assembly are taken into account and the only unified action actually referred to is the common assent of 'Amen'. [7]

The third century

From the point of primary evidence for the third century, the most important figure appears to be Hippolytus (c.170-236). Whilst his relationship with the See of Rome was at times uneasy, writings attributed to him give important evidence for liturgical practice in the Roman liturgical assemblies early in the century. This evidence, admittedly, has been filtered by transmission through Latin, Arabic, Coptic and Ethiopian sources: a consequent problem of terminology occurs. Only fragments of the original Greek texts survive, and for this reason we need to be cautious in definitively equating the rites that Hippolytus describes with the Roman Mass of the early third century. This, unfortunately, has not been the case with much liturgical scholarship in the twentieth century and the outline that Hippolytus describes has been frequently accepted as eucharistic rather than a sacred meal, perhaps the descendent of the *agape*. Mass or not, Hippolytus provides an important insight into functions within some form of Christian liturgical assembly at the time which was conceived as worship and as such is an appropriate quarry for finding information about attitudes to modes of participation.

> And let them arise therefore after supper and pray; let the boys sing psalms, the virgins also. And afterwards let the deacon, as he takes the

mingled chalice of oblation, say a psalm from those in which the 'Alleluia' is written. And afterwards, the presbyter so orders, again from these psalms. And after the bishop has offered the chalice, let him say a psalm from those appropriate to the chalice: always one with 'Alleluia', which all say. When they recite the psalms, let all say 'Alleluia', which means, 'We praise him who is God; glory and praise to him who created the entire world through his work alone'. And when the psalm is finished let him bless the chalice and give of its fragments to all the faithful. [8]

What is important here is the division of ministries that are described. A threefold hierarchical structure is present: bishop, priest and deacon. The responsibility for the psalmody is divided across the assembly. We note both what appears to be specific groups responsible for the singing (the Virgins and the Boys) existing alongside 'individual' use of specific parts of the psalter by individuals. Thus the psalms with 'Alleluias' (probably the final part of the canonical psalter is envisaged) are assigned to a particular office, the Deacon, whilst completing a specific liturgical action: the offering of the Chalice of Oblation.

The only united action that Hippolytus recommends is the communal uttering of 'Alleluia' at the end of the psalms. This action is given a significance beyond its literal meaning. Here a slight digression may give us a better understanding of the nature of the assembly that Hippolytus is describing. The reason for providing a translation for 'Alleluia' is significant in itself and here we move from certainties to apply a hypothesis in the origin of the *jubilus*. We know that in the earliest strata of Christian worship an ecstatic-improvisatory element persisted well into the third century. Do we have here a remnant of the practice of ecstatic song, which Hippolytus terms as 'Alleluia', but actually the starting point for a congregational musical *glossalalia*? By providing a translation of such vocalising is Hippolytus fulfilling the Pauline requirement that ecstatic utterance should be translated? [9]

> *...quid ergo est fratres cum convenitis unusquisque vestrum psalmum habet doctrinam habet apocalypsin habet linguam habet interpretationem habet omnia ad œdificationem fiant sive lingua quis loquitur secundum duos aut ut multum tres et per partes et unus interpretetur si autem non fuerit interpres taceat in ecclesia sibi autem loquatur et Deo prophetœ duo aut tres dicant et ceteri diiudicent quod si alii revelatum fuerit sedenti prior taceat potestis enim omnes per singulos prophetare ut omnes discant et omnes exhortentur.*

1Cor.14:26-28

Such phenomena would not be strange to a contemporary Pentecostal sectarian and the ululations of some of the Oriental churches, and the drones of Byzantine chant, would seem to be descendants from a practice which in the West survived as the *jubilus melisma* now concluding the verses of the 'Alleluias' in the *Graduale*. The corpus of melodic fragments that are assembled to make a single Gregorian composition is remarkably limited for the greater part and the transition from the standardization of improvised elements finally being written down is a hypothesis that merits some attention when considering the origins of the official chant of the Church.

The position, then, that is revealed within the worshipping assembly of the third century is one where a hierarchy of function may be matched to vocalization. It presumes, without any censure, that specific groups and individuals have responsibility for the larger part of the psalmody. The identification of two particular groups in relation to the execution of the psalms is important, and indicates the early admissibility of specialist talent in the worship of the whole assembly. Whilst *participatio actuosa* is not specifically mentioned, the picture given reveals listening as a valid action of participation. If we accept the hypothesis that the 'Alleluia' indicated some sort of ecstatic or improvised vocalization then we may commence to consider the possibility that both internal and external dispositions may have maintained. Whether such a nicety of distinction is something that the third century mind would make cannot be certain.

THE FOURTH CENTURY

From the fourth century it is very difficult to speak in generalizations about the liturgical practice of the laity in the early Church. As we get closer to our own time, the amount of primary evidence extant increases rapidly, and evidence clearly datable to this century is in greater abundance than in the previous centuries. With the growth of Christianity in the Roman world, and the decline of state persecution, the faith came out from its shadowy existence, at least in documentary evidence, into the official records of the culture. From this great diversity however one clear 'development' must be noted: that of the clear existence of the cantor as an official officer of the Church. This development has been well documented by several scholars who have unfortunately commenced from an *'argumentum e silencio'* and neglected identifying the cantor in the earlier centuries.

It is clear from earlier sources that cantors existed, even if they were not called such, and that clear legislation for particular roles in worship is significant in the continuing 'dual understanding' of participation. The common interpretation of the emergence of the cantor at this point is that here we have the beginnings of the clericalization of the liturgy; that the clergy, among whom the cantors are now counted, began to usurp participatory functions from the laity in some way diminishing the proper participation of the latter which was only to be restored 1500 years later. This, we suggest, is a defective reading of the evidence to hand and, rather, the cantor continued in his function during the fourth century much as he had been expected to in the previous centuries.

The problem of interpretation is complicated by difficulties in understanding the large body of references to the singing, by the whole assembly, of psalms. At times these references can be amusing particularly when the complaint is raised that it is difficult to keep the congregation silent during the readings as they seem to be eager for the next psalm to start! These references are a strong body of evidence for the nature of liturgical singing of the psalter at the time, particularly with verses frequently cited as the response that the congregation sang. But the response to what? We have previously noted that there are difficulties in determining the mode of this response and the motivation for such congregational singing is unclear. If one is to read S. Ambrose literally, these responsorial elements belong principally to the Synaxis of the Eucharist [10] serving to keep the attention of the congregation (*Explanatio Psalmorum* I, 9) rather than being an expression of any inner disposition. [11] Such an interpretation is reinforced by St Ambrose's discussion of the soloistic nature of psalmody within the same context and the explicit division of ministries according to ability, including the cantor:

> One is considered better qualified to enunciate a reading, another more pleasing with a psalm, another more solicitous to exorcize those burdened by an evil spirit, and another more suited to have charge of the sacred things. [12]

It is difficult to gauge what actually happened first. A 'traditional' view, certainly behind much twentieth century thought, is that the congregation participated in the psalmody in a responsorial manner from the earliest times; that is, that a particular verse was selected and repeated by the congregation at the end of verses sung by a solo singer. Whilst this might seem the simplest solution to the multiple references to 'responses' throughout the fourth century, several problems with such an interpretation may be observed. The actual origins of such a practice are obscure and whilst certain psalms have repetitive phrases in their structure (e.g. Psalm 135), they are unusual enough within the psalter to disallow the formulation of a principle. The little that we do know about worship from the time of the Second Temple until its destruction, is that professional musicians were responsible for the execution of the psalter and that its performance was considered vicariously sacrificial, the work of an elite, by some reforming groups within Judaism. Alternative theories proposing the influence of Greek theatre, and particularly the chorus, need to be tested.

The fifth century

In the West, the fifth century is dominated by references from the works of St Augustine. I do not propose to examine this seminal corpus here as it really deserves a study in its own right. Sufficient to say that in St Augustine, and the other western authors of the fifth century, the vast majority of references containing participation terminology deal with psalmody and its method of use in the Christian community. In contrast to the East, psalmody appears to have been enshrined in the West as an essential ingredient of the Eucharistic Synaxis only during this century and thus the proliferation of liturgical references probably needs to be interpreted in the light of this 'late' establishment of psalmody in Western rites. Acceptance of the psalter as an ancient way of worship is evidenced by Hilary of Poitiers' extensive examination of the superscriptions in the psalters deriving from the Septuagint; [13] however, the psalms as valid means of participation seem to be a continuing problem in the West if the following passage from Niceta of Remesiana is to read as defending contemporary practice:

> Thus, beloved, let us sing with alert senses and a wakeful mind, as the psalmist exhorts: 'Because God is king of all the earth', he says, 'sing ye wisely' (Ps. 46:8), so that a psalm is sung not only with the spirit, that is, the sound of the voice, but with the mind also (1Cor. 14:15), and so that we think of what we sing rather than allow our mind, seized by extraneous thoughts, as is often the case, to lose the fruit of our labour. One must sing with a manner and melody befitting holy religion; it must not proclaim theatrical distress but rather exhibit Christian simplicity in its very musical movement; it must not remind one of anything theatrical, but rather create compunction in the listeners.
>
> Further, our voice ought not to be dissonant but consonant. One ought not to drag out the singing while another cuts it short, and one ought not to sing too low while another raises his voice. Rather, each should strive to integrate his voice within the sound of the harmonious chorus and not project it outwardly in the manner of a cithara as if to make immodest display... And for him who is not able to blend and fit himself with the others, it is better to sing in a subdued voice than to make a great noise, for thus he performs both his liturgical function and avoids disturbing the singing brotherhood. [14]

Again we find a lot of technical language whose significance is easily missed in translation. That Niceta of Remesiana is concerned with the duality of participation seems likely. Not only is he concerned for the cooperation of 'alert senses' and a 'wakeful mind' but parallels this distinction with a 'spiritual singing' and an 'intellectual singing'. Furthermore, levels of participation determined by ability are explicit. Throughout the fifth century, then, drawing on the clear distinctions discerned in the fourth century, a significant part of the Eucharistic Synaxis is placed into the hands of skilled professionals. This is not without some misgivings, and the excesses of the cantors is criticized in St Jerome, [15] particularly when inner disposition fails to live up to the external skill. [16] However, the united evidence remains in this century of the essential role that solo singing continued to play in the liturgy; indeed, at times, the presence of choral singing seems to be doubtful:

When, therefore, they come together to conduct the aforementioned services, which they call synaxes, all maintain such silence that even though so great a number of brethren assemble, one would believe no man to be present except he who rises in their midst to sing the psalm... [17]

It is clear from Cassian however that this act of singing is considered to be 'congregational activity'. He has to make clear that the attention of the congregation is demanded during such solos and he only begrudgingly allows the congregation to sit during such acts of worship [18] because of weariness.

The sixth century

The Rule of Saint Benedict properly belongs to the sixth Century; however, the liturgical code (Chapters 8-20) reflect the synthesis of ideals from the earlier centuries, monastic and cathedral, adapted for St Benedict's ideal Christian community, which he describes as a 'school of the Lord's service'. [19]

To what extent the Rule is dependent on *The Rule of the Master* has been debated. Earlier scholarship presumed that *The Rule of the Master* was a later elaboration of the Rule—largely because of its greater length and detailed prescriptions—however, since the 1930s serious attention has been paid to the thesis that the longer work is actually a precursor of the *Rule of Saint Benedict* and was indeed a primary source when Benedict set down his rule for the monasteries. The earliest extant texts of the *Rule* are from the ninth century, and given the injunctions within the *Rule* itself, for authority to alter the liturgical code to suit the needs of the community, some care needs to be observed in immediately applying what the *Rule* describes to the time of St Benedict himself.

Outside the liturgical code itself is an important principle which is immediately apposite to our study of attitudes towards participation. In Chapter 47 an interesting principle is given:

> *Psalmos autem vel antiphonas post abbatem ordine suo quibus iussum fuerit imponant. Cantare autem et legere non præsumat nisi qui potest ipsud officium implere ut ædificentur audientes: quod cum humilitate et gravitate et tremore fiat, et cui iusserit abbas.* [20]

One advantage of an examination of the *Rule* for participation is that it presumes a situation which is largely lay, as clerics remain largely an adjunct to the question of the just celebration of the Divine Office. The *Rule* has surprisingly little to say about the regulation of the Mass liturgy. We are dealing, then, with a description of liturgical worship where distinctive functions, because of clerical rank, are largely absent. St Benedict only permits clerics preferential allocation if the abbot has placed them in community order above the date of their entrance to the monastery. [21]

Given this 'level playing field' three points may be noted: (i) That the 'active' participation of certain monks to execute certain items of the liturgy is to be favoured because of their particular musical gifts. (ii) That a quality of performance is required so that it is edifying to the hearer. (iii) That this function is authorized by the abbot and must be undertaken 'with humility, seriousness and reverence'. This style of regulation is not found in the *Rule of the Master* but does seem consistent with the earlier style found in Roman liturgical sources. Do we have here the codification of a Roman Basilican attitude to worship? It seems clear from the earlier documentation that we have covered, that participation in worship did not presume actual verbal participation—or at least the right to do so—for all the faithful. There were certain members that, because of their particular gifts, were assigned certain parts of the liturgy. It is not even a matter of doing it on behalf of the assembly—that is the distinction of a much later age—but rather viewed as part of an integral whole.

The end of the sixth century brings us to an interesting point in liturgical history. It is here that the classical form of the Roman Rite is supposed to have been completed with all the essential characteristics that were appealed to by the liturgical movement at the commencement of this century. It is the interpretation of this 'classical' form which poses problems, as matters are often emphasized which reflect contemporary concerns rather than reality.

Conclusions

I would like to conclude with four points which, I believe, are common to the literary witness of the first seven centuries. This, I suggest, was the heritage surrounding *participatio actuosa* in the period immediately following the regularization of the monasteries and the rise of 'families' of liturgical books.

Firstly, throughout the first seven centuries of Christianity, there is constant witness in the West to the presence of solo material, be it said or sung, within Christian liturgy. This immediately presumes that the Christians in the first centuries understood valid worship both passively and actively. This is true for the East as well.

Secondly, in specifically musical terms, there is no indication that the Christians throughout this period understood solo elements in the Church's liturgy as being in any way exclusive of the Assembly unless the allocation of ministry according to ability is to be considered exclusive.

Thirdly, the presence of professional officials in the liturgy (cantors, lectors, doorkeepers *et al.*) with specific duties, is nowhere described as depriving the Assembly of duties rightly belonging to it. Whilst certain reservations may be observed about abuses amongst these groups the validity of solo singing remains distinct from the abuse.

Finally, the etymological characteristics of terms used in describing participation in worship in the earliest centuries, allow for both an interior and exterior disposition. These were inherited from the worship of temple, early synagogue, and to some degree from pagan worship cults, and are present as a 'dual understanding' of *participatio actuosa* within the earliest stratum of the Christian tradition: an understanding that clearly persisted in the theory and practice of Western Christianity throughout the first seven centuries.

SELECT BIBLIOGRAPHY

—Primary Sources

• *Biblical references*

——, Η ΠΑΛΑΙΑ ΔΙΑΘΗΚΗ ΚΑΤΑ ΤΟΨΣ ῞Ο (Ελληνικη Βιβλικη Εταιρια Οδοσ Εμμ Μπενακὴ. 50 Αθηνα) [*Septuaginta Id est Vetus Testamentum græce iuxta LXX interpretes* ed. A. Rahlfs. (Stuttgart: Deutsche Bibelgesellschaft, 1979)]

——, *Biblia Sacra Iuxta Vulgatem Versionem* ed. R. Webber (Stuttgart: Deutsche Bibelgesellschaft, 1994)

——, *The Greek New Testament* ed. K. Aland et.al. (Stuttgart: United Bible Societies, 1983.)

——, *The Old and New Testaments of the Holy Bible: Revised Standard Version* 2nd edition (Nashville, Nelson, 1972)

• *Patristic references*

Migne, J.P. (ed.) *Patrologiæ cursus completus, Series Græca* (Paris: 1857-1866) 162 vols.

———— , *Patrologiæ cursus completus, Series Latina* (Paris: 1844-1864) 221 vols. repr. post 1868.

McKinnon, James, *Music in Early Christian Literature* (Cambridge: CUP, 1987)

• *Conciliar Documents*

Tanner, Norman (ed.), *Decrees of the Ecumenical Councils Volume I (Nicæa I- Lateran V)* (London: Sheed and Ward, 1990)

Schaff, P. and Wace, H., (eds.) *A Select Library of Nicene and Post-Nicene Fathers of the Christian Church. Second Series. Volume XIV. The Seven Ecumenical Councils.* (Grand Rapids: Eerdmans, 1974)

• *Editions of early texts*

RB 1980 *The Rule of St Benedict In Latin and English with Notes* (ed. T. Fry) Collegeville, Liturgical Press, 1981.

—Secondary Sources

Apel, Willi., *Gregorian Chant* (Bloomington: Indiana University Press, 1958)

Foley, Edward, 'The Cantor in Historical Perspective' in *Worship LVI, No 3* (1982) 194- 213.

Hauck, Friedrich, 'κοινο' in *Theological Dictionary of the New Testament* ed. G.Kittel (Grand Rapids: Eerdmans, 1967) Volume III, 797-809 tr. G. Bromley. Originally published as *Theologisches Wörterbuch zum Neuen Testament* (Stuttgart: W. Kohlhammer Verlag, 1965)

Hayburn, Robert, *Papal Legislation on Sacred Music. 95 A.D. to 1977 A.D.* (Collegeville: Liturgical Press, 1979)

Hiley, David, *Western Plainchant: A Handbook* (Oxford: Clarendon, 1993)

McKinnon, James, *Man and Music: Antiquity and the Middle Ages from Ancient Greece to the 15th century.* (Basingstoke: Macmillan, 1990)

————, *Music in Early Christian Literature* (Cambridge: CUP, 1987)

Nichols, Aidan, *Looking at the Liturgy: A Critical View of its Contemporary Form* (San Francisco: Ignatius Press, 1996)

Skeris, Robert. A, 'Participatio Actuosa in Theological and Musical Perspective- Documentary Considerations' in *Sacred Music Volume 117, Number 4,* (Winter 1990) originally published in *Divini Cultus Studium* (Altötting: Verlag Alfred Coppenrath, 1990)

Werner, Eric, *The Sacred Bridge: The Interdependence of Liturgy and Music in Synagogue and Church during the First Millennium* (London: Dennis Dobson, 1959)

NOTES

1. Skeris, R.A., 'Participatio Actuosa in Theological and Musical perspective-Documentary considerations' in *Sacred Music Volume 117, Number 4,* (Winter 1990) originally published in his *Divini Cultus Studium.* (Altötting: Verlag Alfred Coppenrath, 1990).

2. RSV 'The cup of blessing which we bless, is it not a participation in the blood of Christ? The bread which we break, is it not a participation in the body of Christ?' GNT τὸ ποτήριον τῆς εὐλογίας ὃ εὐλογοῦμεν, οὐχὶ κοινωνία τοῦ αἵματος τοῦ Χριστοῦ ἐστι; τὸν ἄρτον ὃν κλῶμεν, οὐχὶ κοινωνία τοῦ σώματος τοῦ Χριστοῦ ἐστιν;

3. RSV 1Cor. 10:18: 'Consider the people of Israel; are not those who eat the sacrifices *partners* in the altar?' GNT 1Co 10:18 βλέπετε τὸν Ἰσραὴλ κατὰ σάρκα· οὐχ οὐκ οἱ ἐσθίοντες τὰς θυσίας κοινωνοὶ τοῦ θυσιαστηρίου εἰσίν.

4. Pseudo-Ignatius, *Antiochenes* xii, 1-2. Migne, J.P. (ed.) *Patrologiæ Cursus Completus, Series Græca* (Paris: 1857-1866) 162 vols. v, 908. After this as PG.

5. See Foley, Edward, 'The Cantor in Historical Perspective' in Worship LVI, No 3 (1982) 194-213 and McKinnon, James, *Man and Music: Antiquity and the Middle Ages from Ancient Greece to the 15th century.* (Basingstoke: Macmillan, 1990).

6. Ode xvi, 1-2. Cited by McKinnon, James, Music in *Early Christian Literature* (Cambridge: CUP, 1987) pp. 23-24.

7. *Apology* 1, 67: PG vi.

8. *Apostolic Tradition* 25 cited in McKinnon, p. 47.

9. [GNT] Τί οὖν ἐστιν, ἀδελφοί; ὅταν συνέρχησθε, ἕκαστος ψαλμὸν ἔχει, διδαχὴν ἔχει, ἀποκάλυψιν ἔχει, γλῶσσαν ἔχει, ἑρμηνείαν ἔχει· πάντα πρὸς οἰκοδομὴν γινέσθω. εἴτε γλώσσῃ τις λαλεῖ, κατὰ δύο ἢ τὸ πλεῖστον τρεῖς καὶ ἀνὰ μέρος, καὶ εἷς διερμηνευέτω· ἐὰν δὲ μὴ ᾖ διερμηνευτής, σιγάτω ἐν ἐκκλησίᾳ, ἑαυτῷ δὲ λαλείτω καὶ τῷ θεῷ.

[RSV] 'What then, brethren? When you come together, each one has a hymn, a lesson, a revelation, a tongue, or an interpretation. Let all things be done for edification. If any speak in a tongue, let there be only two or at most three, and each in turn; and let one interpret. But if there is no one to interpret, let each of them keep silence in church and speak to himself and to God'.

10. McKinnon, p. 127.

11. Migne, J.P. (ed.), *Patrologiæ Cursus Completus, Series Latina* (Paris: 1844-1864) 221 vols. repr. post 1868.xiv, 924-5. After this as PL.

12. PL xvi, 87.

13. *Instructione Psalmorum* 19, PL IX, 244.

14. *De Utilitate Hymnorum* 13 trans. in McKinnon, p. 138.

15. Epistle LII, *Ad Nepotianum Presbyterum 5;* PL xxii, 532

16. *Commentarium in Epistolam ad Ephesios* iii, v 19; PL xxvi, 528-529.

17. John Cassian, *De Institutis* ii, 10; PL xlix, 97-98.

18. *ibid.* 112; PL xlix, 102.

19. 'Dominici schola servitii'. RB 1980: *The Rule of St Benedict In Latin and English with Notes* (ed. T. Fry) Collegeville, Liturgical Press, 1981. Prol. 45. After this as RB.

20. *RB* XLVII. ' Only those authorized are to lead psalms and refrains, after the abbot according to their rank. No one should presume to read or sing unless he is able to benefit the hearers; let this be done with humility, seriousness and reverence, and at the abbot's bidding.'

21 *RB* LXI, 12

LAY PARTICIPATION IN THE EUCHARISTIC LITURGY OF THE LATER MIDDLE AGES

Joseph A. Gribbin

Dr Joseph Gribbin was born in 1967 and graduated in history at St Mary's College, Middlesex. Following a period as Master of Ceremonies at the English National Shrine of the Blessed Virgin at Walsingham, he obtained a Master's degree in history at Cambridge University as a student of Christ's College and later completed his doctoral thesis on the English Premonstratensians during the high Middle Ages. Dr Gribbin's works on the Carthusian liturgy were published in the Analecta Cartusiana *and he has written numerous articles on the subject. At present, Dr Gribbin is preparing publication of various liturgical manuscripts in pursuit of his works on monasticism, liturgy, and English and Scottish mediæval church history*

INTRODUCTION

IN the *Assertionum Regis Angliæ Defensio,* St John Fisher (d.1535), Bishop of Rochester and future Catholic martyr, wrote the following in defence of the Mass: 'He who goes about to take the Sacrifice [of the Mass] from the Church plots no less a calamity than if he tried to snatch the sun from the universe'.[1] The centrality of the Eucharist in the mediæval Church, so evident in Fisher's words, is beyond dispute. Nevertheless it is generally believed that the role of the mediæval laity in the *Mysterium Fidei,* was, at best, largely minimal, and, at worst, completely absent. One liturgist expressed the view that:

> The Mass, in the course of time - not only because of the language barrier, but primarily as a result of it - had become purely the priest's Mass. The people were silent spectators, by no means lacking in devotion, but unliturgical... In the cathedrals, chapters and foundations with their own clerical worship, services increasingly divided the clerical liturgy from that of the people, so that the stone screen in front of the choir strikingly documented the situation... Mediæval liturgy had, for the most part, lost

its power to exercise influence on popular, private devotion.

Another author wrote that,

> The infrequency of communion was not the only sign of the progressive
> decline through the Middle Ages in active participation of the faithful in
> the Eucharist...[for example] the abandonment of a donation of the gifts
> by the faithful...the multiplication of private Masses...the use of a lan-
> guage increasingly different from that spoken by the people...[etc.] All
> these factors turned the laity into onlookers so passive that the liturgical
> books no longer even mentioned their presence. [2]

Though most of these conclusions were reached many years ago, largely by
scholars with sincere intentions, they seem to have gained greater credibility
recently, in an era when the Church's desire for *actuosa participatio* in the
liturgy is often subjected to inappropriate interpretations.[3] In other words,
mediæval liturgy and lay participation are frequently seen solely in the light of
modern liturgical perspectives, which may not be entirely well-founded and
can be limited by an incomplete knowledge, or handling of historical sources.
It is also the case that historical research continues to make progress, building
upon and sometimes modifying previous scholarly endeavours. This paper will
propose that the role of the laity in the Roman Rite Mass in mediæval Europe
was not 'spectator-orientated' or generally characterized by inactivity, but
mainly participatory.[4] The evidence which will be presented here will largely,
though not exclusively, originate from English late mediæval sources. Admittedly this calls for several caveats. Certain European regions possessed forms
of spirituality, culture and mentality which characterized those areas. As well
as linguistic differences, one must allow for individual devotional preferences.
However apparent drawbacks can be illusory. Devotional texts used in England circulated elsewhere in Western Christendom, which shared a common
faith and religious practices.[5]

THE EXPOSITIONES MISSÆ

We must first establish how mediæval theologians and liturgical commentators
understood the Eucharistic liturgy, and thus how the laity were to understand
and participate in the Mass. Allegorical interpretations of each liturgical prayer,
vestment and ceremony, mainly aligned to events in the life and Passion of
Christ, predominated the popular *Expositiones Missæ*. This is apparent in the
influential writings of Amalarius of Metz (775-852), and later, for instance, in
De Divinis Officiis of Rupert von Deutz (d. 1129), who stressed the narrative of
Christ's life, and John Beleth (d.1165) in his *Summa de Ecclesiasticis Officiis*,
which was influenced by neo-platonism. Viewing the Mass in terms of Christ's
Passion is apparent in the *Rationale Divinorum Officiorum* by William Durandus
(1230-96), who was the greatest compiler of Mass allegory in the middle ages.
Durandus and other authors owed much to another important work, *De Mysteriis*

Missæ (c.1195) by Cardinal Lothar of Segni, the future Pope Innocent III. [6]

Aside from allegorical methods, other writings interpreted the Mass within the context of the liturgical texts, especially in the thirteenth century. This is exemplified in St Albert the Great's (c.1200-80) *De Sacrificio Missæ* (1270). Albert divided the Mass into three parts : firstly the *Introitus,* from the beginning until the collects; the *Instructio,* which ended after the Credo; and lastly the *Oblatio.* Albert's speculative approach to the Mass had moral and even mystical overtones, but spurned allegorical explanations.[7] Some works gave literal and 'spiritual' interpretations of the *Canon Missæ,* including Gabriel Biel's (c.1412-95) *Canonis Misse Expositio.* [8] Other authors interpreted the Mass allegorically, but also paid varying degrees of attention to the purpose or actual meaning of the liturgical texts. For instance, Aquinas explained that the invocations of the *Kyrie* can refer to each person of the Holy Trinity, and that the Alleluia signified spiritual exaltation. He also says that in the *Credo* the people assent to Christ's teaching, and that by the reading of the Epistle and Gospel, and the singing of the *Credo,* they are instructed and prepared, and can move on *'ad celebrationem mysterii'.* [9] However it must be emphasized that interpreting the Mass allegorically held sway until the end of the middle ages.[10]

As regards the laity, most writers therefore placed the Mass liturgy before them as a *'memoria passionis'* and essentially a sacred action done by the priest. They proposed that Mass was also offered on their behalf, whether or not they were physically present. In addition the laity were expected to pray during Mass in a form akin to 'affective' prayer. As early as Amalarius, the *Orate Fratres* was re-interpreted to become an 'exhortation' to the people. [11] In his *De Mysteriis Missæ* Pope Innocent III explained that:

> Although only one offers the Sacrifice [i.e. the priest], nevertheless he speaks in the plural: 'We offer', since the priest sacrifices not only in his own, but in the person of the entire Church'.[12]

John Burchard in his *Ordo Missæ* (1502) proposed that even if the people did not understand the priest's words or any Latin they should

> …not say any other prayers but should pay attention to what the priest is saying and doing and should in spirit offer up, supplicate and plead along with him except during the time when the Sacrament is adored, and at that place in the Canon where he (at the *Memento*) prays softly by himself: then one could likewise freely pray for oneself and for all those whom one wishes to commend to God.

Burchard even desired the congregation to answer the liturgical responses, which had generally fallen into disuse: though silent prayer during Mass was insisted upon from earlier times. [13]

Comprehension of Liturgical Language

A wide degree of latitude was allowed to the laity concerning the methods or aids which they could use to pray and meditate during Mass. Before examining these we ought to consider the following question: while lay participation in the mediæval Mass was not generally viewed as entailing complete comprehension of the Latin liturgical words, or answering the liturgical responses, to what extent was liturgical language a barrier to lay participation when the vast majority of people could not possibly speak Latin fluently or possess a satisfactory knowledge of it? Surely the unintelligibility of the liturgical texts meant that they were a 'closed book'? While Latin was, indeed, largely incomprehensible, there is evidence which indicates that the laity probably possessed varying degrees of Latin comprehension. Though Margery Kempe (fl. 1373-1438), a devout woman from King's Lynn in Norfolk, was illiterate, she possessed the ability to recognise and speak some Latin words. For example in one chapter of her dictated biography it is related that a priest was willing to hear her confession, and that she should go to him '...in the name of Jesus and say her *Confiteor*...'. [14] It also seems that members of the lower classes understood the significance of certain Latin liturgical words. Eamon Duffy has shown that the Office of *Dirige* and *Placebo* from the Office of the Dead, would have been familiar to lay people, considering the emphasis on praying for the dead in the middle ages. Evidence in English wills indicates '...provision for lettered paupers [and laymen] to recite both the Little office [of our Lady] and the *Dirige*...' and that poor men could be found capable of reciting all or part of the primer offices for the dead. Liturgical words became well known because of the ceremonies they were attached to, even if not entirely understood, and Latin texts were looked upon as sacred. The prologue of St John's Gospel ('*In Principio*'), was a familiar text to the laity, as it was recited after Mass.[15] Due to the repetition of liturgical texts, the acquisition of a very basic knowledge of key liturgical texts and phrases is likely to have been a reality. This would afford the laity with varying degrees of familiarity with the liturgical ceremonies, especially as many lay people attended Mass daily. As in ancient times, mediæval men and women apparently had a greater capacity for memorizing texts as there was greater emphasis on aural listening in that period.[16] As education and literacy levels appeared to increase in Europe in the later middle ages and printing made reading material more accessible, varying degrees of comprehension of Latin texts increased.[17]

It is likely that catechesis and preaching also made a contribution to the people's limited knowledge of Latin. Some sermons actually contained explanations and vernacular translations of the Latin liturgy and, as we shall see, biblical texts. A very popular English book of sermons called the Festial, by John Mirk, a canon of Lilleshall in Shropshire (c.1380's?), not only gives moral interpretations of biblical and liturgical texts, but also aspects of the liturgy. In a sermon for Septuagesima Sunday, for instance, Mirk says the following about the introit:

...to meditate on death inwardly, Holy Church provides an example thus in the office [i.e. introit] of the Mass. There it says... *Circumdederunt me gemitus mortis,* which is in English, 'The lamentations of death have embraced me'.

On the penitential nature of Septuagesima, Mirk writes that,

...Holy Church...sets aside Alleluias and other melodious songs, and brings out tractus, which are songs of mourning, and searching, and longing. [18]

Individuals with greater literacy levels, such as Margaret Beaufort, mother of Henry VII of England, and Richard Hill, a grocer from London (c.1520), probably knew more Latin than those further down the social ladder. A Christmas poem in Hill's commonplace book cited the first lines of several seasonal liturgical hymns. St John Fisher commented that Margaret Beaufort possessed

...a little understanding [of Latin], especially of the rubrics of the ordinal in order to say her prayers ['servyce'], which she well understood.

Though Margaret's Latin was not fluent, it did not prevent her from using Latin prayers and offices, and she apparently made efforts to improve her Latin. [19]

BOOKS OF HOURS AND LAY MASS BOOKS

How would lay people have prayed during Mass? Those who were literate could have chosen a variety of devotional books. Amongst these were the Latin *Primer* or *Book of Hours,* also known as *Horæ* in England. Although their content often reflects their place of origin they mainly contained liturgical and quasi-liturgical prayers such as the Office of Our Lady, the seven penitential psalms, the fifteen gradual psalms, and the Office of the Dead. A variety of Latin and vernacular prayers were often added to the Horæ by their owners. [20] The accessibility of this literature increased with the advent of printing. It has been estimated that, before the 1530s, 114 editions of the Latin *Horæ* were printed for lay use in England alone, and that two generations prior to the Reformation, there were in the region of 57,000 printed Latin *Horæ* in circulation. Sarum Use *Horæ* were printed in London, Paris, Rouen, and Antwerp. [21]

Another variety of books were specifically designed for use during Mass, or for preparation beforehand. These enabled lay people to follow the liturgical ceremonies, and to express appropriate devotional sentiments. Allegorical *Explanations of the Mass* were made available by Simon of Venlo. Gherit vander Goude's *Dat Boexken vander Missen,* first printed in Antwerp in c.1507, was mainly allegorical, but was still extremely useful. It contained woodcuts illustrating each stage of the Mass, with directions for the reader's instruction. [22] More advanced forms of lay Mass books are apparent in the *Missale Vulgare* produced in Germany (early 15th cent. onwards), with translations of liturgical texts and scriptural readings. [23] Various *Lay Folks' Mass Books* and Mass guides existed in England. Examples of the latter are John Audelay's lengthy poem, *De Meritis Missæ, Quomodo Debemus Audire Missam* (c.1420); the *Interpretation and Virtues of the Mass* (c.1430-40's) by the Benedictine author John Lydgate; and *Meditations for Ghostly Exercise, in the Time of Mass* (late 1520s), now thought to have been composed by William Bonde, a Bridgettine of Syon Abbey. [24] Lydgate's *Interpretation*, for instance, recommended the lay reader to

> ...anticipate and understand the action of the altar... [Lydgate] directs his explanation of the significance of clerical gestures, vestments, words, to an active and well-informed participant, who is led from moment of entry into the church and until the *Ite*, with a clear high-point at the consecration. Priest and lay participant are exhorted here as they receive cues from and keep a vigilant eye over each other's actions.

It encouraged the reader to pray, and properly dispose himself during Mass. [25]

Of particular interest is the *Lay Folks' Mass Book*, which was originally written in French for an English readership in the late twelfth or early thirteenth century. It was translated into English and exists in several versions, and was still used during the later middle ages. [26] This book also allowed one to follow the basic Mass ceremonies and to pray during low Mass, for which it was mainly designed. In many respects the *Lay Folks' Mass Book* brought lay readers into even closer union with the liturgical texts and ceremonies than other methods of Mass participation, though it was not entirely divorced from methods of prayer which the illiterate used and provided plenty of scope for private prayer. It also gave directions on when to stand and kneel. At the Offertory, for example, the reader is exhorted to

> Take care that you are saying the Our Father whilst the priest is privately praying; afterwards the priest will move himself a little distance in that place, until he comes to the middle of the altar. Stand up, when he summons men in heart and body...Then he begins *Per omnia*, and next 'Lift up your hearts'. At the end he says *Sanctus* three times...

Though the Mass book's prayers do not entirely reproduce the priest's words verbatim, many of them clearly derived from the liturgical prayers, and in places were translations of the Latin text. The *Confiteor* was written in this way:

> I acknowledge to God almighty, and to his mother, the bright Virgin, and to all the saints here, and to you spiritual father, that I have sinned greatly, in many different sins, of thought, of speech, and of delight, in word and in action...Therefore I beg St Mary and all the holy saints...and you, priest...to pray for me.

The Confiteor in a missal of the Sarum Use reads,

Confiteor Deo, beate Mariæ, omnibus sanctis, et vobis, quia peccavi nimis cogitatione, locutione et opere, mea culpa. Precor sanctam Mariam omnes sanctos Dei, et vos, orare pro me. [27]

There is also evidence which suggests that in some areas, vocal, liturgical responses, apart from vernacular prayers, were still expected of the laity to a certain degree. After the priest recited the *Pater noster,* the reader is exhorted to,

> ...answer at 'temptation' 'But deliver us from evil Amen'. There should be no need to instruct you on this for those who do not know it are ignorant people. When this is done, say privately another prayer together with it. Our Father first in Latin, and then in English. [28]

One should add here that the custom of intercessory prayers on Sunday, known as 'prone', were widely attested in England, France, Germany and Italy. [29]

The reader of the *Lay Folks' Mass Book* was also instructed that

> When the priest speaks, or if he sings, you should listen well to him: when he prays privately, that is a time for you to pray.

This makes an interesting liturgical distinction, albeit a broad one, between the private and public prayers uttered by the priest. We should also note that these Mass books contain indications that the laity followed the actions of the priest at close quarters. Not only was Mass celebrated in the chancel/sanctuary, but also at side altars, especially during the week, which were often at arms length from the congregation. Though we must make allowances for screens where these existed - especially at the entrance of the chancel and designs peculiar to certain regions, they did not entirely remove the altar from the people's view.[30] For instance the *Lay Folks' Mass Book* relates that during the canon the reader was to

> Make sure you are saying Our Father until he [i.e. the priest] is making a cross over the chalice: then the time for the sacring [i.e. the consecration/elevation] is near. People usually ring a little bell; then you shall pay reverence to Jesus Christ's own presence [in the Host]...Kneeling, hold up both your hands, and so behold the elevation.

Symbols were extremely important in the middle ages. They

> ...convey knowledge...are emotionally packed...communicate information, and induce moods which cannot always be expressed in words.

This is applicable to the affect that liturgical ceremonies would have had on the laity. [31]

POPULAR METHODS OF LAY PARTICIPATION

We must now turn to other ways of lay participation, especially methods taught to illiterate people. Before and after the Fourth Lateran Council (1215) a whole range of vernacular and Latin pastoral literature was provided for the education of priests and to enable them to teach the Catholic Faith to their flocks. Some manuals helped the priest to understand liturgical practice and Eucharistic theology, thus equipping him to say Mass better and disseminate knowledge to the laity: for example the *Oculum Sacerdotis* (c.1320-30) of William of Pagula, the *Manipulus Curatorum* (1333) written by Guy of Montrocher, and the *Alphabetum seu Instructio Sacerdotum*. [32] John Mirk's vernacular *Instructions for Parish Priests* (early fifteenth century), and other works, gave guidance on how lay people were to be taught to behave during Mass, and paid particular emphasis to gesture, indicating that a degree of external unity was envisaged for the congregation. These gestures allowed the laity to externalise their devotions, and thus harmonise the worship of their bodies with the worship offered by their souls. Mirk says that the laity were to refrain from earthly vanity and to

> ...say here [a] *Pater noster* and there [an] *Ave*...kneeling upon the ground, to pray to God with a humble heart, that they may each be granted grace and mercy...[At the Gospel they were to]...Stand up, and bless themselves and when [the] *Gloria tibi* is begun, to kneel down...

At the Elevation 'both young and old' were to kneel and raise their hands, and pray. The *Paters* and *Aves* were recited on strings of beads akin to the modern rosary. The laity could also gaze on woodcuts, particularly those of Christ's crucifixion. We should take into account what we related earlier about a basic familiarity with liturgical procedures and the wide scope for private prayer. [33] Much lay devotion which both literate and illiterate laity used, and evidence for the use of literature by all classes of society, strongly suggests that despite individual preferences and the occurrence of private chapels in many upper class households, distinctions between 'learned' ('elite') and 'popular' religion are highly questionable. [34] To some extent external activity by the laity during Mass weakens arguments that lay participation was purely internal.

What about lay participation by listening to sermons? [35] Though the use of written sermons, especially those in Latin, has to be viewed cautiously—some sermons were probably only devotional texts—many of them appear to reflect the methods used in preaching sermons and their content, which mainly concerned moral conduct and *caritas* within the Christian community. Sermons were preached during Mass and outside it, throughout mediæval Europe, perhaps frequently, especially on Sundays and feasts. [36] John Mirk's popular Festal sermons were tailor-made for the liturgical year, and provided explanations of the epistles and gospels for Sundays and feast days. [37] Sermons of this nature, in the vernacular, allowed more lay comprehension of the scriptures. To some extent they lifted the Latin veil over the proclamation of the *Verbum Dei*.

Another series of sermons, called the *Miroir,* were translated into a local vernacular dialect by a Premonstratensian canon of Welbeck Abbey in Nottinghamshire in 1432. It contained sermons on the Gospel texts used from Advent to the 24th Sunday after Pentecost, and their format implies that they were probably designed for delivery during Mass. As well as commenting on each Latin Gospel text, translations were also provided. For example, the Gospel for the seventh Sunday after Pentecost, from St Matthew, concerns false prophets who are wolves in sheep's clothing

> *Attendite a falsis* [*'salsis'* in ms.] *prophetis...*Jesus said these words to his disciples: 'keep yourselves from false prophets that suddenly come to you clothed white as sheep, but are ravishing wolves within'. [38]

When one takes into consideration the other methods the Church employed in conveying her biblical message, such as stained glass and wall paintings, and paraphrases of the life of Christ, like *The Mirror of the Blessed Lyf of Jesu Christ* by the English Carthusian Nicholas Love, one cannot consider that the lack of vernacular bibles in England in the late middle ages - and the rest of Europe for that matter - was such a 'major weakness'. [39]

At this point some may wonder whether citing texts written by the clergy on the gestures and prayers expected of lay people during Mass mirrored reality. One can respond to this by indicating that the creation of these texts could not have been done in a complete vacuum from contemporary lay liturgical practice and Eucharistic piety. Their production throughout the middle ages would surely have discontinued had there not been some kind of clerical and lay demand for them. They must, therefore, have not been entirely innovative in content, and to some extent reflect the methods of prayer and gesture that the laity utilized. There is also pictorial and written evidence apart from the material we have discussed, illustrating lay Mass piety, such as kneeling and the raising of the arms at the Elevation, the use of beads and the reading of devotional books. [40] This is corroborated by eyewitness accounts, such as Margery Kempe's biography and the *Relatio* written by an Italian visitor to England in the early sixteenth century. [41]

While much of this paper has so far indicated genuine sentiments of piety among the laity, sometimes individuals and even congregations behaved inappropriately, mainly due to slovenliness or simply human frailty. One can find such cases in English episcopal parish visitation records, such as the misbehaviour recorded among the congregation at Wymondham and Kirkby Bellars in Leicestershire, and talkative parishioners at Rossendale and Trawden in Lancashire.[42] Nevertheless such instances should not be exaggerated. These and other cases of lay misbehaviour, which were worthy of note, were presented to the bishop or his officials by other laity, who were clearly disturbed by them. Despite the outbreaks of heresy at various times in mediæval Europe, or anticlericalism - which was relatively rare in any case - such records are not necessarily indicative of heretical activity and dissatisfaction with the clergy: the latter was usually connected with lay concern for the correct ministration of the sacraments and the liturgy and not with priestly status.[43]

THE ELEVATION OF THE HOST AND THE LAITY

We must now turn to the vehicle of mediæval lay participation *par excellence:* the Elevation of the Host. The consecrated Host was raised by the priest, above his head, for the adoration and gaze of the faithful. Bells were rung in order to signify that the consecration was either imminent or that the Elevation was in progress. Torches were used and curtains sometimes drawn behind the elevated Host in order to aid the people's visibility. Hundreds of Latin and vernacular prayers were composed to 'greet' and adore Christ in the holy Eucharist, and to ask for graces. The following is an example:

> May you be loved king; and may you be blessed, king; and may you be thanked, king, for all your good gifts. Jesus, all my delight, who spilt your blood for me, and died upon the…[cross], you give me grace to sing the song of love for you.

The elevation was clearly instituted in order that the real presence of Christ under the species of bread be acknowledged. It has been recently suggested that it was possible to use the 'Elevation' prayers, and other compositions, and thus pray in a proper 'liturgical spirit'. These prayers were '…in quite a defensible sense, liturgical.' [44] To 'view the Host' was an important part of lay piety during the Mass, and led to longer expositions of the Host in special vessels and repositories in some regions. These 'expositions' increased Eucharistic adoration outside Mass. [45] Miri Rubin highlights the communal and participatory nature of the elevation:

> …by the early thirteenth century a focus for eucharistic awareness, a moment designed to encompass and communicate every aspect of the message which the church wished to convey, one which provided space for participation and for submergence in a ritual-communal moment, was in place. [46]

Unfortunately, despite the Church's best intentions, many superstitious 'benefits' were thought to be obtained by looking at the elevated Host and hearing Mass, which led to numerous *Merita Missæ* lists. These practices frequently went beyond the boundaries of sound devotional practice. Individuals, and sometimes congregations, ran from altar to altar, from church to church, just to see the elevated Host. One priest—who was actually a Lollard—complained in 1407 that while he was preaching a number of his congregation quickly left him upon hearing an elevation bell elsewhere in the church. This problem was noted in the thirteenth century by Durandus, and in the sixteenth century by Erasmus and Thomas Cranmer. [47] Superstitious promises attached to seeing the Host may even be found in John Mirk's Instructions:

> …glad may that man be, that once a day he may view the Host ['may hym see']. For so much good comes from seeing…for on the day that

you see God's body you shall secure these benefits: food and drink when you require it...You will not fear dying suddenly that day'.

On the day one saw the Host, one would not grow old and would be cured of various ailments. [48] Methods of celebrating Mass, such as 'staggering' elevations when several masses were in progress at side altars, so as not to coincide with the elevation at Mass on the high altar, deliberately fostered the misdirected attitude of viewing as many elevations as possible. [49] We should be left in no doubt that such practices were a frequent occurrence in the middle ages. Indeed references to the laity being required to hear entire masses by Church authorities is indicative of this, and certain ceremonies at the Sunday parish Mass—namely the distribution of blessed bread and perhaps the recitation of St John's Gospel prologue after Mass—were used in order to dissuade people from leaving after the consecration and Elevation, the high point of the mediæval Mass. John Lydgate and other writers, while extolling the benefits of hearing Mass, were most emphatic that the laity remain in church until the *In principio* was concluded. Only then—ironically—could one accrue the Mass's benefits. [50]

John Huizinga's view that

> The excesses and abuses resulting from an extreme familiarity with things holy...are generally characteristic of periods of unshaken faith and of a deeply religious culture,

contains a grain of truth. However it would be fair to say that there has been a tendency to universalise aspects of the undesirable elements of lay mediæval piety, and the criticisms voiced by men such as Jean Gerson, Pierre d'Ailly and Nicolas de Clemanges. [51] It is surely inaccurate to suppose that everywhere the laity were continuously rushing around the church, from altar to altar to gaze at the Host, despite the frequency of this problem. The practice should be recognized, but not stereotyped. It may have been more common in large cities and towns with numerous churches and altars than country parishes. The last verse of a Latin ditty, which was reproduced in Lydgate's Interpretations, circulated as a proverb:

> *Qui vult audire missam, non debet abire, Donec dicatur et totum perficiatur! Si primo fueris et non in fine manetis, Pars tibi nulla datur, quia laus on fine probatur'.* [52]

In fact the ceremonies which are thought to have acted as inducements to lay people to remain until the end of Sunday Mass, could be said to have been effectual in many instances. On the other hand their popularity within existing lay religious culture indicates that individuals leaving Mass was less problematic in some locations. The distribution of blessed bread after Sunday Mass was highly esteemed by the laity, and became an established custom by the twelfth century: this pre-dates the introduction of the elevation (from the late twelfth century). [53] The prologue of St John's Gospel was popular among the laity as a 'blessing', and was frequently recited after Mass, more so towards the end of the middle ages. According to the *Hortulus Animæ* (1503) this Gospel passage was recited in some areas by everyone present at Mass. In the 1520s William Tyndale scornfully remarked that

> During the recitation of St John's Gospel in Latin over the heads of thousands [of people], they bless themselves with a legion of crosses,

perhaps in order to gain an indulgence attached to the words *'et verbum caro factum est'*. One can infer from these references that people remained for entire masses, and that this was commonplace. [54] The same impression is given in the *Lay Folks' Mass Book* and in references to laity hearing daily Mass, sometimes several masses, particularly among the upper classes. The parishioners of Spalding in Lincolnshire, even complained that they were disturbed during Mass by the stipendiary and fraternity priests saying their own masses at the same time instead of taking their place in choir at the service, which chantry priests were obliged to do. These parishioners were concerned with participating in the parish Mass, free from distractions. [55] While the elevation was at the centre of lay Mass devotion, the liturgy of the priest and people did not converge '...only at the climactic moment when Earth and Heaven met in the fragile disc of bread he [i.e. the priest] held above his head'. [56] This proposition appears to define lay participation too narrowly, when considering the modes of participation which we have discussed. Modern observers, at least, would criticise the mechanical approach to the Mass which is particularly evident in the *Merita Missæ* lists: though we should not doubt people's sincerity and genuine devotion, so apparent, for example, in the elevation prayers.

THE RECEPTION OF HOLY COMMUNION

It should be asked why the laity generally did not receive communion—by then solely under the species of bread—more frequently than the stipulated annual reception, as the Holy Eucharist was so popular. Fear of an unworthy, sinful, reception; the requirement for sexual abstinence; the belief that the priest received on behalf of the entire congregation, and greater regulation by the Church to ensure worthy receptions, have been suggested. [57] The disinclination to receive the Eucharist because of 'fear' and the steps taken to be free from sin before the Easter communions, should not be viewed as indications of morbidity. Ironically, 'fear' was based upon the reverence and love in which the Holy Eucharist was held, which was manifested in a particular manner during the feast of Corpus Christi. 'Fear' was a consequence of reverence, albeit disproportionate, and not a primary motivation. Here we should make additional allowances for the fact that infrequent reception was a long established custom. [58] It is also noteworthy that the desire to receive the Host, if not the actual reception, was clearly prevalent among the laity, as implied in the 'communion substitutes' which were available, such as the blessed bread, the kissing of the 'pax' instrument by the congregation, and above all, by gazing at the elevated

Host. Many of these substitutes were recognized by authors such as John Beleth and Durandus. 'Spiritual Communion' was also proposed, for instance, by Alexander of Hales and St Bonaventure. [59] Though we might suggest, in hindsight, that the mediæval laity may not have derived the full benefits afforded by frequent sacramental communion, they were clearly not deprived of grace by their veneration of the *Sanctissimum*. It should be indicated that the faithful were not explicitly prohibited from receiving more than once a year, and that a few people, especially devout women and members of the nobility, communicated with greater regularity. [60]

THE LAITY AND THE SACRIFICE OF CALVARY

Before concluding this paper, one point requires critical comment. Although writers such as Pope Innocent III and John Burchard, and, indeed the liturgical texts, proposed that the laity played a role in offering Christ's sacrifice, one may be surprised to learn that some have proposed that the notion of sacrifice was obscured by emphasis on adoration of the Host in the middle ages, and questioned the extent to which the laity were conscious of participating in the offering of Christ's sacrifice. [61] We cannot, of course, delve into the thought processes of the vast majority of lay people in late mediæval Europe in order to consider these propositions. Nevertheless external evidence for eucharistic piety strongly indicates that most laity must have possessed some consciousness of being present at the re-presentation of the sacrifice of Calvary during Mass, even if this was unlikely to have been a sophisticated theological understanding. For instance: the crucifix over the screen separating the chancel/sanctuary area from the nave made a graphic theological point about the connection between the Mass and Christ's sacrifice, which was emphasized when a suffering Saviour was portrayed on the cross in the later middle ages; sacrificial imagery in paintings, manuscripts and books made a similar connection, especially the popular 'Mass of St Gregory' image; [62] the numerous allegorical interpretations of the ceremonies of the Mass as a *'memoria passionis'*; the elevation of the Host, which naturally suggested the raising of Christ on the cross; the numerous bequests for Masses to be offered for the souls in purgatory; the references to Christ's passion, explicit or otherwise, in many of the Eucharistic prayers which many laity used during Mass; [63] references to Christ's sacrifice and the Mass in literature; [64] and allusions and explicit references to the passion in sermons, and dramatic reconstructions of the passion, which often alluded to the Mass, especially during the popular Corpus Christi plays. [65] With such a wide dissemination of the notion of sacrifice at all levels of mediæval society, and the importance of the passion in contemporary spirituality, it would be true to say that the laity had no reason to be unaware of Christ's sacrifice on the Cross and its connection with the sacrifice of the altar.

CONCLUSION

It is clear that existing historical evidence from the middle ages indicates that the laity who participated at Mass, did so actively, and not as passive spectators, largely by means of personal prayer, which was sometimes directly influenced by the liturgical texts, and communal forms of prayer; by viewing and being spiritually united with the ceremonies of the Mass; by performing gestures which gave external expression to their inner dispositions and emphasized the communal aspect of the assembled lay people of God at the Holy Sacrifice. [66] When pondering the restrictive view of the altar that the basilican-church design had upon the early Roman Christians, perhaps it would not be too conjectural to propose that aspects of mediæval devotion and architecture, including side altars, actually facilitated more participation for the laity at the Mass, and not less. [67]

The 'external' participation of the faithful in the middle ages was clearly no less participatory for the absence of vocal liturgical responses, or complete comprehension of the Latin liturgical texts. While it generally lacked certain developed characteristics of the kind of participation encouraged by the modern Liturgical Movement and Magisterium, the participation envisaged in the middle ages was, still, fundamentally *actuosa participatio*. Let us recall Pope Innocent III's opinion:

> Not only do priests offer [the Holy Sacrifice] but all the faithful offer too; what is performed in a special way by the ministry of the priests is done in a general way by the desire of the faithful.

This quotation is actually included in Pope Pius XII's encyclical *Mediator Dei*. Sections of this encyclical on the manner of the laity's offering of Christ's sacrifice, through the priest, and, in a certain sense, with him, are truly applicable to the middle ages:

> ...they [i.e.the laity] are said to offer with him inasmuch as they unite their sentiments of praise, entreaty, expiation, and thanksgiving with the sentiments or intention of the priest...

While the Pope highly commends the use of lay missals, and vocal responses and chants by the faithful - which the Instruction *De Musica Sacra* sought to implement - he emphasises that '...they are by no means necessary to give it [i.e. the Mass] its public and communal character...'. With great pastoral sensitivity, Pope Pius says that

> A great number of the faithful are incapable of using the Roman Missal even in a vernacular translation; nor are all equal to a proper understanding of the rites and formulas of the liturgy. People differ so widely in character, temperament and intelligence...spiritual needs and dispositions are not all the same...Are we therefore to say...that all these Chris-

tians are unable to take part in the Eucharistic Sacrifice or to enjoy its benefits? Of course they can…for example by devoutly meditating on the mysteries of Jesus Christ…and saying other prayers which, though different in form from the liturgical prayers, are by their nature in keeping with them. [68]

While knowledge of the liturgical texts and rites, and pronouncing the liturgical responses, are the vehicles of lay participation par excellence—though not the only vehicles [69]—and recognising the infrequency of Holy Communion and undesirable elements and abuses in mediæval lay Eucharistic devotion and liturgy, noted by the Council of Trent,[70] to doubt the *actuosa participatio* of the mediæval laity, is not only to ignore the evidence of history, and the Eucharist's centrality in the middle ages; but surely to question certain fundamental notions of participation enunciated by the Magisterium.[71] In a wider perspective, to quote Eamon Duffy, 'For townsmen and countrymen alike, the rhythms of the liturgy on the eve of the Reformation remained the rhythms of life itself'. The assimilation of liturgical themes amongst the laity make any '…notion of general lay alienation from the liturgy untenable. [72]

NOTES

1. '*Quo fit ut quisquis hoc sacrificium ab ecclesia tollere moliatur, nihilo minorem ei jacturam intentat, quam si mundo solem eripere studuerit*': *Assertionum Regis Angliæ Defensio* vi. 9: cited in T.E. Bridgett, *Life of Blessed John Fisher,* London, 1888, p.40.

2. J.H. Emminghaus, *The Eucharist: Essence, Form, Celebration,* (revised and edited by T. Mass-Ewerd), Collegeville (Minnesota), 1997, pp.70-73; R. Cabié, The Church at Prayer: The Eucharist, vol. 2, London, 1986, p.139.

3. G. Diekmann, 'Popular Forms of Participation and the History of Christian Piety', *Participation in the Mass: 20th North American Liturgical Week,* University of Notre Dame, Notre Dame, Indiana, August 23-26, 1959, Washington, 1960, pp.52-53. On *actuosa participatio* and Vatican II see J. Ratzinger, *The Feast of Faith: Approaches to a Theology of the Liturgy,* San Francisco, 1981, pp.68-75.

4. This paper agrees with many points made in the important work undertaken recently by Eamon Duffy, and that of T.E. Bridgett, C.SS.R. from the nineteenth century, whose endeavours have perhaps been largely obscured. I am indebted to their research: E. Duffy, *The Stripping of the Altars : Traditional Religion in England, 1400-1580,* New Haven and London, 1992; T.E. Bridgett, *The History of the Holy Eucharist in Great Britain,* 2 vols, London, 1888.

5. R.N. Swanson, *Religion and Devotion in Europe, c.1215-1515,* Cambridge, 1995, pp. xiii-xiv.

6. *Primum in Ordine,* ed. A. Wilmart, *Ephemerides Liturgicæ,* vol.50, 1936, pp.133-39; Amalarius, *Amalarii Episcopi Opera Omnia,* ed. J.M. Hanssens, 3 vols, *Studi e Testi,* vols. 138-40, Vatican City, 1948-50. The *Expositiones Missæ* are vol.1, 283-338; John Beleth, *Summa de Ecclesiasticis Officiis,* ed. H. Douteil, 2 vols, *Corpus Christianorum: Continuatio Mediævalis,* vols 41-41A, Turnholt, 1976; William Durandus, *Rationale Divinorum Officiorum,* ed. V. d'Avino, Naples, 1859; Pope Innocent III, *De Sacro Altaris Mysterio,* P.L. 217, col.774-914; J.F. White, 'Durandus and the Interpretation of Christian Worship', in *Contemporary Reflections on Mediæval Christian Tradition: Essays in Honor of Ray C. Petry,* ed. G.H. Shiver, Durham (N. C.), 1974. pp. 41-52.

7. J.A. Jungmann, *The Mass of the Roman Rite,* 2 vols, Blackrock (co. Dublin), 1986: vol.1 pp.113-14; St Albert the Great, *De Sacrificio Missæ* in Albert's Opera Omnia, ed. A. Borgnet, 38 vols, Paris (Vivès), 1890-99: vol. 38, 1-189.

8. *Canonis Misse Expositio,* ed. H.A. Oberman and W.J. Courtenay, 5 vols, *Veröffentlichungen des Instituts für Europäische Geschichte in Mainz,* vols 31-34, 79, Wiesbaden, 1963-76.

9. St Thomas Aquinas, *Summa Theologiæ,* 3a.83, 4.

10. *Vide* A. Franz, *Die Messe im Deutschen Mittelalter,* Freiburg 1902 (repr. Darmstadt 1963), esp. p.460 sq.

11. Note that some rites used the formula *Orate fratres et sorores,* and that in some cases the people responded to it vocally: J.A. Jungmann, *The Mass of the Roman Rite,* vol.2, pp.82-90.

12. J.L. Murphy, 'The Church Offers the Mass', part one, *American Ecclesiastical Review,* vol.141, 1960, p.168.

13. J.A. Jungmann, *The Mass of the Roman Rite,* vol.1, pp.74-76, 85-86, 235-38, 243-44.

14. *The Book of Margery Kempe,* ed. B.A. Windeatt, Harmondsworth, 1985, p.117. On the influence of German spirituality upon Margery: U. Stargardt, 'The Beguines of Belgium, the Dominican Nuns of Germany, and Margery Kempe', *The Popular Literature of Mediæval England,* ed. T.J. Heffernan, Tennessee Studies in Literature, vol.28, Knoxville, (Tenn.), 1985, pp.285-308.

15. E. Duffy, *The Stripping of the Altars,* pp.114, 219-22, 215-16.

16. M.J. Carruthers, *The Book of Memory: A Study of Memory in Mediæval Culture,* Cambridge Studies in Mediæval Literature, vol.10, Cambridge, 1990.

17. R.N. Swanson, *Religion and Devotion in Europe,* pp.78, 82; J.A.H. Moran, *The Growth of English Schooling, 1340-1538 : Learning, Literacy and Laicization in Pre-Reformation York Diocese,* Princeton, 1985, esp. pp.171-82.

18. John Mirk, *Mirk's Festial,* ed. T. Erbe, Early English Text Society, extra series, vol.96, 1905; R.N. Swanson, *Catholic England: Faith, Religion and Observance before the Reformation,* Manchester, 1993, pp.58-64. Note that I modernise mediæval English texts or use the translations given in Swanson's book *ut supra* .

19. M.K. James and M.G. Underwood, *The King's Mother: Lady Margaret Beaufort, Countess of Richmond and Derby,* Cambridge, 1992, pp.15, 184; Songs, Carols and other Miscellaneous Poems from the Balliol MS. 353, *Richard Hill's Commonplace Book,* ed. R. Dyboski, Early English Text Society, extra series, vol.101, London, 1908, p.12; E. Duffy, *The Stripping of the Altars,* pp. 222-23.

20. H. Leclercq, 'Livres d'Heures', in *Dictionnaire d' Archéologie Chrétienne et de Liturgie,* eds. F. Cabrol and H. Leclercq, Paris 1930, vol.9, part 2, cols. 1836-82.

21. E. Duffy, *The Stripping of the Altars,* pp. 50-52, 212-15, 222-25. For examples of *Horæ* see *Horæ Eboracenses: the Prymer of Hours of the Blessed Virgin Mary According to the Use of the Illustrious Church of York,* ed. C. Wordsworth, Surtees Society, vol. 132, 1919; *The Prymer or Prayer-Book of the Lay People in the Middle Ages,* 2 vols, ed. H. Littlehales, London, 1891, 1892.

22. M. Smits van Wæsberghe, 'De Misverklaring van Meester Simon van Venlo', *Ons Geestlijk Erf,* 1941-42, vol.15, pp. 228-61, 285-327 : vol.16, pp. 85-129, 177-85 ; Gherit vander Goude, *Dat Boexken vander Missen,* ed. P. Dearmer, Alcuin Club Collections, vol.5, London, 1903. Some Book of Hours have illustrations of the Mass and instructions. See F. Wormald, 'Some Pictures of the Mass in an English XIVth Century Manuscript', Walpole Society, vol.41, 1966-68, pp. 39-45.

23. K. Gamber, 'Missale Vulgare : Ein Deutsches Volksmessbuch aus dem Mittelalter', *Musik und Kirche,* vol.14, pp.121 ff. ; K. Gamber, *The Reform of the Roman Liturgy : Its Problems and Background,* California and New York, 1993, p.14.

24. J. Wickham Legg, *Tracts on the Mass,* Henry Bradshaw Society, vol.27, London, 1904, pp.19-29; *The Poems of John Audelay,* ed. E.K. Whiting, Early English Text Society, vol. 184, London, 1931, pp.65-79; John Lydgate, *The Minor Poems of John Lydgate I,* ed. H.N. MacCracken, Early English Text Society, extra series, vol.107, London, 1909, pp.87-115.

25. M. Rubin, Corpus Christi: *The Eucharist in late Mediæval Culture,* Cambridge, 1991, pp.103-4.

26. *The Lay Folks' Mass Book,* ed. T.F. Simmons, Early English Text Society, original series, vol.71, 1879. For convenience I use the earlier 'B' text, edited in R.N. Swanson, Catholic England, pp.83-91.

27. *Missale ad Usum Insignis et Præclare Sarum,* ed. F. H. Dickinson, part 1, Burntisland, 1861, col. 580. That the laity in southern Europe recited the liturgical responses is indicated in G. Ellard, *The Mass of the Future,* Milwaukee, 1948, p.103. However evidence presented in this paper suggests that Ellard's claim that the laity generally did not hear the priest's voice at low Mass in northern Europe - sotto voce masses -appears to be misplaced.

28. For evidence that many of the faithful recited the *Confiteor,* see R.N. Swanson, *Catholic England,* p.84; F. Clément, 'The Liturgical Rites of Meal and Sacrifice', *Altar and Sacrifice: the Proceedings of*

The Third International Colloquium of Historical, Canonical and Theological Studies of the Roman Liturgy, (C.I.E.L.), London, 1998, p.97.

29. J.B. Molin, 'L'Oratio Fidelium ses Survivances', *Ephemerides Liturgicæ,* vol.73, 1959, pp. 310-17.

30. P.J. Cobb, 'The Architectural Setting of the Liturgy', *The Study of the Liturgy,* eds. C. Jones, G.Wainwright and E. Yarnold, London, 1980, pp. 476-77; E. Duffy, *The Stripping of the Altars,* pp. 111-12.

31. M. Rubin, *Corpus Christi,* pp. 6-7.

32. *ibid.* pp. 82-108.

33. John Mirk, *Instructions for Parish Priests* by John Mirc, ed. E. Peacock and F.J. Furnivall, Early English Text Society, old series, vol.31, London, 1902, pp. 8-10 ; J.A. Jungmann, *The Mass of the Roman Rite,* vol.1, pp. 239-45. The laity also took part in liturgical processions and other activities, e.g. Candlemas (Feast of the Purification of the B.V.M.) and Palm Sunday.

34. R.N. Swanson, *Religion and Devotion in Europe,* pp. 26-27, 184-88 ; E. Duffy, *The Stripping of the Altars,* pp. 121-23, 130-54.

35. In addition to hearing the largely incomprehensible liturgical texts, one could add here sacred music, which has more than one level of comprehension: C. Burgess 'For the Increase of Divine Service': Chantries in the Parish in Late Mediæval Bristol', *Journal of Ecclesiastical History,* vol.36, 1985, pp. 54-59. Abbot Whethamstede of St Albans remarked in 1423 on the installation of *organistæ* who would sing the Lady Mass in his abbey that 'Wherever the Divine Service is more honourably celebrated the glory of the church is increased and the people are aroused to much greater devotion': C. Burgess, 'For the Increase of Divine Service', p.59.

36. R.N. Swanson, *Religion and Devotion in Europe,* pp. 64-71 ; J.A.F. Thomson, *The Early Tudor Church and Society,* 1485-1529, London and New York, 1993, pp. 271-72, 315-18 ; E. Duffy, *The Stripping of the Altars,* pp. 57-58 and plates 17-18.

37. John Mirk, *Mirk's Festial,* passim.

38. J.A. Gribbin, *The Premonstratensian Order in Late Medieval England,* Ph.D., Cambridge, 1998 (unpublished), pp. 180-82 ; John Rylands University of Manchester Library MS. Eng. 109, ff. 81-82v; Mt 7:15-21.

39. E. Duffy, *The Stripping of the Altars,* p.80; N.Love, *The Mirrour of the Blessed Lyf of Jesu Christ,* ed. L.F. Powell, Oxford, 1908. On the limited use of vernacular bibles: R.N. Swanson, Religion and Devotion in Europe, pp. 73-78.

40. For a selection of manuscript illustrations see M. Rubin, *Corpus Christi,* passim ; P. Dearmer, *Fifty Pictures of Gothic Altars,* Alcuin Club Collections, vol.10, London, 1910, pp. 86-87, 122-23, 194-95. On Elevation prayers see note 44 below.

41. *The Book of Margery Kempe,* p.257 ; C. Harper-Bill, *The Pre-Reformation Church in England 1400-1530,* London and New York, 1989, p.97.

42. J.A.F. Thomson, *The Early Tudor Church and Society,* p.314.

43. R.N. Swanson, *Religion and Devotion in Europe,* pp. 249-52, 256. For particular studies on the clergy and parochial life in Scotland and England, see D. McKay, 'Parish Life in Scotland, 1500-1560', in *Essays on the Scottish Reformation* 1513-1625, ed. D. McRoberts, Glasgow, 1962, pp. 82-115 and P.Marshall, *The Catholic Priesthood and the English Reformation,* Oxford, 1994, passim, esp. p.99.

44. R.N. Swanson, Catholic England, pp. 88-89 ; J. Bossy, 'Christian Life in the Later Middle Ages: Prayers', *Transactions of the Royal Historical Society, 6th series, vol.1,* 1991, pp. 144-46. For other examples of prayers recited during the Elevation, including the *Adoro te Devote* and the *Anima Christi,* see R. Rubin, *Corpus Christi,* pp.155-63 ; A. Wilmart, 'Pour les Prières de Dévotion', *Auteurs Spirituels et Textes Dévots du Moyen-Age Latin : Etudes d'Histoire Littéraire,* Paris, 1932, pp.13-25. The elevation of the chalice did not capture the popular imagination as the elevation of the Host did.

45. C-P. Chanut, 'Concerning Exposition of the Blessed Sacrament', *The Veneration and Administration of the Eucharist: The Proceedings of the Second International Colloquium on the Roman Catholic Liturgy Organized by the Centre International d'Etudes Liturgiques,* Southampton, 1997, pp. 95-111.

46. M. Rubin, *Corpus Christi,* pp.62-63.

47. J. Bossy, 'Christian Life in the Later Middle Ages', p.146; E. Duffy, *The Stripping of the Altars,* p.98; P. Adam, *La Vie Paroissale en France au XIVe Siècle,* Paris, 1964, pp.249-51.

48. J.Mirk, *Instructions for Parish Priests,* p.10. Some people went further in believing that consecrated hosts could be used for practical things, such as an insect repellent. However these beliefs should not be exaggerated ; R. Swanson, *Religion and Devotion in Europe,* pp.182-83.

49. E. Duffy, *The Stripping of the Altars,* pp.97-98.

50. John Lydgate, *The Minor Poems of John Lydgate I,* pp.88, 89; M. Rubin, *Corpus Christi,* p.152; E. Duffy, *The Stripping of the Altars,* p.124.

51. J. Huizinga, *The Waning of the Middle Ages,* New York, 1959, pp.151-77; cf. R.N. Swanson, *Religion and Devotion in Europe,* pp.182-90, 249-52, 256.

52. 'He who wishes to hear the Mass, ought not to leave while it is said, and he will profit from it all. If you are there at the start but do not remain till the end, the part [i.e. the Mass's benefits] will not be granted to you, because the benefit accrues at the end'; M. Rubin, *Corpus Christi,* p.152; John Lydgate, *The Minor Poems of John Lydgate I,* p.89.

53. M. Rubin, *Corpus Christi,* pp.73-74.

54. J.A. Jungmann, *The Mass of the Roman Rite,* vol.2, pp. 447-51 ; T.E. Bridgett, *The History of the Holy Eucharist in Great Britain,* vol.2, pp.37-38, 50-51; E.Duffy, *The Stripping of the Altars,* pp.124-25, 215-16.

55. J.A.F. Thomson, *The Early Tudor Church and Society,* p.312; *The Book of Margery Kempe,* p.108.

56. E. Duffy, *The Stripping of the Altars,* p.118.

57. M. Rubin, *Corpus Christi,* pp.64-65, 147-50; R. Cabié, *The Church at Prayer,* p.138.

58. M. Rubin, *Corpus Christi, passim.* Evidence from Flanders may suggest large-scale non-attendance of parish churches, and non-reception of Holy Communion at Easter, but clearly cannot be taken as typical: J. Toussært, *Le Sentiment Religieux en Flandre à la fin du Moyen-Age,* Paris, 1963, pp. 128-41, 160-94; cf. E. Duffy, *The Stripping of the Altars,* pp.93-94, 99.

59. M. Rubin, *Corpus Christi,* pp. 63-82, 147-55. I would argue that the view, held by some, that gazing at the elevated Host led to a decrease in communion, simply does not follow, for non-frequent communions pre-date the Elevation: hence Lateran IV's stipulation of annual reception (*Omni Utriusque Sexus,* 1215).

60. Margaret Beaufort received communion twelve times a year, and her devotion to frequent reception is also apparent in her efforts to produce a translation of the fourth book of the *Imitation of Christ:* M.K. Jones and M.G. Underwood, *The King's Mother,* pp.15, 200. Margery Kempe eventually received communion weekly: *The Book of Margery Kempe,* pp. 72, 117, 120, 144. In some areas it was believed that communion could be received twice or three times a year, after preparation: M. Rubin, *Corpus Christi,* pp. 147-48.

61. W. J. O'Shea, *The Worship of the Church,* London, 1960, pp.129, 399-400; G. Donaldson, *The Faith of the Scots,* London, 1990, p. 50.

62. E. Mâle, *The Gothic Image: Religious Art in France in the Thirteenth Century,* London, 1961, p. 188. The 'Mass of St Gregory', '...was a highly compressed theological image, teaching the real presence and the unity of Christ's suffering with the daily sacrifice in every church in Christendom': E. Duffy, *The Stripping of the Altars,* pp. 108-9.

63. J. Bossy in 'Christian life in the Later Middle Ages' (p. 146) argues that 'The worshipper is joining in the sacrifice of praise and thanksgiving...is he not?...There is a comparable French prayer...which was to be recited between the elevation and the pax, 'Lord Jesus Christ, who assumed this your most holy flesh in the womb of the glorious virgin Mary, and shed your most precious blood on the tree of the Cross for our salvation, and in this glorious flesh rose from the dead and ascended into Heaven and art to come in this flesh to judge both the living and the dead - deliver us by this your most Holy Body which now is held on your altar from all impurities of mind and body and from all evil and danger, now and forever. Amen'.

64. 'When Abraham rescued his brother from his enemies, he met Melchisedech making his offering of bread and wine, as our priest now does, confirming the precedent...daily at the altar the priest offers nothing less than the Son [i.e. Christ] to the Father': *Songs, Carols and other Miscellaneous Poems,* ed. R. Dyboski, pp. 68-69.

65. D. Bevington, *Mediæval Drama,* Boston, 1975, passim, esp. pp. 225-658.

66. One should not forget that Mass was said for the whole Church, whether or not there was a congregation present.

67. K. Gamber, *The Reform of the Roman Liturgy,* pp. 82-84, 157-66.

68. Pope Innocent III, *De Sacro Altaris Mysterio,* III, 6; Pope Pius XII, Encyclical letter *Mediator Dei,* 1947, nn.96-115 (numbering from the Catholic Truth Society edition, 1967); The Sacred Congregation of Rites, *Instructio De Musica Sacra et Sacra Liturgia ad Mentem Litterarum Encyclicarum Pii Papæ XII Musicæ Sacræ Disciplina et Mediator Dei,* Sept. 3rd 1958, cap. III, *'Normæ Speciales',* esp. n.28ff. ; Second Vatican Council, *Constitution on the Sacred Liturgy, Sacrosanctum Concilium,* Dec. 4th 1963, cap.I, n.19.

69. 'It is true that liturgical prayer being the public prayer of the august Bride of Christ, is superior to private prayers; but this superiority does not mean that there is any conflict or incompatibility between them. The two are harmoniously blended because they are both animated by the same spirit...' : Pope Pius XII, *Mediator Dei,* nn.41, 111-115, 125; *Sacrosanctum Concilium,* cap. II, n.48.

70. R. Knittel, 'Deformata Reformare: Pratiques Liturgiques Erronées et Préoccupations de Réforme Liturgiques dans les Décretes des Réforme du Concile de Trente', *Liturgie Trésor de l'Eglise: Actes du Premier Colloqui d'Etudes Historiques, Théologiques, Canoniques sur le Rite Catholique Romain,* (C.I.E.L), Paris, 1996, pp.43-59. The Council of Trent must be given credit from its efforts to enhance the dignity of Eucharistic celebrations. However the list of liturgical abuses compiled for the Council should not be viewed as entirely representative of the liturgy of the late mediæval period.

71. Concerning liturgical responses, gestures (etc.), Pope Pius XII says, importantly, 'Their chief purpose is to foster the devotion of the faithful and their close union with Christ and His visible minister...': Pope Pius XII, *Mediator Dei,* nn.111-115; The Sacred Congregation of Rites, *Instructio De Musica Sacra et Sacra Liturgica,* cap. III, nn.22, 28, 29.

72. E. Duffy, *The Stripping of the Altars,* pp.52, 111. On cognizance of the liturgical rites amongst English gentry and nobility, and other laity in England, see for instance E. Duffy, *The Stripping of the Altars,* passim, esp. pp.114-16; M.A. Hicks, 'The Piety of Margaret Lady Hungerford' *Journal of Ecclesiastical History,* vol.38, 1987, pp.1-38.

THE ROLE OF THE PRIEST IN THE LITURGICAL RITES

Bernward Deneke

Fr Bernward Wilhelm Deneke was born in 1968. A member of the Confraternity of St Peter since 1988, he was ordained priest in 1993 by Alfons Maria Cardinal Stickler SDB. At first, Fr Deneke was Professor of Spirituality before becoming Vice-Rector of the seminary of the Confraternity of St Peter at Wigratzbad where he continues to teach.

INTRODUCTION

NEW insights into exegesis, the history of dogma, or liturgy should not be expected from this contribution. It is also not possible to give a comprehensive and exhaustive account of the role and significance of the priest in the distribution of the sacraments. In view of the abundance of new and old literature, which now stretches to infinity, on this subject, be it Catholic or anti-Catholic, conforming to the Magisterium or critical of the Church, scientific or devotional, to claim new insights would be too ambitious.

We propose to discuss the priest from only one point of view; as the *minister Christi:* in biblical terms, as 'the servant of Christ and steward of the mysteries of God'. [1] Certain present day circumstances are not least among the reasons for this; circumstances that affect the way Catholics experience their faith and thus in not a few cases affect their faith itself. This cannot be regarded by the theologian with indifference.

To make this clear, let us use an illustration which any believer can observe in our present-day liturgical situation: the fact that the behaviour of the priest determines to a large extent the effect that sacramental rites have on those attending. Certainly the Church teaches that the effect of the sacraments is not dependant on the personality of the minister, but the evidence tells a different story.

Sometimes a sacrament is not immediately recognizable as such, and with some celebrations, the faithful feel like the original hearers of the Sermon on the Mount, who appeared amazed, even shaken and upset by the words of Jesus (the Greek word εκπλεσσειν has all these meanings), because he taught them 'as one with authority, and not as their scribes'. [2]

Applied to our situation, sometimes when a priest baptizes, absolves sins, assists at a marriage, distributes Communion, or anoints the sick, it becomes clear to the faithful who are present that here is someone who is not just acting as a private individual or as the representative of a particular group of people; The acts of the priest reveal, rather, a position and authority that come to him from a supernatural source.

On another occasion the opposite impression is given. In performing the sacramental rites the priest appears to be only too human; he may intentionally seem to avoid any appearance of holding a special position based on office and supernatural gifts in relation to the congregation. Consequently, those present have to make a determined act of faith to believe in the possibility of anything more than the human person of the priest being involved.

The relationship between the ordained minister of the sacraments and his priestly authority is not irrelevant to the way the faithful perceive the sacraments. This has been shown over recent decades, since the changes that have taken place in the area of liturgy have made variations possible in the area of the sacraments to an extent hitherto unknown. The official liturgical renewals were perceived by many to be the go-ahead for unofficial experiments. The outcome of these experiments often seriously obscures priestly authority. For this reason a look back to former practices can only be helpful to a renewal of sacramental life and priestly ministry in the administration of the sacraments.

Our question is as follows: how does traditional theology see the relationship of the priest, the subject administering the sacraments, to his objective authority, and how is this relationship expressed in the sacramental rites that have been handed down to us?

CLASSICAL QUESTIONS

Certainly, we do not direct our attention solely towards the Catholic teaching with respect to the minister of the sacraments. Yet we can only deal with our subject against the background of expressions of revelation and their proclamation through the Church's teaching office, and its penetration of theology. For this reason, we must, at least briefly, consider the dogmatic context of our question.

Priestly authority has in itself been the subject of many heated controversies in the history of theology. We need only think of the views of the Donatists in the fourth and fifth centuries, the Waldensians in the Middle Ages and the followers of Wycliffe and Hus at the beginning of the Renaissance, who made the effectiveness of the sacraments dependant on the worthiness of the minister, as well as the Protestant teaching which denies the existence of actual authority belonging to the minister of sacraments by virtue of his priestly ordination.

The Church's Magisterium has clearly demonstrated its position with respect to these opinions: for instance, at the Council of Trent where, in opposition to the Protestant novel ideas, it was declared that authority to administer the sacraments belongs not to all Christians, but only to the specific [ministerial] priesthood, authorized by ordination and commissioning.

In the question of the relationship between the personal holiness—or lack of it—of the *minister sacramenti* and the sanctifying effect of the sacrament, the Church has long known that it is bound by the teaching of St. Augustine. Augustine led the struggle against the Donatists and in doing so arrived at some remarkably acute and audacious statements. He wrote as follows in his commentary on the Gospel of St. John:

> Those whom John the Baptist baptized, John baptized; but those Judas baptized, Christ baptized. Those whom a drunkard, murderer or adulterer baptized, Christ baptized, so long as it was a baptism of Christ' [4]

And:

> Even if many ministers, just or unjust, baptize, the holiness of the baptism originates with the one of whom it is said: This is he who baptizes in the Holy Spirit (Mt. 3:11). Let Peter baptize—this is the one who is baptizing; let Paul baptize—this is the one who is baptizing; let Judas baptize—this is the one who is baptizing. [5]

Later St. Thomas Aquinas presents the same teaching in a less poetic but theologically more precise manner. In his explanation, the priest is to be seen as the *causa instrumentalis,* the instrument in the administration of the sacraments. Such an instrument works through the power of the one that moves it and not from itself, not *secundum propriam formam.* Accordingly, for Aquinas, the priest no more needs to be worthy for a merely valid administration of the sacrament, than the body of a doctor (the instrument of a 'healing soul') needs to be healthy to treat a patient, or a water pipe needs to be of a particular material. [6]

In the controversies about the *minister sacramenti,* the Magisterium made its own the pioneering work of St. Augustine and its development by St. Thomas. Thus in 1208 Pope Innocent III required an anti-Waldensian profession of faith from Durandus of Huesca, in which he had to promise not to refuse the sacraments administered by a sinful priest, but on the contrary to receive them 'with a willing heart as if from the most just of people' [7]

In 1415 the Council of Constance condemned the views of Wyclif, a precursor of the so-called Reformation. Wyclif had revived the old heresies by maintaining that the sacraments of a minister in a state of mortal sin were without effect. [8] The Council of Trent spoke in the same way as the Council of Constance when it condemned the same error. [9]

The question of how the subjective worthiness or unworthiness of the minister of the sacrament relates to the objective holiness of the sacrament, and how the two relate, one to the other, has thus been unambiguously answered. In fact in the present day the question hardly occurs. The horizons of thought and experience have shifted so much in theology that a question like this is rarely discussed with the degree of passion it aroused in the religious disputes of the early Christian period, the Middle Ages or the early Renaissance.

PRESENT DAY QUESTIONS

Such questions have long been replaced by others. These do not concern matters of detail but rather fundamental issues. For although theology has not escaped the modern trend to fragmentation into even more specialities, it is only superficially concerned with single questions. Theological disputes are concerned with first and last questions about the relationship between God and man, nature and grace, reason and faith, individual and community etc.

• *The accusation of objectivism*

The way the relationship between the subjective and the objective has become a problem in the official acts of the Church plays a role also in our own area. Recent theology, which presents itself under the sign of an anthropological shift and a turning to the human subject, has many difficulties with the markedly objective understanding of the sacraments in the Catholic tradition. That neither the person of the recipient nor that of the minister has been sufficiently considered in the Church's declarations on this question up to now, is the complaint that is heard everywhere.

Let us briefly call to mind the requirements the Church makes of the *minister sacramenti,* the active subject of the administration of the sacraments, so as better to understand the starting point of contemporary criticism.

For validity, as we have already seen, the state of grace, a living bond between the priest and Christ, is not required: 'Let Peter baptize - this is the one that is baptizing; let Paul baptize - this is the one that is baptizing'. [10] Where the founder of the sacrament is himself at work, the human instrument retreats into the background.

But to go into the background does not mean to completely disappear. In respect of the Catholic tradition, it is also without question that the minister/ dispenser, however unimportant his spiritual condition may be, in the sacramental rites has to act in a specifically human manner, i.e. based on cognition and interior purpose. This means: a minimum of attention and willing affirmation of 'intention' is required for validity. In the classic formulation, if the minister does not at least intend to do what the Church does, the sacrament does not take place. [11]

This clearly applies to the personality and acquiescence of the minister. As previously understood, all other subjective elements were supposed to be lost in the objectivity of the prescribed *actio liturgica*. Only in this way, priests are taught by the pre-Vatican II liturgical ascetic books, may the transparency of the sacramental act, pointing to the acts of the Lord, be preserved from subjective additions, obscurity and distortion.

A consequence of this, is that guided by such principles, the Church used to reject any kind of spontaneity in the liturgical and particularly the sacramental area. The earlier (1917) *Codex Iuris Canonici* accordingly, insisted on observing rites and ceremonies accurately, as laid down in the books authorized by the Church. [12] In this the Church's law was on the same footing as the Council of Trent which had strictly forbidden contempt of ecclesiastically approved rites, making arbitrary omissions in them, or changing them into new and different rites. [13]

The administration of the sacraments is thus a strictly objective process according to the old understanding. The human instrument has totally to conform himself to this. The subject is only considered insofar as it is needed and inwardly agrees to being used.

It could be added, that even in the old Canon Law the Church called its servants to exercise *'summa diligentia et reverentia':* highest care and reverence in liturgical actions. [14] In making such recommendations the Church had in mind the holiness of priests and the edification of the Christian people. But care and reverence are again only concerned with faithful fulfillment of prescriptions, with being subject to what is laid down. As a consequence the official recommendations did not loosen the predominant objectivism but insisted on it.

The impression is gained that the individual person is reduced to his higher, assenting spiritual faculties and the limbs necessary for the administration of the sacraments. His personality appears to be an unavoidable obstacle rather than an instrument in the saving work of God with its own worth. Is there not in this a degradation of the person, who is after all called by God and through the sacrament of Holy Orders been made to resemble Christ? Is the person not being regarded as a thing? Does not the Church's teaching on the sacraments in this promote a de-humanizing de-personalizing objectivism?

The fathers at the last Council seem to have sensed the problem and struggled with an answer. At least such a perspective makes the following extract understandable, which firstly fits in seamlessly with the above described traditional line on sacramental validity, but then, as a counterpoint, gives it a shift towards the personal and subjective:

> Although, the grace of God can complete the work of salvation even through unworthy ministers, God normally desires to manifest his wonders through those who have made themselves particularly open to the impulse and guidance of the Holy Spirit. Because of their intimate un-

ion with Christ and their holiness of life, these men can say with the Apostle: 'it is now no longer I that live, but Christ lives in me' (Gal. 2:20). [15]

But even with this statement, theology, after the 'anthropological shift' will not be able to declare itself satisfied. Does it not just repeat the old familiar call to priestly sanctity? Looked at carefully it says nothing about the actual performance of the sacraments. Again the minister should conform himself inwardly to the prescribed rite. At most he will give the *actio liturgica* a certain lustre that derives from a certain, personal piety, which is reflected in the actions and edifies the assisting faithful.

• *The shift to the subject*

In the view of many contemporary theologians the former 'objectivism' is on the same lines as 'validity-minimalism', which only enquires after what is strictly required for the sacrament to take place. Because the sacrament was only considered from the point of view of its effect and this was massively objectified, the personal and interpersonal dimensions of the Church's signs of salvation were lost from view; such is the criticism.

As an example of this new perspective let us consider the work of Alexandre Ganoczy, Professor of Dogma in Wurzburg. He has developed a sacramental theology making considerable use of modern communicative sciences and so has different requirements for the minister of the sacraments than one could find in the older works of moral theology or practical liturgy:

> The standard for a sacramental celebration, which is to be not merely 'valid' but a genuine response to the divine call, is found in the state of mind of the celebrant, who activates his personal faith, existentially commits it and expresses it in the genuine attitude of a witness. This means not merely piety, conscientiousness and serious awareness of the situation of the recipients. This ethos for the administration of the sacraments also includes, in my view, material and professional (e.g. psychological and didactic) skills, at least a lasting intention to appropriate these in the best possible way. Otherwise it may happen that the rite is performed by a pious person and remains under the permanent guarantee of God's promise of salvation, but hardly speaks to those for whom it is intended; a gap arises between the intention of the sacrament and the particular experience of the target group or person. [16]

These observations may remind one of the advice a famous pianist once gave to a young pianist, not just to concentrate on playing the piano, but also to deepen his general knowledge of history, literature and natural science, as the inner wealth of a person is clearly reflected in his musical interpretation. Similarly, in the view of the above-mentioned theologian, the human formation and competence of a *minister sacramenti* cannot stay hidden in liturgical action.

But does Ganoczy mean just that? Does he only want to give the good piece of advice, 'You priests, continue your professional education'? Or does bridging the apparent gap between 'the intention of the sacrament and the particular experience of the target group or person', concerned with making sure that the participants feel involved, make specific interventions in the liturgical action necessary ?

In a rite such as the traditional Roman rite, which prescribes the actions of the minister in the smallest detail, and so hinders his own personality from appearing, it will in any case not be easy to attest to 'psychological and didactic skills' without making arbitrary changes in the liturgy. .

To return to the comparison with the virtuoso pianist: were he Ganoczy, he would not just send his pupil on his way with the recommendation to continue his education, he would advise him to adapt the classical composers to the horizon of his audience, perhaps to let elements of jazz or oriental music mingle with Beethoven and Chopin - possibly testimony to psychological or didactic competence - but what about fidelity to the work?

Present-day theology often shows a serious lack of genuinely theological consideration of its subjects. An all-too-strong emphasis on the subjective and horizontal plane relegates the vertical and objective dimension to the background. For this reason the human competence of the minister of the sacrament becomes concerned to replace the divine empowerment that is no longer considered. Present-day practice confirms that the attempt does not succeed.

In teaching sacramental theology, the one-sided approach which attempts to respond to an apparent or genuine objectivism, is all the more regrettable. This is because it is precisely the newer theology that provided some new approaches that could bring the vertical and horizontal, the objective and the subjective in the sacraments, successfully into harmony. We propose making them the starting point for the following considerations.

REPRESENTATION OF JESUS CHRIST

In 1976 the Common Synod of the German Dioceses formulated the correct proposition: 'sacraments are actions, in which God meets human beings; this occurs in a visible sign in the encounter between the minister of the sacrament and the recipient'. [17] Accordingly, in the liturgical action the minister of the sacrament is in the place of God, or more precisely in the place of Jesus Christ, the eternal high-priest. He is fully the representative, the one who makes his Lord present.

• *Personal Representation*

Exactly how this representation of Christ is to be understood, is not entirely without dispute. In the case of the Mass, there is unanimity that the Son of God is most closely connected with the celebrating priest. In the words of the last council:

> He is present in the sacrifice of the Mass, not only in the person of his minister, the same one now offering, through the ministry of priests, who formerly offered himself on the Cross, but especially under the eucharistic species. [18]

In connection with the other sacraments the same Church council could not arrive at such far-reaching statements. So it simply said that: 'By his power he is present in the sacraments, so that when a man baptizes it is really Christ himself who baptizes'. [19] A presence in power appears to be more a virtual than a personal presence.

Even so the wording raises a question; if Christ is present by his power in the sacraments, how are Augustine's words true 'Every time someone baptizes, it is Christ who baptizes'? Without the personal presence of Christ in the minister of the sacrament—as in the offering of the sacrifice of the Mass—the statement remains incomprehensible.

Also the 'Constitution on the Ministry and Life of Priests', which even mentions a kind of presence of the bishop in the priest, [20] expresses itself very cautiously on the subject of the representation of Christ by the *minister sacramenti*. After it was said of the sacrifice of the Mass, that the priests offered it *in persona Christi,* it is said of the sacraments 'they are joined to the intention and love of Christ when they administer the sacraments'. [21]

This time there is only a moral union and representation of the Lord! And the 'Constitution on the Church' of the last council stresses again in connection with the eucharistic sacrifice, 'Acting in the person of Christ, he (i.e. the priest) brings about the Eucharistic Sacrifice, and offers it to God in the name of all the people' [22] There is, however, no mention in the document of the sacraments that places the priest *in persona Christi.*

In my opinion there is a regrettable shortcoming in all this. The council could, without difficulty, have found texts in plenty which could have evidenced more than a mere basic attitude or simple instrumental connection of the administrator of the sacraments with the Son of God. Even the sacramental rites themselves give us a clear signal in this connection. Let us consider the 'Ego' which equally belongs to the formulations for baptism and absolution, [23] which the priest, incontestably, pronounces *in persona Christi.*

Whatever the precise nature of the representation of Christ by the *minister sacramenti,* it is unanimously held that ordination makes priests 'living instruments of Christ the eternal priest'. [24] The altogether high demands that the Church's leadership has so often made of priests, [25] must be understood in the light of the truth of their representation of Christ.

• *Vertical representation*

In sharp contradiction to many current notions, traditional teaching considers this representation of the Saviour's work primarily in its vertical, other-worldly dimension. Through this sacraments are not assigned to the 'cultic' part of the liturgy, whose main content is the glorification of God, but rather to its 'soteric' part that continues God's loving approach to the human race. This can be seen in a statement well-known statement of Pius XII in his encyclical on the liturgy:

> Faithful to the commission she received from her Founder, the Church continues the priesthood of Jesus Christ above all in the sacred liturgy. In the first place she does this at the altar, where the sacrifice of the cross is continually offered and renewed...then through the sacraments, particular ways in which men become sharers of supernatural life...[26]

The Divine life flows down to earth through the sacraments! Even so, the Jesuit Otto Semmelroth rightly stresses that even the sacraments do not have only a horizontal and vertical 'descending' direction to the human race. In the liturgy, according to Semmelroth, the horizontal dimension is always in truth broken through by the transcendence from which Christ comes, and leads into the transcendence into which he returns. Thus the sacraments have 'as a cultic exercise of the priestly office of the Church a trend from below to above, from the human race to God' because Christ takes us here coming 'from above to below' to take us with him on his way to the Father 'from below to above'. [27]

• *Representation of Christ in the sacramental rites*

That Jesus Christ is the *primus agens,* the primary agent in the sacramental action, is proclaimed in various ways in the traditional rites. When the priest in baptism says *'Ego te baptizo'* and in giving sacramental absolution says *'Ego te absolvo',* he does not give room for the slightest doubt, that here the Son of God is using him, even through him, with him, and in him Christ works the miracle of grace, even if the priest can only do so through him, with him and in him.

What the *minister sacramenti* could never say and never do from human ability, flows into him in the moment of the sacramental action, from the saving work of Christ, mediated by the grace of the sacrament of Order. He becomes a representative of Christ in matters of salvation.

Various aspects of this realization are illuminated clearly in the sacramental rites. For example, the baptizing priest represents Christ, not just as the Redeemer and caller to a new life, but also as the victor over Satan, the evil one, and as the one who brings the Holy Spirit. This becomes evident when he pronounces the exorcism over the candidate and then breathes three times into his face. [28]

This symbolic *insufflatio,* the *Ephphatha*-rite, recalls the Lord's action, as it is handed down in the Gospel: he healed the deaf and dumb person by putting his finger in his ears, touching his tongue with spittle and, looking up to heaven, saying 'Be thou opened'. [30] Similarly, the liturgy instructs the minister of the sacrament of baptism to place his index finger moistened with spittle on the ears and nose of the person to be baptized and say the words '*Ephphetha,* which is: Be thou open - to the sweet fragrance about you. As for thee, Satan, get thee gone; for God's judgement is upon thee.' [31]

Representation of Christ extends thus into the dimension of the senses. This is also evident in the exorcism over the salt which is then put on the catechumen's mouth. [32] By the authority of the incarnate Son of God made man, the priest tears away visible things from the power and influence of the prince of darkness, to put them in the service of God. He participates in the cosmic priesthood of Christ, whom he represents, which brings all the elements of the world into the glorification of the Father.

The rites for the anointing of the sick show the same 'wholeness'. Eyes, ears, nose, mouth, hands and feet are here each anointed with holy oil, [33] to purge the sins committed with the body, to raise up the inner person through the outward senses and to prepare completely for the final restoration. Here the priest takes the role of Christ the healer, who mercifully turns to the sick person to heal him.

The same is true of the sacrament of penance. As it is a kind of 'tribunal of penitence' it includes the dimension of divine justice. The sitting position, which the confessor takes according to the directions of the Church [34] represents in this moment Jesus Christ as the future judge, who, through the confessor in the sacrament of penance, in a sense anticipates the judgement. Only in the name and power of the Son of God can the priest grant mercy and forgiveness to the sinner who accuses himself.

REPRESENTATION OF THE CHURCH

As the *minister sacramenti* the priest is the image, representative, and steward of Jesus Christ. *In persona Christi* and acting with his authority, he represents the Lord as the victor over Satan and bringer of the Holy Spirit, as healer and as judge who absolves us from guilt. These are vast and important perspectives for an understanding of the sacraments and their minister. But the essential aspect of the representation of Christ does not stand by itself. According to Catholic faith the mediation of Jesus Christ is continued in the Church he founded, which is visible and hierarchically ordered. She teaches at his behest, and in his infallibility guides people in the power of the Good Shepherd and continues his saving work in the holy sacrifice and in the sacraments for those who partake in them, so that they may share his grace.

Though the priest, being human, stands before God, as does every Christian, he also has to take the place of God before his fellow humans. He relies on the Church, as the continuing Christ, and needs her, as does every Christian, for his eternal salvation. However, in his official actions he takes her place, becoming the personal representative of the Church acting *in persona Ecclesiæ.*

In this connection the thinking of Matthias Joseph Scheeben, a very significant German theologian of the last century, should be mentioned. Like few others he knew how to uncover the interconnections of the mysteries of the faith in his organic presentation of the mysteries of Christianity. Scheeben explained the aspect of the representation of the Church—particularly the Church as mother —by the priest in the following way:

Starting from the Church as bride and body of Christ and as mother of his children, Scheeben discusses a particular 'marriage' of the bridegroom and head of the Church with the priest, which goes much further than the general 'marriage of Christ with his church and her members'. At their ordination priests are empowered to cooperate, through the power of the Holy Spirit, in the re-birth of Christ in the womb of the Church and in human souls, and to lead the baptized to an ever more intimate union with Jesus Christ. This happens essen-tially through the sacraments, which therefore appear as the Church acting as mother towards the faithful, and the priesthood is seen as a motherly service: 'everywhere this is expressive of the exalted motherhood of the Church'. [35]

Scheeben's thoughts lead to a somewhat unusual and strange, but not un-founded way of seeing the priest. We are clearly used to seeing him as a father as the forms of address *Pater, père, padre* etc. show. But if we look away from the individual priest, who stands before us as a man, and see in him an execu-tive organ within the Church, then it will be easier for us to see in him not just one who represents the Redeemer by supernatural power, but also the repre-sentative of mother Church.

The extent to which priestly service stands under the sign of motherly care for the people entrusted to the priest, who are to be guided, and catechized, fed and supported, can be read from the words of Pope Pius XI;

> The priest is appointed as the 'steward of the mysteries of God' to be a blessing for the members of the mystical body of Jesus Christ. He is the ordinary minister of almost all the sacraments, which are the channels through which the grace of the Redeemer flows to us for the salvation of the human race. At almost every decisive step on his earthly journey the Christian finds the priest at his side ready, through the authority given him by God, to give or increase that grace which is the supernatural life of the soul'. [36]

Pius XII, who sees priesthood more from the viewpoint of an ecclesiology of the Body of Christ, shows, at least indirectly, the way ordained ministers share the motherliness of the Church, when he writes:

Just as the human body is obviously equipped with its own organs, with which it ensures its own life, health, and growth and that of its various parts, so the Redeemer of mankind has wonderfully provided for his mystical body in his infinite goodness, by enriching it with sacraments so as to maintain its members in an unbroken succession of graces from the cradle to their last breath, and also to provide generously for the social; needs of the whole body. [37]

The priest is an instrument and representative of the motherly love of the Church, who provides for and nourishes and nurses her children! This concept of the priestly office would be beyond doubtless be instrumental in removing many misunderstandings, which have given rise to the criticism of a 'man's church'. We cannot dwell on this further, for we must now turn our attention to how the representation of the Church is presented in the traditional rites.

• Representation of the Church in the sacramental rites

The representation of the Church, like that of Christ, is unambiguously expressed. It is not as representative of the Lord but of the Church that the priest questions the catechumen before baptism. [38] When he has led the catechumen to the baptistery and—usually through the godparents—makes him repeat the Lord's prayer and the Apostles' Creed, [39] when he asks if he rejects the devil and believes in God, [40] and finally when he gives the neophyte a white garment and a lighted candle, [41] as a mother clothes her child and equips it for life, then, in a sense, the Church is visible in him.

In the sacrament of penance the representation of the Church by the priest is seen in his kindly approach to the penitents, whom he is to encourage to make an full confession of their sins and to speak to them with fatherly love 'paterna caritate'. [43]

The absolution given in persona Christi is preceded in the traditional rite by a formula of reconciliation spoken in persona Ecclesiæ. [44] This order is also kept in cases of danger of death. [45] It is thus made clear that reconciliation with God in Christ presupposes reconciliation with the Church, and that the priest must first act as the Church's representative in order to complete the sacrament as the representative of Christ.

Finally the priest represents the motherly Church when he brings Viaticum to the dying and gives them the papal blessing, which is linked to a plenary indulgence. [46] Mother Church on earth survives her children and shows her care to accompany them on their pilgrim journey in their supernatural life through the ministry of her priests.

CONCLUSION

From these necessarily brief comments it should have become clear how the Catholic tradition understands the task of a priest as *minister sacramenti*. This is founded not in personal competence or holiness of life, but in the act of representing Christ and the Church.

The traditional liturgy of the sacramental rites clearly shows the priest first as representative of Jesus Christ and then as representative of the Church. In both the verbal and non-verbal areas the Church attests, almost without exception, that the minister of the sacrament, as the representative of the Lord and the Church, comes 'from above' from another world to appear to people. Consequently the sacred actions need no subjective additions on the part of the priest to demonstrate his competence to those present.

Even so, there is no question of the priest being used as a 'matter of fact' impersonal instrument. The minister of the sacrament can always be replaced by another. That has to be the case, otherwise the redeeming work of Jesus Christ through the Church would be handed over to human subjectivity and have its continued existence endangered. The rites, however, require that the priest should involve his whole personality so as to share the authority of Christ in the Church, and to let it come to a fruitful effect in the receiver of the sacrament. This is an authority, which extends far beyond any 'didactic and pedagogical competence' and yet, when incorporated in the objective rite, will always bear rich fruit.

The modern problem of the subjective and objective in the area of sacraments finds in the old rites that answer that was given long before by St. Paul; 'This is how one should regard us, as servants of Christ and stewards of the mysteries of God'. [47]

NOTES

1. 1Cor. 4:1

2. Mt. 7:28 et seq.

3. Council of Trent, sess. VII (DS 1610) : *'Si quis dixerit, Christianos omnes in verbo et in omnibus sacramentis administrandis habere potestatem: anathema sit.'*

4. *In Joann.* V.18.

5. *ibid.* VI.7.

6. S.T.III 64.5.

7. *'...benevolo animo tanquam a iustissimo amplectimur'*(DS 793).

8. *'Si episcopus vel sacerdos existat in peccato mortali, non ordinat, non consecrat, non conficit, non baptizat'*(DS 1154).

9. DS 1612

10. as note 3

11. cf. Trent sess. VI *'Si quis dixerit, in ministris, dum sacramenta conficiunt et conferunt, non requiri intentionem, saltem faciendi quod facit Ecclesia: anathema sit.'*(DS 1611)

12. C.I.C. (1917) can. 733 1

13. *Si quis dixerit, receptos et approbatos Ecclesiæ catholicæ ritus in solemni sacramentorum administratione adhiberi consuetos aut contemni, aut sine peccato a ministris pro libito omitti, aut in novos alios per quemcumque ecclesiarum pastorem mutari posse: a.s.* (DS 1613)

14. cf. C.I.C. (1917) can. 731 1

15. Presbyterorum ordinis, no. 12

16. Alexandre Ganoczy, *Einfuehrung in die katholische Sakramentenlehre,* Darmstadt (2) 1984, pp. 46 -47

17. *Beschluesse der Vollversammlung, Offizielle Gesamtausgabe I,* Freiburg 1976, 241

18. *Sacrosanctum Concilium,* no. 7

19. *ibid.*

20. *Presbyterorum ordinis,* no. 5

21. *ibid,* no. 13

22. *Lumen Gentium,* no. 10

23. *Ego te baptizo...ego te absolvo....Hoc est enim corpus meum.*

24. *Presbyterorum Ordinis,* no. 12

25. cf. Apostolic exhortation of Pius X to the Catholic clergy of 4th August 1908, *Hærent animo,* the encyclical of Pius XI of 20th December 1935 *Ad catholici sacerdotii,* the encyclical of Pius XII on advancing the holiness of priestly life *Menti nostræ* of 23rd September 1950, and many passages in *Presbyterorum Ordinis.*

26. Pius XII, encyclical of 20th November 1947, *Mediator Dei et hominum.* (AAS XXXIX , 1947, pp. 521-525, no. 214

27. Otto Semmelroth, *Gott und Mensch in Begegnung,* Frankfurt a.M.(2)1958, p. 286

28. *Ordo Baptismatis Parvulorum* (OBP; sacramental rites are quoted according to the Rituale Romanum. no3, see also nn. 7 and 12 (with invocation of the Holy Spirit)

29. Jn. 20:22

30. Mk. 7:33

31. OBP no. 13

32. OBP no. 6

33. *Ordo administrandi Sacramentum Extremæ Unctionis* nn. 8-12

34. *Ordo Pænitentiæ* in the introduction no. 8 speaks of the *'sedes confessionalis'*

35. Matthias Joseph Scheeben, *Die Mysterien des Christentums,* 79, (=GS) vol. ii. Freiburg 1941 p. 449 et seq.

36. Pius XI encyclical of 20th December 1935 *Ad catholici sacerdotii* (AAS XXVIII, 1936, 5-35)

37. Pius XII *Mystici Corporis,* 29th June 1943 in AAS XXXV, 1943, no. 768

38. OBP no. 1

39. OBP no. 10

40. OBP nn. 14 and 17

41. OBP no. 22 -23

42. *Ordo ministrandi sacramentum poenitentiæ:...proinde fiduciam ei præbeat, et humaniter suggerat, ut omnia peccata sua rite et integre confiteatur...*(*Rituale Romanum,* tit. III. Cap. 1. no. 15)

43. ibid. no. 18

44. *'Dominus noster Jesus Christus te absolvat: et ego auctoritate ipsius te absolvo ab omni vinculo excommunications, suspensionis et interdicti, in quantum possum, et tu indiges'* Then, *'Deinde ego te absolvo a peccatis tuis' ibid.* no. 2

45. *'Ego te absolvo ab omnibus censuris, et peccatis, in nomine.....' ibid* no.5

46. *Rituale Romanum,* tit. V. cap vi.

47. 1Cor. 4:1-2

WHAT IS CONVEYED BY LITURGICAL SYMBOL?

Alain Contat

Father Contat, born in Geneva in 1955, is a Doctor of Philosophy and a Licentiate in Theology. He is a corresponding Member of the Pontifical Academy of St Thomas Aquinas and currently teaches at a university in Rome. Dr Contat is the author of a monograph on Truth according to St Thomas Aquinas, published by Libreria Editrice Vaticana.

T HE aim of the present study is two-fold: in the first part we shall try to bring out the nature of liturgical symbolism; and in the second part, we shall briefly demonstrate its dogmatic foundations. As our purpose is neither exegetic nor historical, but speculative, we shall rely principally on the doctrine of St Thomas Aquinas, [1] the Common Doctor of the Church, whose systematic perspective and precise language will permit us to delimit more carefully the objects of our study. This is not to deny that there could be a place here for integrating the specific contributions of the history and phenomenology of religions, and disciplines which have known a great blossoming in the twentieth century; [2] but the distinctions and the critiques which would be required if one were to take such factors into account would need to be developed in such a way that it could not be justified in a simple presentation of this kind. Therefore we shall limit ourselves to a 'plan', which will allow us to place in a proper context the principles which determine what is at stake in sacramental symbolism.

THE NATURE OF LITURGICAL SYMBOLISM

A sacrament is defined as the sign of a sacred reality which causes, sacramentally, what it signifies so that *sacramentum est in genere signi* ('sacraments fall under the general category of signs'). [3] As for the liturgy, it prepares, makes explicit, and prolongs the conferring of the sacraments, and hence it also constitutes a system of signs which are ordered to the sanctification of the faithful. [4] If we wish to understand what is the symbolism proper to the liturgy, we must therefore seek to discover what it consists of; precisely, the signs to which it has recourse, and whether this be in the strictly sacramental order or in the ceremonial order. To do this we shall bring out the specificity of the sacramental signs, then of those signs which are purely liturgical, making comparisons with the linguistic signs with which we are most familiar, and also form part of the liturgy.

• *The linguistic sign*

In a famous passage in the *Peri Hermeneias* Aristotle establishes the status of the linguistic sign as follows:

> Sounds emitted by the voice are symbols of the passions in the soul, and written words are symbols of the words emitted by the voice. And just as writing is not the same with all men, spoken words are not the same either; [on the other hand] the passions in the soul of which these expressions are the signs, are the same for everyone; and the things of which these states of the soul are similitudes are also the same for everyone. [5]

The analysis of these most basic facts of language, and words, bring to the fore three instances: the linguistic sign considered in itself, that is to say; primarily the spoken utterance, then the 'passion in the soul' to which the uttered word relates, and finally the thing aimed at by this word and the 'passion' which corresponds to it 'in the soul'. Between these instances, speech sets up two relations of signification which are quite different, one from the other: one which links the spoken word to the 'passion in the soul', and the other which unites the latter to the thing, which is normally exterior to the soul.

Let us make more explicit the status of these three instances and of the two relations which they imply. The spoken word, in the sense which Aristotle understands it here, is a sound effectively pronounced by a speaker, and at the same time endowed with signification: by extension, it can also refer to the acoustical image which accompanies every idea and thought by the mind, even if the mouth of the person who thinks it remains closed. In the two examples referred to, the sound which is under discussion here is always a signifier for the person who says it, exteriorly or interiorly because it is always posited in relation to a 'passion in the soul', that is to say to a concept, thanks to which our intelligence expresses in itself and for itself an aspect of reality. In contrast to the word which is a sense-perceptible phenomenon totally different from the thing which ultimately signifies the concept—this is a mental word, hence not sense-perceptible, which is identified intentionally to the thing itself, which it makes present to the mind: it is that very thing which the intelligence actually comes to know about the thing.

Words are not the same for all, as is witnessed by the fact that they differ from one language to another. On a deeper level we must note that there is not, in contemporary language, any intrinsic similarity, even remote, between the spoken word or its acoustical image on the one hand, and the notion conceived concomitantly by the intellect, on the other. The relation of the linguistic sign to the mental word is therefore arbitrary as to the respective natures of the extremes which it connects, while nevertheless remaining necessary as to its very existence, since indeed, there could be no concept without an acoustic image: if I can eventually come to think successively in different languages, I must nevertheless always think in one language [at a time]. By contrast, the 'affections of the soul' which here are our concepts, are the same for all, whatever the idiom in which they are, as it were, inscribed. The reason for this identity is to be found in the relationship of similitude which exists, independently of our will, between the mental word, which expresses intelligibly the thing, and the thing itself which is thus expressed. In total, the linguistic sign therefore consists of three features: the word, which is a pure signifier; the concept, which is at the same time both the primary 'signified reality' of the word and the similitude of the thing; and finally the thing signified by the word and made present to the mind by the concept. The word signifies the concept without resembling it, whereas the concept, by contrast, is the intentional similitude of the thing which it signifies:

> *Litteræ autem ita sunt signa vocem et voces passionum quod non attenditur ibi aliqua ratio similitudinis, sed sola ratio institutionis, sicut et in multis aliis signis, ut tuba est signum belli; in passionibus autem animæ oportet attendi rationem similitudinis ad exprimendas res, quia eas naturaliter designant, non ex institutione.* [6]

> Letters are signs of utterances, and utterances of 'passions in the soul', in such fashion that there is not to be expected there any natural aspect of similitude, but only the aspect of an arbitrary arrangement, as indeed is true of many other signs, such as a trumpet being a sign for battle; but where the passions of the soul [the concepts] are concerned there is to be expected an aspect of similitude with the things being expressed, because the concepts express these by their very nature, and not by an arbitrary agreement.

In the perspective which we are considering here, it is this opposition between the natural character of the conceptual signification and the conventional character of the linguistic signification which we must underline. It follows that ordinary language says things, through the intermediary of concepts, but does not give them a shape; or if you prefer, it presents them but does not represent them, at least in so far as the delicate notion of representation implies a similitude with what it represents.

• The sacramental sign and its symbolic dimension

The most cursory analysis of the notion of sacrament easily discovers there, *mutatis mutandis*, the three features which we have just isolated in the linguistic sign: like the latter, the essential rite of the sacraments includes a sense-perceptible exterior signifier, a 'signified reality' interior to the soul of the minister, the recipient, or the other participants, and finally a sacred reality which is aimed at jointly by the signifier and its intra-mental 'signified reality'. In baptism, for example, the signifier is effectuated by the conjunction of the ritual form *'ego te baptizo in nomine Patris et Filii et Spiritus Sancti'*, and the pouring of the water on the head of the one to be baptized. The primary 'signified reality' of this rite consists in the understanding that the celebrant and the baptized (or his representatives) have of it, at the moment in which baptism is administered, and without which the baptism would be neither a human act nor a human sign. As for the *res sacra* ('sacred reality') which the baptismal rite and its intelligible apprehension attain, it is a question, assuredly, in the first place, of sanctifying grace and the sacramental character of which the sacrament of baptism is the instrumental cause.

At the same time as we perceive the analogy of the three-fold structure which allows us to place the sacraments *in genere signi* ('in the category of sign'), after the model of linguistic signs, we also grasp the profound differences which separate them. First of all, faith teaches us that the sacramental signs are distinguished from every other human word by this; that they alone have the power to cause, instrumentally, what they signify: *verba sacramentalia significando efficiunt* ('sacramental words are effective in their signifying'), as a neatly-turned phrase of the Common Doctor sums it up. [7] In a sacrament, the global relationship of signification is such that it enjoys the exclusive power to produce, simultaneously, the reality in which it finds its term.

But the originality of the sacraments within the category of sign, affects also each of the instances which make them such, as Christ has instituted them. Let us examine them in succession, beginning with the *res* ('thing') which the sacrament causes by signifying it. Our human concepts are characterized by the unity and accessibility, at least relative, of their objects: to one idea corresponds directly and formally one aspect of things, univocally or at least analogically one; and this segment of reality finds a home in the natural amplitude of our intellect, if only through being handled by analogy, as in the case of theological language. Sacramental signs, on the other hand, signify, at the same time, and jointly, the formal cause of our sanctification, which is habitual grace, and the whole supernatural organism, its primary instrumental cause, which is the passion of Our Lord - and its final cause, which is eternal life. [8] In truth, these three causalities are signified simultaneously in so far as they are united in the one order, defined by the sanctification of the subject who receives the sacrament; but it remains true that the richness of signification of the sacramental signs surpasses the natural genius of simply spoken language. This transcendence appears quite clearly, if one considers the origin of the gifts which the sacraments signify and communicate, which is to be found in God alone, beyond all created efficient power. This is why, on the epistemological plane, the actual reality of the justification signified by the sacraments is not within the reach of the purely natural exercise of the human intelligence: full consent to sacramental teachings is possible only under the impulsion of theological faith.

The most visible difference for us between the linguistic sign and the sacramental sign is to be found in the case of the signifier. From the strictly physical point of view, the words of language all fall into the same category, since they are always articulated sounds which have no wider variety than the phonemes which make them up; and from the properly significatory point of view, they are totally dissimilar to their corresponding 'signified realities'. Under those two aspects, the sacraments present clearly opposed characteristics. Their sense-perceptible being, first of all, is by definition heterogeneous, since it includes words and actions, or 'elements', according to the celebrated Augustinian definition: *accedit verbum ad elementum, et fit sacramentum* ('the word unites with the action, and there is made a sacrament'). [9] The signifier in the sacraments is thus a whole, but a complex whole, and this will allow it to unite in an ordered sheaf several layers of signification. For example, in the baptismal rite, the water evokes principally a certain purification, whereas the sacramental word *ego te baptizo...* determines the exact sense of this purification by linking it to the Holy Trinity and so to the remission of sins. The initial disparity, on the purely physical plane, between action and word, is therefore assumed through their aspects as matter and form into the unity of a single sign with multiple, but ordered dynamisms.

It is because a visible rite, and not a word alone, belongs constitutively to the significative being of the sacrament (*sacramentum tantum*) that this sacrament is not, like the words of the language, reducible to a simple conventional sign, but that it is, in all the fullness of the term, an efficacious symbol of the sacred reality which it causes by symbolizing it. Unlike what happens, in fact, in the linguistic sign, the sacramental action embodies a certain similitude with the thing which it signifies. In the case of Baptism the symbolism will consist in the application to spiritual regeneration of all the functions which water provides for bodily life: since water washes by reason of its wetness, cools by reason of its freshness, and transmits light by reason of its transparency, we can say that baptism removes the stain of original sin; that it calms the fire of concupiscence; and that it opens the soul to the light of revelation. [10] Taking notice, in faith, of the material rites, will therefore lead the faithful to interpret their spiritual effect. On what does this interplay of correspondences between the sense-perceptible signs and their corresponding 'signified realities' rest? In its natural root, sacramental symbolism calls upon a relationship of participation between the visible world of signs - which it sets in motion - and the invisible world of spiritual realities which it evokes; in the concrete economy of salvation the symbolic sign sends us back to an exactly specified object, of which it is destined to be the instrument. Nevertheless, this participation is not inscribed in the ontology of the sense-perceptible realities involved in the sacraments, except from a distance, and merely dispositively: by nature and according to its own inner properties, water will indeed wash bodies, but it could not be, of itself, the efficacious sign of the sanctification of the soul; for the sense-perceptible element to have, in general, a symbolic significance, the mediation of the spirit must intervene: for this mediation to be properly sacramental, and therefore efficacious, it must benefit from divine institution. [11] At this point we must go beyond the two opposing extremes of a platonizing approach, which is happy to see the physical reality of the symbols melt into their significative value,[12] and a nominalist functionalism which would deny them any ontological roots and reduce them to merely linguistic structures, deprived of true signification. [13] In this regard the very structure of the sacramental rite speaks to us directly, because thanks to the visible action, the sacramental sign possesses a certain similitude to the sacred 'thing' which it causes; but this similitude is not effective except by virtue of the words which, by assuming the action as matter under form, confers on it thereby its being as a sign:

> *ad perfectionem significationis sacramentalis necesse fuit ut significatio rerum sensibilium per aliqua verba determinarentur.* [14]
>
> Hence in order that the communication of meaning through the sacraments might achieve its full perfection, it was necessary to give precision to the meaning that sensible materials have the power to convey as signs, by adding certain words to them.

If the words which the priest pronounces constitute the form of the sacrament, clearly they do not exercise this role of determinative principle except by reason of the signification which makes them ordered, building on the intellectual apprehension of their object, to the *res sacra* (sacred thing). The two elements which comprise the external sacramental rite are not united except by, and in the interior meaning which the objective faith of the Church assigns to them.

How does one then formulate how the integration of sense-perceptible symbolism in the median feature of the sacramental sign, that is to say in the apprehension of its ultimate 'signified reality, by the believing intelligence? In other words, how is the symbolical scope of the sacrament itself proportioned to the immaterial and supernatural gift which it must, at the same time, both signify and cause? On this point, St Thomas likens the visible aspect of the sacraments to the language of scripture:

> *Signum autem est per quod aliquis devenit in cognitionem alterius. Unde, cum res sacræ quæ per sacramenta significantur, sint quædam spiritualia et intelligibilia bona quibus homo sanctificatur, consequens est ut per aliquas res sensibiles significatio sacramenti impleatur: sicut etiam per similitudinem sensibilium rerum in divina Scriptura res spirituales nobis describuntur.* [15]
>
> A sign is something through which a person arrives at knowledge of some further thing beyond itself. Moreover the sacred realities signified by the sacraments are certain spiritual and intelligible goods by which man is sanctified. And the consequence of this fact is that the function of the sacrament as signifying is implemented by means of some sensible realities. The case here is similar to that in the Holy Scriptures where, in

order to describe spiritual realities to us, corresponding sensible realities are used to illustrate them.

At the outset therefore, sacramental symbolism must be rooted in the external perception of the ritual action in the same way as biblical symbolism is founded on the internal representation ('phantasma' in the thomistic lexicon) which is aroused by the metaphor inspired in our imagination. In the two cases the intellect transfers spontaneously (in virtue of the meta-phora) on to the transcendent register which God, the primary source and end of the symbol, had sealed in a particularly evocative spatial or even temporal complex. [16] In this way, the ontological resemblance—real indeed but radically insufficient—which links the sacramental action to the grace of Christ, founds on the noetic level a relationship of analogy which must be interpreted after the model of the divine names. Since the symbolic sign belongs indisputably to the world of bodies, it comes into the same category as terms such as the stock and shoots of the vine, or again the shepherd and the sheep, the definition of which includes finitude and materiality. Like these, sacramental symbols will therefore signify a *res sacra* in a very imperfect way by means of what is conventionally called an only improper or metaphorical analogy of proportionality, because their direct signification is of an essentially corporal order: and this because it is not open of itself, to the divine realities. When the faithful person understands that Christ justifies the soul of the baptized, just as water in the same instant purifies his body, what he believes surpasses what he sees; not only because the light of faith is above the light of reason but also because the physical symbol has not, strictly speaking, a common measure with its meta-physical 'signified reality'.

• *Liturgical symbolism*

We have explained in summary fashion the three factors around which is structured the sacrament, integrally considered, namely; the sacramental sign, the sacred reality which the sign causes by signifying it, and the presence of this thing to the mind which perceives the sign of it. On this basis we can define sacramental symbolism as the relationship of metaphorical similitude which the form of the sacrament inaugurates, by virtue of the divine institution, between the totality of the sacramental action on the one hand, and the entirety of its significations on the other. [17] But since the human intelligence is rational, and therefore discursive, it is necessary that all the riches enclosed in the essential rite of the sacraments be expressed in their ceremonial rite, as precisely and as intensely as possible.

When we bear in mind here, that the essence of a thing, far from abolishing its accidental qualities, demands them, we will be able to avoid the reductive minimalism so common in our day, which considers them as mere accessories —and therefore subject to 'pastoral' manipulations—everything in the liturgy which is not required for the validity of the sacrament being celebrated. On the contrary, we are convinced, that the purely ceremonial rites are indispensable for the manifestation of the multiple aspects which lie hidden within the essential symbolism. This flowering of meaning will not happen without the multiplication of formulas and actions, which thereby do not become superfluous, provided that each time they make explicit a different dimension of the mystery.

In the traditional rite of baptism, for example, the three exorcisms which precede the sacrament, properly so called, have slightly different objects: the first concerns the salt (which itself will symbolize wisdom), the second expels from the person about to be baptized the devil taken in the singular, *exorcizo te, immunde spiritus* ('I exorcise thee, unclean spirit...'), while the third generalizes this banishment, *exorcizo te, omnis spiritus immunde...*('I exorcize thee, every unclean spirit...'). [18]

One might object that all these repeated exorcisms are superfluous (and especially ill adapted to 'the man of today', since the water in the essential rite already signifies our regeneration in the death of Christ, and hence victory over the gates of hell. St Thomas had already provided the reply that exorcism is a sacramental which possesses its own proper effectiveness, and that what is to be sanctified, whether it be a person or a thing, must first of all be withdrawn from the empire of Satan. [19] Starting out from this particular case, we can easily understand that liturgical symbolism respects two crucial requirements of the economy of the sacraments. In the first place, in the line of efficacy, it has the value of a sacramental which prepares or completes the pure *opus operatum*, (the saving work which is performed) of the sacraments, in the same way as the Church unites its intercession to that of Christ. In the second place, in the line of signification, the symbols used in the ceremonial rites make explicit all that the essential rites contain but cannot express, given the limits of the human mind.

The Foundations of Liturgical Symbolism.

Now that we have shown in what sacramental and liturgical symbolism consists, we must seek to establish its raison d'être. When he asks himself why Christ instituted visible sacraments to communicate his invisible grace, St Thomas proposes two series of motives of which the first is of the anthropological order, while the second is of the Christological order. By analysing them briefly, we will come to understand better the role of symbolism in the Church's liturgy.

• *The anthropological foundations of symbolism*

From the perspective of the person who must be sanctified by the grace of Christ, recourse to sense-perceptible instruments is justified for two principal reasons. There is first of all an arcane disposition of human nature whose function it is to ascend to spiritual realities starting from sense-perceptible data, as the naturally and constitutively abstractive character of our intellectual knowledge makes particularly clear. [20] This argument provides the basis for a strict requirement in the order of ascent according to which man owes worship to his creator in strict justice; and that is why the virtue of religion demands external actions, [21] among which we must count the gestures of bodily adoration [22] and sacrifices: [23] all of which flows from the natural law. On the other hand, in the descending order in which we receive gifts from on high, the principle which we have just stated is not quite sufficient: it would be unwise if one were to consider the rational animal in himself, for God to sanctify the nobler part from the vantage point of the inferior part. In itself, our nature calls for a worship linked to the senses, but in strict rigour it does not demand sense-perceptible sacraments; consequently the anthropological justification for the sacraments and their symbolism requires a second reason. This concerns the concrete condition of nature in relation to its final end (state) and not only its constitutive notes. In the state of original justice it was illogical that spiritual grace should come to us via the detour of a corporal sign; [24] but in the state of fallen nature which we have inherited from Adam, our sensory appetite is in revolt against our spirit which itself is in some way distanced from God, the beginning and end of our being; that is why it is, henceforth, fully in conformity with the divine pedagogy, that we should be healed by that in which we have sinned:

> *Secunda ratio sumenda est ex statu hominis, qui peccando se subdidit per affectum corporalibus rebus. Ibi autem debet medicinale remedium homini adhiberi ubi patitur morbum. Et ideo conveniens fuit ut Deus per quædam corporalia signa hominibus spiritualem medicinam adhiberet: nam, si spiritualia nuda ei proponerentur, eius animus applicari non posset, corporalibus deditus.* [25]

The second reason is taken from man's own state. For by sinning he incurred an affection for physical things and so made himself subject to them. Now the remedy designed to heal man has to be applied to that part of his nature affected by his sickness. Hence it was appropriate for God to apply spiritual medicine to men by means of certain physical signs. For if he were to be confronted with spiritual realities pure and unalloyed his mind, absorbed as it is in physical things, would be incapable of accepting them'.

We cannot overemphasize this medicinal value of sense-perceptible symbols in the Christian scheme of things. Even prior to its instrumental efficacy, and in order to prepare the soul for this efficacy, the sacramental sign and all the liturgical actions which unroll its varied potentials must purify the sensory part of our nature, which is turned in on itself by sin and so predisposes it to let itself be straightened out by the moral virtues and the life of grace. Here beauty must totally fulfil its office as ambassador of the true and the good: *pulchrum splendor veri'* ('beauty is the radiance of truth'), so that a beautiful celebration may be for the participants and the congregation like a sense-perceptible reflection of the glory of the risen Christ. This symbolic catharsis is today repudiated in practice, by the covertly iconoclastic mania for 'stripping down', which under the cloak of poverty, makes every well-structured liturgical solemnity unbelievably suspect to the mass of the clergy. Such drabness which likes to consider itself as being close to this false abstraction, which is 'contemporary man', serves rather only to leave him sunk in his wretchedness, because in practice it refuses him all sensory presence of the sacred, which is nonetheless one of the major benefits of the Incarnation.

• *The Christological foundations of symbolism*

By becoming incarnate, the Word made himself accessible to our sense of hearing, our sight, and even, St John tells us, our sense of touch. [26] After the Ascension, and thanks to the sending of the Holy Spirit, the Church continues the mystery of Christ and his triple messianic function of priest, prophet and king. As the prolongation of the Incarnation, the Church analogically reproduces its structure, since it unites a human element to a divine principle. [27] That is why its sacraments have a theandric (divine-human) character, which assimilates them to the Incarnate Word:

> *Primo enim possunt [sacramenta] considerari ex parte causæ*
> *sanctificantis, quæ est Verbum incarnatum: cui sacramentum quo-*
> *dammodo conformatur in hoc quod rei sensibili verbum adhibetur, sicut*
> *in mysterio incarnationis carni sensibili est Verbum Dei unitum.* [28]
> Thus the sacraments can be considered first from the aspect of the sanctifying cause which is the incarnate Word. There is a certain conformity with this in the constitution of the sacrament consisting in the fact that just as in the mystery of the Incarnation, the Word of God is united to the flesh which we can perceive with our senses, so too in the sacraments words are applied to sensible elements.

The joining in the sacramental sign, of a word to an action, mirrors the joining of the Word and of the flesh in Christ. In this comparison, the sacramental word is taken in its totality, to include its signification as well as its efficacy: just as the subsistent Word of the Father becomes visible in the flesh, so his redeeming Word comes into effective contact with us through a visible sign.

It seems valid to develop still more deeply the analogy which Aquinas puts before us here. Christ conjoins in the single person of the Word the two natures, divine and human, and in turn his human nature unites these two really distinct principles, the body and the soul. In a similar way the sacrament binds grace into a single efficacious action, which is a participation in the divine nature, and a properly human sense-perceptible sign, which comprises a soul, which is its signification, and a body, which is a corporal element specified by a word. By thus analysing the relationship of exemplarity, which connects the sacraments to Christ, we can understand clearly that it provides the foundation for liturgical symbolism: for if the Incarnate Word reveals the Father because he is the 'brightness of his glory' and 'the exact imprint of his very being', [29] the sacramental action must be in the image of the three realities which it signifies; the grace which it confers, the Passion which it applies, and the beatitude which it prefigures. A liturgical symbol will be so much the more adapted to its object as it allows this triple signification to shine through: especially the first which is the principal.

The two foundations of symbolism, anthropological and Christological, come together over the salvation which Christ has come to bring to mankind, as is made easily perceptible by the etymology of the term 'συμ-βολον', 'symbol'. This word comes from 'συν-βαλλειν', 'to throw together', and in antiquity designated a sign of recognition composed of the two parts of a token, which one joined back together to constitute a claim to hospitality. In the sacramental and liturgical context, the symbol makes possible, by analogy, the restoration of the unity with God which is required for the perfection of human nature, and which the disobedience of our first parents caused to be broken. In so far as it conjoins a sense-perceptible action to a meaningful word, the liturgical sign repairs, as we have seen, the break, at the heart of our nature, between flesh and spirit; in so far as it is the bearer *ex opere operato* ('by the very fact of the action being performed') or *ex opere operantis* ('by the very fact of the action of the minister'), of the grace which it signifies, it reorders this very nature to its ultimate end by the gift of the shared divine life; and in so far as it is in the image of Christ, it anticipates the gathering up of the members of the mystical body in their head. [30]

NOTES

1.   We quote St Thomas according to the Leonine edition (except for the Commentary on the Sentences) and after the following fashion:

1 Co	*Expositio et Lectura super Primam epistolam ad Corinthios*
CG	*Summa contra Gentiles*
EPH	*Expositio libri Peryermenias*
Io	*Lectura super Ioannem*
QDP	*Quæstiones disputatæ De Potentia*
QIDV	*Quæstiones disputatæ De Veritate*
Sn 1, 1, 1, 1, c	*Scriptum super Sententiarum, Book 1, Distinction 1, question 1*
I, 1, 1, c	*Summa Theologica, 1st part, question 1, article 1, corpus*
ag 1 - 1m	first objection - reply to the first objection
quia	*quæstiuncula*
sc	*sed contra*
sol	*solutio*
un.	*quæstio unica*

The English translations from the Tertia Pars are from the Blackfriars Latin/English edition of the *Summa Theologica.*

2.   We are thinking especially of Mircea Eliade, whose copious output is often closely related to our theme. cf. for example *Images et Symboles, Essais sur le symbolisme magico-religieux,* Paris, 1952; *Aspects du Mythe,* Paris, 1963; *Le sacre et le profane.* Paris, 1965.

3.   Ill, 60, 1, c. cf. also *Catechism of the Catholic Church.* n. 1131; Sn 4, 1, 1, sol. 2, c; 4, 14, 1, 1, sol. 1, c; III, 60, 2. c.

4.   cf. for example *The Second Vatican Council, Constitution on the Sacred Liturgy Sacrosanctum*

Concilium n. 7.

5.   Aristotle, *Peri Hermeneias*, 1, 16 a 3-8. The term symbol here has no symbolic connotation, in the sense which we are examining here, where water symbolises the purification of the soul.

6.   EPH 1, lect. 2, n. 19 [9], 1, 202-208.

7.   1 Cor. 11, lect. 6, n. 673

8.   cf. III, 60, 3, c; Sn 4, 1, 1,1, qla 1, 4m

9.   cf. III, 60, 4, sc.

10. We are summarizing here III, 66, 3, c. cf. also Sn 4, 3, 1, 3, sol. 1, c; CG 4, 59, n. 3976.

11. cf. III, 60, 5, 2m.

12. This is, in our opinion, the fundamental error of the otherwise extremely seminal book of Jean Borella, *La crise du symbolisme religieux*, Lausanne, 1990, especially pp. 45-51 and 130-132. By contrast, pp. 208-212, dedicated to the liturgical reform flowing from the second Vatican Council, seem to us to be extremely relevant. We gladly make our own, his conclusion, p. 212: 'In a word, the old sacred forms, of a prodigious richness, have been destroyed; in their place has been produced an abstract symbolism, verbose and arid, So it is not only in Africa, in America, in Asia, that cultural murders are being carried out, and that millennia of beauty and splendour are disappearing, treasures of imagination and sensitivity; but it is also in the West that this is happening, under our very eyes, at this very moment, in the fare of total incomprehension and perfect indifference'.

13. We are thinking here, as is clear, of *L'Anthropologie structurale* of Claude Levi-Strauss, Paris, 1958, passim.

14. III, 60, 6, c.

15. III, 60, 4, c.

16. cf. III, 60, 5, 1m.

17. cf. Sn 2, 1, 4, sol. 1, c: *'sacramenta sunt signa remedii ad quod ordinantur. Sunt autem signa repræsentia effectus spirituales ex similitudine sensibilium rerum, quarum in sacramento est usus'* ('sacraments are signs of the remedy to which they are ordained. They are signs which represent spiritual effects in the likeness of the sense-perceptible things of which the sacrament makes use').

18. cf. *Rituale Romanum Ssmi D. N. Pii Papæ XII auctoritate ordinatum et auctum*, Rome, 1952, Titulus II, Caput II, nn. 6, 7 et 11.

19. cf. SN 6, 2, 3, sol. 1, c and 3m, also sol. 2, c.

20. cf. III, 60, 5, c.

21. cf. II-II, 81, 7, c.

22. cf. II-II, 84, 2, 2rn.

23. cf. II-II, 85, 1, c.

24. cf. III, 61, 2, c.

25. cf. III, 61, 1, c. The same doctrine was already proposed in Sn 4, 1, 1, 2, sol. 1, c.

26. cf. I Jn 1, 1

27. cf. *The Second Vatican Council, Dogmatic Constitution on the Church, Lumen Gentium*, no. 8; *Constitution on the Sacred Liturgy Sacrosanctum Concilium*, no 2.

28. III, 60, 6 c. cf lo 3 lect. 1, n. 443: *'Congruit ergo quod in sacramentis quæ efficacium habent ex virtute Verbi incarnati, sit aliquid correspondens Verbo, et aliquid correspondens carni, seu corpori'* ('It is fitting therefore that in the sacraments, which have their efficacy from the power of the Word incarnate, there should be something corresponding to the flesh or the body').

29. Heb 1.3

30. cf. Eph 1.10. To this sym-bolism is opposed the dia-bolism of the rites, social or pseudo-religious, which divide man and God, instinct and reason. A 'concert' of rock 'music', for example, where the pounding beat is very similar to the rhythms which accompanied human sacrifices among the Aztecs, has no transcendent meaning, but drugs the sensitive part of our nature and blinds the intelligence. It is striking to observe the chronological parallelism which exists between the desacralization of the Roman liturgy which has been underway for the past thirty years, and the proliferation of those paraliturgies of whose demonic inspiration only the advocates of inculturation seem to be unaware.

LITURGICAL LANGUAGE AND COMPREHENSION OF THE RITES

Seán Finnegan

Fr Finnegan, born in 1961, is a priest in the diocese of Arundel and Brighton and currently Catholic Chaplain to the University of Surrey in Guildford. He is a Master of Arts (St Andrews) and a Bachelor of Theology (Southampton); and the founder of the Priestly Association of St John Fisher.

U PON consideration of the matter in hand—not so profound, perhaps, as some of the other matters treated of in this colloquium, but none theless capable of exciting all sorts of strong and contrary opinions, even among those who broadly agree—it appears that the subject under discussion within this paper could well occupy an entire colloquium. Hence one must, perforce, confine oneself to an overview at best; a consideration of the broad picture that will repay further, more detailed investigations in the future. I have, therefore, broadly grouped the aspects of this paper under three headings; historical considerations, theological/philosophical reflections, and practical and pastoral implications.

HISTORICAL CONSIDERATIONS.

It is one of the faults of our modern age to think that the present is the sum and crown of all the past. The Church knows better. As Newton, the great English scientist said 'we are merely the pygmies that stand on the shoulders of giants'. History is the window that sheds light upon the condition of the present and teaches us to see things in their true nature. Such is evidenced by the Church's insistence that sacred tradition is a true and authentic organ of divine revelation itself. In this spirit, while preparing this talk, it seemed congruent to consult, among many other documents, the *Acta* of Preparation and Sessions of the Council of Trent. While reading through the minutes of the preparatory sessions, I found myself deeply impressed by the manner in which both tradition and history truly lay at the very foundation of those Fathers' investigations and discussions, as well as the thorough and systematic methods they employed. There was an evidently strenuous effort when examining each doctrine and practice to establish just what the Church has always practised, understood and believed in her tradition, and to regard this as normative and even legislative for what was then proposed as being, or assessed as having been, the modern day practice. Naturally, every ecumenical council is protected from error in its doctrinal formulations, but one is very certain that at Trent it did not happen by accident. In a similar manner, when one is conducting any examination of Catholic faith or practice, it is always fitting, indeed essential, to establish what precedents there are in our history to establish whether these shed light on the present and, indeed, what may be in the future.

Ever since the Renaissance, and the rediscovery of the ancient learning, which included the study and, to an extent, the revival of the ancient languages of Hebrew and Greek, there has been among Christians a fantasy for the rediscovery of the initial fervour of the early Christian Church. There is a sort of shared delusion, commonly found even in our day, of what is called 'Gospel Simplicity'. All development, ornamentation, elaboration—dare one say it, even beauty —is said to belong to a later, more decadent, age. Thus it is that both Luther and those who would modify Catholicism in our own age have, as it were, been bitten with the bug of paring down, simplifying, 'getting back to' some sort of a golden age before the accretions of the middle ages obscured the presumed rational and noble simplicities of the early Christian ideal of worship. But we must ask whether the presumptions that underlie this are correct. Indeed, most of the evidence suggests the contrary to be the case. It appears that our earliest Fathers in the faith, far from conducting simple Gospel services with the aid of a guitar and a bible, on the contrary celebrated the sacraments in an atmosphere of the very greatest reverence and mystery.

The very first celebration of the Mass, begun at the last Supper, and finding its fulfilment and meaning in the sacrifice of our Lord himself upon Calvary, was almost certainly not a vernacular celebration. The vernacular of the time, as we all know, was Aramaic, and almost certainly the language of the prayers and psalms was Hebrew, a language long dead even by the time of our Lord, and used, by and large, only in prayer. But within the Christian era, before too long, it appears that some form of commonly understood language was being used: at least this is the implication of both the Didache and the writings of St Hippolytus. [1] The use of a language other than Hebrew was building, presumably, on the practice of Jews within the Diaspora using Greek for even the sacred texts; witness their already ancient translation of the scriptures, known as the Septuagint.

One should add, however, that to call Greek, and thereafter Latin, vernacular tongues, is not really accurate. There was no one Latin vernacular tongue but many variations, as in modern Italy where, whereas the *lingua Toscana in bocca Romana* remains the official language of the country, nevertheless, at least until recent times, every region had its own dialect. Greek, and subsequently Latin, had, like modern Italian, a similar character of being not vernaculars through the empire, but *linguæ francæ;* tongues mutually intelligible to a number of distinct vernacular language groups, in the same way that modern French and

English nowadays serve many nations and tongues in Africa. The status of, initially Greek, and then also Latin as languages of culture went unchallenged until very modern times; at the beginning of this present century it was still not uncommon for even secular scholars, native speakers of mutually unintelligible vernaculars, to converse in Latin.

So, once the prayers of the Mass and Office had been codified and written down, perhaps around the time of the settlement of the Church under Constantine, they tended to remain in circulation in precisely the language in which they were first written. When Pope St Gregory the Great sent St Augustine to evangelize England, he sent Latin service books with him, and though he suggested the possibility of modifications, should these seem sensible to St Augustine, there was never any question of changing the language of public worship to a true vernacular. In the same way, when Winfrith or Boniface left Crediton in Devon to evangelize the pagan Germans, it was the Latin books that he took with him. In addition to this, it was often asserted through the early period, and right up to the deliberations of the Council of Trent, that there were only three appropriate languages in which to celebrate the Mass: Hebrew, Latin and Greek, since these were the three languages affixed to the Cross itself.

As far as I can understand, this situation broadly went unchallenged in the Latin Rite until the Reformation. The Eastern Rites, however, were a notable exception to the general principle. When Saints Cyril and Methodius brought the Gospel to the Slavs, they did so, and worshipped too, in the Slavs' own tongue. In this they were initially encouraged by Pope Hadrian II, and then in 879 reproved by his successor, John VIII, for celebrating the Mass neither in Latin, nor Greek tongue, *sed barbara, id est Sclavina lingua*. [2] In the following year, however, after an appeal, the same Pope rescinded this rebuke and actually encouraged the missionaries in their work, requiring only that the Epistle and Gospel should be read in Latin (presumably meaning the formal, liturgical proclamation, together with a Slavic translation). One should note in this context that the contemporary attitude was not that the scriptures demand a vernacular proclamation, but that their integrity demanded the retention of sacred language. This attitude contrasts with the modern idea, espoused by modern liturgists, and (arguably) also by the Fathers of the Second Vatican Council in their prescription of a wider selection of God's word for Mass, [3] and even by many adherents of the traditional liturgy, that the reading of the scriptures at Mass has a didactic purpose, and therefore ought to be in the vernacular. The ancient idea, on the other hand, seems to have been that in the reading of the scriptures we have a kind of an 'epiphany' of God the Word, corresponding by analogy with the coming of the Lord in Flesh and Blood during the Mass of the Faithful: the place for actual instruction in the faith was not in the liturgy, but elsewhere, in catechetical classes. This reminds one of the comment made by Pius Parsch in the introduction to his *Jahr des Heils* that

> During the Gospel, it is Christ who appears and who speaks to us. We should not think of the Gospel specifically as a teaching, but much more as an epiphany of Christ'. [4]

The liturgy itself was seen as being something else; a humble reflection of the worship of heaven, gazing, though through a veil, at the face of God, and not to be used for more mundane things.

To resume: In 885, the Pope changed his mind again, and permitted only a rough translation and exposition of the Scriptures (presumably after Latin reading, and with the sermon) into Slavonic. This was the manner reported to be used throughout the East, for example in Jerusalem at the time of the visit of the famous fourth century peripatetic nun Egeria (who heard the readings first in Greek, then a translation into Syrian), and to this day among the Copts (first Coptic, then Arabic). It is, of course, a method familiar to us today, though in the Roman Rite vernacular reading of the scriptures does not form part of the liturgy, but is usually an adjunct to a homily. It was not long after this that most of the Slavs went into schism together with the greater part of the remainder of the Christian East.

The prohibition of Slavonic was renewed by Pope Hildebrand, St Gregory VII (1073-1085) and was then permitted once more by Innocent IV (1243-54) who allowed Slavonic to continue in those places where it had somehow survived; Croatia, Istria, Dalmatia, Bosnia and Slavonia. This latter use, let us be clear, was not the liturgy of St John Chrysostom or any other Eastern rite, but the Roman liturgy in Slavonic. It flourished, under the title *Missa Glagolitica* until the seventeenth century when, simply, the books became hard to come by and a certain hybridization called derisively *schiavetto* took place. Thereafter, somewhat in the manner of the adaptation of the Roman Missal in 1965, the parts of the Mass that the congregation sung or answered were done so in Slavonic, everything else being taken from the Latin Missal. In the reign of Pope Leo XIII a brief revival was undertaken of the Glagolitic Mass, and this has continued sporadically since, the only interruption being the general reforms of the last thirty-five years. The Glagolitic Mass is perhaps known best to the world through the famous setting of its common in this century by Leos Janácek. Curiously, the Ritual offices have been celebrated in modern Croatian, a true vernacular, since the seventeenth century.

The Carolingian movement in Western Europe aimed at the revival of a kind of Roman Empire, and hence encouraged Roman stability throughout it. So it is not surprising that when it came to the liturgy, Latin was perpetuated and encouraged as the language of formal worship. Vernacular was not entirely excised, however; Jungmann recounts that a kind of Credo-song might be sung by the faithful in their various vernaculars [5] throughout the Carolingian empire, and a form of this survived into comparatively modern times in parts of France as a kind of congregational counterpoint to the Latin recitation by the priest at the altar.

St Thomas Aquinas has very little to say on the subject of vernacular liturgy. He merely discusses mispronunciations and other possible invalidating acts or accidents. [6]

There had been a certain amount of the vernacular admitted into the liturgy probably during the later middle ages, at least in the Sarum Use, celebrated *mutatis mutandis* throughout the greater part of the British Isles. A prayer known as the 'Bidding of the Bedes' which corresponds very approximately to our modern 'Prayer of the Faithful' (or, in English usage 'Bidding Prayers') was made at each Sunday or greater feast day celebration, commanding prayers of charity to be made for various benefactors of the Church and individuals. Opinions differ as to the point within the Mass when this occurred: perhaps, indeed, it varied from one part of the country to another. Some authorities place it in the same position that the 'Prayer of the Faithful' occupies today, that is, after the Creed, together with the sermon. [5] Many continental uses had something similar, called the 'Office of Prône' at this point. Most authorities, however, place the Sarum Bidding of the Bedes as a kind of extra-liturgical rite at the end of the customary Festal Procession which preceded Solemn Mass, and which paused at the rood-screen for a versicle, collect and, probably, the Bidding of the Bedes.

The new learning of the Renaissance, inclined always to see education as being essential if human nature is to achieve its full potential, saw anything else as obscurantism and superstition. Catholic pre-Reformation reform began the study of the scriptures in the original languages the better to understand them. One may instance Cardinal Ximenes de Cisneros' remarkable Complutensian Bible prepared between 1502 and 1517 and the textual restoration (as they saw it) of New Testament and Patristic texts undertaken by Erasmus, who produced a new Latin version in 1516, and Lefèvre d'Etaples who actually translated the New Testament into contemporary French between 1516 and 1524. From this beginning, it is not surprising that, from Tyndale (English, 1526,), Luther (German, 1534), and Olivetain (French, in 1535), all the reformers produced or used vernacular translations of the bible. As the Reformation spread, however, positions became rapidly entrenched, and in England the counter-attack against the vernacular scriptures was championed by no less a figure than the great St Thomas More, himself a friend of Erasmus, and a Catholic Humanist, spurred into action by the publication of Tyndale's New Testament in Flanders during 1526. [8] Countless copies had been imported with merchant's goods, and the discovery of a large cache of them in the Hanseatic German merchants' warehouses, together with a number of other Protestant tracts in English, led to a great burning of books at St Paul's Cross accompanied by a sermon from St John Fisher. These men, who had so championed the Renaissance and the rebirth of learning had seen that learning, or rather a form of that learning, turned against the Church itself.

From the translation of the scriptures into the vernacular, it is but a small step to the translation of the liturgy. Lutheranism retained a Latin liturgy, at least in part, for over a hundred years, but all the other variations of Protestantism, based so strongly on the reading of, and preaching upon, the scriptures, adopted vernacular forms. It is well known that the Council of Trent gave serious consideration as to whether the liturgy could be fruitfully celebrated in the vernacular. Nobody seemed very keen to have it so. Francisco de Sanctio (a Spaniard) in the Theologians' Congregation of 31st July 1562 commented that the use of the Latin tongue in the Mass for the evangelization of France and Germany was useful, 'lest one should throw pearls before swine' (!) The council eventually concluded that:

> Although the mass contains great instruction for the faithful people, nevertheless, it has not seemed expedient to the Fathers, that it should be every where celebrated in the vulgar tongue. Wherefore, the ancient usage of each church, and the rite approved of by the holy Roman Church, the mother and mistress of all churches, being in each place retained; and, that the sheep of Christ may not suffer hunger, nor the little ones ask for bread, and there be none to break it unto them, the holy Synod charges pastors, and all who have the cure of souls, that they frequently, during the celebration of Mass, expound either by themselves, or others, some portion of those things which are read at Mass, and that, amongst the rest, they explain some mystery of this most holy sacrifice, especially on the Lord's days and festivals. [9]

One may note with interest the requirement for (presumably vernacular) commentary upon the Mass 'frequently', which was even permitted to be given by a non-ordained person. This has interesting developments in the twentieth century. The following canon was also promulgated: 'If any one should say that the Mass ought to be celebrated in the vulgar tongue only, let him be anathema'.[10]—a canon also having interesting resonances in our own time.

Given the fact that the Church in China (in both its underground form and in the so-called 'Patriotic' communities) even today is notable for its adherence to the use of Latin in the liturgy, it is remarkable that in the past, China was felt to be a particular case requiring the vernacular. The first example was one Jean de Montcorvin, a Franciscan missionary to Tartary, who simply informed the Pope that he celebrated the Latin Rite in the local language. This does not seem to have alarmed the Holy Father, who in 1307 created him Archbishop of Peking. A more famous example, however, was that of Matteo Ricci, the seventeenth-century Jesuit missionary to China, who received considerable latitude from the Vatican in 1615 for the use of Chinese in the Latin-rite liturgy, along with many of what we would today call inculturational experiments. His work did not last, however, foundering on the rock of the dispute over ancestor-worship, and after his death the use of Latin was once more mandated.

In Austria-Hungary, the reign of the unhappy son of Maria Theresa, Joseph II brought many failed attempts at reform, among which was the attempted partial vernacularization of the liturgy, at least within his own dominions. In practice, this meant the congregation singing vernacular, metrical versions of the common of the Mass while the priest celebrated in Latin at the altar. The tradition endured, and the *Deutsche Messe* settings of both Schubert and Haydn, made at the time, are still to be heard in both Austrian and German parish Churches, having acquired a new impetus in the context of the modern re-formed liturgy.

It is now worth considering a non-Catholic movement which is known only imperfectly outside England. Most Europeans are aware that the Church of England is not doctrinally homogenous; within the Anglican Communion you will find people who call themselves Anglicans and yet hold the teachings of Calvin in all their fullness, and people who, while professing the same Angli-can Communion, hold all the Catholic doctrines, including that of Papal Infal-libility and, in at least one case, to my own certain knowledge, extraordinarily, a secret disbelief in the validity of Anglican Orders. You will also find all shades of difference between these poles. The Oxford Movement of the nine-teenth century gave rise to a number of 'Anglo-Catholic' variations, of which perhaps the strongest was the 'Papalist' movement which held, together with all the Anglo-Catholics, that the Church of England was a true part of the Catho-lic Church, though sadly severed from the main body of the Church by the unfortunate accident of the Reformation; but added that the best way to reunite with the Catholic Church was to make familiar to the English all the doctrines and practices of the Catholic Church as they had continued to develop from the counter-Reformation onwards. Hence, the 1570 *Missale Romanum* was, in the late nineteenth century, translated into the most beautiful English, and, though often interleaved with extracts from the *Book of Common Prayer,* continued to be used until the recent reforms of the liturgy, when those churches formerly accustomed to using the *English Missal* simply substituted the 1970 *Roman Missal* in its familiar English ICEL and ICET translations with the *Jerusalem Bible* lectionary. Why this *English Missal* is important is that it is the only truly vernacular translation [10] of the traditional Missal that sprang from an effort to inculcate traditional Catholic dogma and practice, and was implemented in a thoroughgoing way. The 'Papalist' Anglicans often took appointments in the most unpromising districts, long abandoned by the mainstream Anglican Church, most notably in the East End of London, among the poorest of the poor. They took lads off the street, dressed them in cassocks and cottas, and taught them to serve Mass, and answer Psalm 42, like any boy on the continent, only in Eng-lish instead of Latin. The effect was remarkable: whole districts of the poorer parts of England were won back to the Church of England, albeit in a rather unique way, and, of course according to the singular manner in which they perceived the Church of England. The fruits of this can be seen today. A friend of mine is the rector of one of these churches, now using the modern *Roman Missal,* and in most respects the church and congregation are in externals and in most internal matters indististinguishable from our own: including the fact—remarkable in the modern non-evangelical parts of the Church of England—that it actually has a substantial congregation. Clearly in some form, the people have been sanctified and nourished by a vernacular form of the Mass, though of course the grace received has not been directly sacramental, owing to the probable defect in the validity of most Anglican orders.

The twentieth century saw a growth in the movement for the use of the vernacular, perhaps associated with the growth in the methods of communication, and, indeed, of the entertainments industry. This vernacular enthusiasm seemed to be, in the main, a variant—though a small minority one—of the Liturgical Movement. The efforts of the Liturgical Movement to actively involve the people in the action of the Mass and other sacraments inevitably increased the modes of this participation and led to 'revivals' and 'rediscoveries' of what was believed, or at least asserted, to be the practice of earlier, more enlightened ages. One might observe that this appeal to an earlier age has been shamelessly abused at times. In England and Wales, when lay ministers of the Blessed Sacrament were introduced in the nineteen-seventies, Catholics were told that this was a revival of the practice of the early church, and the truly traditional thing to do. In the context of the traditional Mass, the introduction of the dialogue Mass was presented in many quarters as being a 'rediscovery'. I am not aware of any historical context before this century where the entire congregation would answer psalm 42 with the server. The whole idea of low, or spoken, Mass is a relatively recent—that is, mediæval—creation. But, anyway, it is a small step from having the people answer the priest, and stumbling awkwardly over the Latin, to wondering why they cannot do so in their own tongue. And if the laity were being encouraged to pray the breviary in the vernacular, why could not a priest, finding the readings of Matins difficult, or the hymns and collects, do the same?

The movement grew, and there were many experiments, both authorized and unauthorized. The vows at marriage had been in the vernacular since at least the middle ages. Now, in the 1950s, the dialogue at baptisms was permitted to take place using the vernacular. Monsignor Ronald Knox, the well-known English wit and scholar acidly remarked when asked to use the new version 'The baby knows no English, but the Devil understands Latin'. In France and, I believe, in Germany, vernacular experiments took place with the Mass itself. I know people who had attended Sunday Mass in a French parish church in 1960, to find the Mass largely in French, and facing the congregation. Maybe this was a product of the Worker-Priest movement. In many places, the readings and other texts of the Mass would be read in the vernacular, often by a lay person, while the priest was quietly reading them in Latin at the altar. It was quite clear that the situation was reaching the position that required a resolution.

Those in any doubt about what the position of Good Pope John was on the subject of Latin need only be shown the remarkable Apostolic Constitution *Veterum Sapientia* issued 22nd February 1962, on the very eve of the Second Vatican Council and intended, presumably, to spike the guns of any vernacularists that might attempt to use the council to further the cause of the vernacular.

The employment of Latin has recently been contested in some quarters, and many are asking what the mind of the Apostolic See is in this matter. We have therefore decided to issue the timely directives contained in this document, so as to ensure that the ancient and uninterrupted use of Latin be maintained and, where necessary, restored. [12]

This is stern stuff. However, as it turned out, the enterprise was ill-conceived, its effect was in the long term negligible and perhaps, for Latin, was the kiss of death. It made no liturgical prescriptions, but concerned itself with the compulsory academic study of Latin. I know little of how it was implemented on the continent, but, in my own seminary, each lecture for a year or more was given in Latin for the first half and then repeated in the vernacular immediately afterwards. The result was that the law was seen to be an ass: students whose knowledge of Latin did not run to following complicated theology or philosophy were left bored and confused by the first half of a lecture and in the end had been supplied with only half the quantity of information that they formerly received when the entire lecture was in the vernacular. Latin was clearly seen to be a bar to knowledge and an anachronism: exactly the opposite effect to that intended by Pope John. Hence the evident relief when Latin was sidelined almost entirely such a very little time after.

The history of Latin and the vernacular during the last thirty five years is all too familiar to us all, and so I do not propose to go over it here. Instead, I would like to turn to some internal considerations.

PHILOSOPHICAL AND THEOLOGICAL CONSIDERATIONS

As we are all aware, even the august and holy Sacrifice of the Mass is not an end in itself, but only a means to an end, or rather ends: these ends being the glory of God and the salvation of man, as Pope Pius XII in his Encyclical *Mediator Dei* has reminded us. It follows, then, that any question of how we celebrate the Mass will be evaluated on how well it achieves the ends towards which the Mass is directed. Clearly, *ex opere operato,* the Mass validly celebrated in any language achieves the ends perfectly, but there remains still the question of the effects *ex opere operantis.*

I would suggest that for most of us the reason that we adhere to the traditional rite of Mass is not firstly and formostly, *a priori,* because of theoretical considerations but rather of experiential ones. We have, in other words, been moved spiritually by the celebration of Mass in its traditional forms, and feel that the end of our salvation is better helped in this form than in any other. Naturally our study of the Mass will lead us to the same conclusions for intellectual reasons, but these may be said—at least for most of us—to be *a posteriori.* I am aware that when I celebrate, or assist at a Mass that is celebrated in Latin, my devotion, my awareness of the divine, my sense of spiritual replenishment is so much stronger than when I assist at or am required to celebrate a Mass in the vernacular. Now to this I would adjoin the further observations that it is also important for the same reasons that the Mass be celebrated facing liturgical East, wearing the appropriate vestments that bear no relation to street dress, and with an atmosphere of recollection and devotion. These things speak to me of God and of his Kingdom which I await and to which I pray to be admitted. The word that sums up something of this attitude or experience is 'transcendence'. A liturgy that does not have these elements—in other words one that adopts an imminentist attitude—will not achieve the same ends as one that adopts a transcendent attitude. Those who champion the imminentist forms of worship see this as itself desirable. When one is in dialogue with these theologians and liturgists, they will point to the more physically active congregation, to the heightened sense of community, in whom our Lord is undoubtedly present, to the absence of 'passenger' Catholics who used to attend Mass with the air of a cow looking over a gate, being in no way 'involved' in what was going on.

They forget, of course, that the very purpose of the Mass is to point beyond itself. They are so busy admiring the sign that they fail to see the very thing to which the sign is pointing. And so the sign itself loses its meaning, and becomes empty. A sign that points to nothing is meaningless. It becomes an end in itself: mere theatre. Within the traditional forms of Mass there are several elements, as outlined above, each of which contribute to this transcendent 'pointing beyond'. The use of a non-vernacular language is one. The sense of transcendence can survive without it, providing most of the other elements are there, as in the case of the Anglican *English Missal* (setting aside, however, the question of its effectiveness *ex opere operato*). The fewer transcending elements, the more the Mass resembles the worldly and mundane, the less will it achieve the ends for which it was instituted, at least *ex opere operantis*. It may entertain, but it will not fascinate; it may socialize, but it is less likely to sanctify. And it will not encourage us to seek those things that are above, as the apostle reminds us to do.

And so, I would suggest, that whereas the use of a non-vernacular language is certainly infinitely preferable, it is not absolutely of the essence.

• *The apostrophic voice*

I should like now to investigate this idea of language and transcendence a little more. Recently, in fact this year, a remarkable new book has been published in Great Britain. It is called *After Writing: The Liturgical Consummation of Philosophy* [13] and is by one Catherine Pickstock, a young academic of Cambridge University. Her field of study is the philosophy of language and its relationship with theology, in particular, liturgy. In this particular, and undoubtedly seminal work, she examines the notions of language that we have nowadays, particularly with reference to the work of the post-modernist philosopher Derrida, and finds the whole contemporary approach to language fundamentally empty. Beginning from Plato, she investigates a truer notion of language, particularly as it pertains to the relationship between the Creator and his creation. She finds that one of the finest expressions of correct and truly meaningful divine-human dialogue is that found in the traditional Roman rite. It may therefore surprise you to know that Doctor Pickstock is not a Catholic, but an Anglican, albeit an Anglo-Catholic. It is her opinion that language has become increasingly manipulative as the centuries have gone on. Now, manipulation can have both good and bad effects, in the same way that indoctrination can have good and bad effects: we 'manipulate' children not to run out onto the street or be selfish; we manipulate them to say their prayers and love God and their neighbours. And clearly manipulation can have bad effects. Language is almost always used to change the person to whom we are speaking in some way: to inform, perhaps or challenge: we press a button and a communicated response is expected. Liturgical language is of a very particular kind. For a start, it is non-manipulative. Consider those great Roman collects which say everything and nothing. Why do we ask God things? Because he is our Father who knows better than we what we need anyway. We are, in the end, like those little chicks in the nest with their beaks open, waiting for the mothering hen bird to fill us. The liturgy is simply an expression of the creature waiting for his loving Creator and Redeemer to save him: even the specific requests that the liturgy makes of God are symbolic of our general need of him, are an awareness of our relationship of utter dependence on God as the utter ground of our being.

Liturgy is the greatest, most powerful way to do this, because it is free of the manipulative nature of modern language: it simply addresses God as God because that is Who He is: the One Who Is. It is useless to attempt to manipulate him with our chatter: this has its place, but the liturgy is the utter, wordless cry of love of the Church for her bridegroom, and her longing for the consummation of that love at the nuptial banquet of heaven, prefigured so perfectly in the reception of Communion. In the Holy Spirit we cry out 'Abba, Father'. What else is there to say? This is the purpose of what Doctor Pickstock calls the *apostrophic voice*. It is language that has a different mode, a different purpose from everyday speech. It is utterly non-manipulative but essentially transcendent. Even when a familiar language is used, the apostrophic voice is precisely and very importantly non-vernacular. Language that constantly tells God about himself and then demands particular things of him is manipulative, and in the end does not maintain any sort of meaningful or proper relationship between Creator and Creature. The god who is harangued is a god who can be manipulated. That is not our God, the only God, and he has made possible this transcendent mode in which we can, as it were, glimpse the hem of his garment.

Perhaps the closest other example of this apostrophic voice is the rosary. As we all know, when one has prayed the rosary for a time, the literal meaning of the prayers becomes increasingly unimportant, and even the discursive meditation on the mysteries fades into the background. One is left simply as the creature looking, hand in hand with our Lady, at our Creator. The rosary is, as it were, the liturgy *par excellence* of the laity. Perhaps those who pray the rosary at Mass sense the appropriateness of this in a way that those of the liturgical movement keen on more active participation would not approve.

PRACTICAL CONSIDERATIONS

I think that though we have established that while there is *some* precedent for the use of the vernacular on historical grounds, there is not a great deal, and though we also have established that epistemologically it is preferable to address the Deity in a non-vernacular way, in the end, one has to come to terms with the nitty-gritty of implementation. It is all very well theorizing about these matters, but the practical aspects seem now to be very thorny indeed. People, Catholic people are simply no longer used to Latin, nor even to a liturgy with any sense of transcendence. Latin, for many of today's Catholics, particularly the younger generation, is no longer about nostalgia but about innovation: introducing something that they might never have associated with worship. Why Latin, rather than Norwegian or Innuit?

Secondly, it is undoubtedly true that the vernacular rites are a great deal more approachable than Latin for those encountering them for the first time. Non-churchgoers and non-catholics coming to weddings, baptisms or funerals are not entirely puzzled by what is going on when they can at least understand the words. There is some correlation between their lives—television, for the most part—and the efforts of the priest to communicate with them. A priest who quite obviously is spending most of his time talking to God in an arcane language and making no effort to amuse the congregation at all is not going to make much impact on those who do not already understand what he is doing.

It seems to me that what we are talking about is the difference between fast food and a really nourishing meal. Fast food may have short-term appeal, but in the end frustrates the very purpose for which food was created, which is to nourish. A child fed on nothing but ice cream will die in the end of malnourishment, though paradoxically with a full stomach. In England, and probably elsewhere in the world, there are many Protestant communities that spring up overnight, attract hundreds of young people with an up-beat message, loud music and fast talking, but within five years they have collapsed; unable to sustain all those who first flocked to them. This is, in our Lord's terms, the seed that fell in shallow soil. In the liturgy, the Christian people must learn the skills that they will need for eternity: they need to relate as creatures to the God who created them. The seed needs to be planted in deep soil where it will produce its crop.

I think that it is undoubtedly true that the Catholic liturgy *can* do its job in the vernacular, providing that the other things (for example; eastward orientation in the case of the Mass, and 'sacred' rather than colloquial speech) are sufficiently strongly maintained. On occasion, some use of the vernacular may even be desirable, as the Fathers of Vatican II commented. I might instance the sacrament of the Anointing of the Sick, or Extreme Unction, where an individual who is sick or dying, together with those assisting are more directly concerned with the action and the prayers constituting the sacrament, and the distress of the moment, to say nothing of the practical conveniences of the situations in which this sacrament is usually administered may obviate the use of the full texts with translations for all who participate. But certainly those sacraments which are more visibly ecclesial—those celebrations where clearly the Church is manifested, and especially where ecclesial Communion itself is so essential, such as the Mass, or the conferral of Holy Orders, perhaps also in the case of Baptism—in these cases, the use of a common non-vernacular liturgical language is, for all the reason outlined in this paper, very strongly desirable.

Thirdly, there is the problem that Latin has really ceased to play a prominent role in our culture during this century. A hundred years ago, it was not unusual, at least in England, for seminarians to be taught to converse in Latin, and not just to have a reading knowledge of it. These days, despite the prescriptions of the Church on the matter, it is a rare seminary in the West that has Latin on the curriculum at all. Any programme attempting the re-introduction of Latin would, at the same time, have to concern itself with the education of a highly reluctant clergy! Either that, or simply accept that the re-introduction of a Latin liturgy is something that cannot be achieved in this present generation, and begin to make longer-term plans for its re-establishment in the next.

Fourthly, it must be observed from the entire history of the Church that vernacular experiment has almost always gone hand-in-hand with doctrinal heterodoxy. In a very real sense, the use of the sacred language has been a sort of bastion, or at least a companion of orthodoxy. We have to confront the fact that in the Church today there are issues of far greater moment than the language in which the sacraments are celebrated; in many places the very sacraments themselves are under attack. I suspect that if the use of the sacred languages had been continued, the damage would not have been as great, nevertheless the mere restoration of Latin will not be sufficient in itself to restore everything else.

Conclusion

There is no doubt that in the history of the Church, liturgical *volte-faces* have come about. The Quignonez breviary, used so extensively, curiously, by the English reformer, Cranmer, in his *Book of Common Prayer* was replaced not long after its introduction. And the drastic pruning of the calendar made after the Council of Trent gave way rapidly to a burgeoning of the old feasts once more. It is far from impossible that, as the number of people increase who are concerned that our tradition is gravely in danger, that some official effort may be made to reinstate Latin as truly the language of the Church. But, for all the reasons that I have outlined, though I believe that Latin should be restored, with so much else that has been lost, I do not believe that the time for Latin has come yet; I honestly believe that it will be the most difficult of the restorations to make. When the first English Mass was celebrated in my home parish: in essence still, of course, the Mass of St Pius V, my Father commented that he felt that he had not been to Mass; the shock and sense of unfamiliarity were simply too great. But at that time, the sense of obedience and respect for the Church was still strong, and most people coped with the change. The reversion of the liturgical language to Latin, attempted too suddenly, may well produce the same effect, without the sense of obedience to carry it through. One might have simple anarchy (which might, though, please some). In any contemplated reform or restoration of the present rites, other things such as eastward celebration, kneeling Communion, even the traditional Mass itself will, I believe, be more readily accepted than an entirely Latin Mass. When these other things are in place, then will be the time to crown these things with the restoration of the sacred language. And by the grace of God, perhaps we will not have to wait too long.

NOTES

1   Both the *Didache* and Hippolytus seem to imply that the celebrant improvised the Canon of the Mass. When considering these as normative texts, the point should be made that Hippolytus, though ultimately canonized as a martyr, was a man with rather a chequered history when it came to relationship with the Church, and the writer has also heard the question being raised of whether the *Didache* be truly a Catholic document, or one belonging to a heretical sect.

2.   P.L. tom. CXXVI col. 849-850

3.   *Sacrosanctum Concilium* 35 (1)

4.   Pius Parsch Jahr Des Heils *10 Aufl., Klosterneuburg, 1932, p.16 quoted in Mgr Klaus Gamber* La Réforme Liturgique en Question, *Éditions Sainte-Madeleine 1992 p.61*
    During the delivery of this paper at the colloquium, the point was made by a participant that one must also take into account the earlier tradition of catechesis through the liturgy as evidenced by the homilies of St Augustine and St Cyril of Jerusalem. One must, however, observe that it is only in modern times that the sermon has been perceived as being part of the liturgy itself.

5.   Jungmann gives a German example of the Credo song, quoted by Berthold of Regensburg (*Predigten,* ed. Pfeiffer, I, 498):

> *Ich gloube an den Vater,*
> *ich gloube an den Sun*
> *miner frouwen sant Marien,*
> *und an den Heiligen Geist. Kyrieleys.*

6.   ST III q60 art.7

7.   In the Sarum use, the sermon is preached after the *Credo*.

8.   Tyndale was living on the continent at the time, in and around Switzerland and Germany. The authorities had discovered what he was up to, and John Cochläus warned William Warham, Archbishop of Canterbury who did his best to stem the flood of books by having them bought up on the continent, at source. In order to avoid prosecution, Tyndale took refuge with Philip of Hesse: the man to whom Luther gave permission to commit bigamy.

9.   Session 22, 17th September 1562. The preparatory commission of 6 August 1562 Ch. IV expresses it thus:

> *Ita enim et huius ineffabilis mysteriis maiestas rectius conservatur, et populus excitatur vehementius ad præclare de hoc sacrificio cogitandum. Lingua etiam latina, qua missæ in occidentali ecclesia celebrantur, maxime congruit, si quidem ea pluribus nationibus communis est, neque videtur esse dubitandum, quin, si missæ vulgari cuiusque gentisque idiomate peragerentur, divina mysteria minori reverentia colerentur. Esset etiam magnopere periculosum, ne varii in multis translationibus errores nascerentur, qui facerent, ut fidei nostræ mysteria, quæ simplicia sunt, viderentur esse diversa.*

There followed a prescription that the Epistle and Gospel might be read on Sunday and other feasts in a vernacular tongue. It will be seen that the eventual decree somewhat softened the findings of the preparatory text.

10. *Si quis dixerit, missam nonnisi in lingua vulgari celebrari debere: anathema sit.* Preparatory text of Canon 10, *de Sacrificio Missæ* 6th August 1562. The text in the main part of the paper is a translation of the actual canon.

11. The *Missa Glagolitica* used Church Slavonic and not vernacular Croatian.

12. §13 *Veterum Sapientia*

13. Blackwell, Oxford, 1998.

The writer is grateful for assistance given by Rev. Kenneth Macnab of Pusey House Library, Oxford, in the gathering of material.

HOMILY
AT THE SOLEMN OPENING MASS

Mgr Gilles Wach

Mgr Wach is a Doctor of Theology (Pontifical University Angelicum in Rome) and Superior General of the Priestly Institute of Christ the King Sovereign Priest, the mother house and seminary of which are established in the diocese of Florence, Italy.

Your Excellency, dear confrères, my beloved brethren,

Omnia instaurare in Christo. Thus was the motto of Pope St Pius X, at the dawn of our century. Today, more than ever, this motto seems to me not only of a burning relevance, but even more so a grave necessity, at this end of both a century and of a millennium. The restoration of all things in Christ will not happen unless the sacred liturgy is reinstated in its rightful place, that is the first place, since the liturgy is of paramount importance for the life of the Church, for the Christian life, and for our life as a society.

The liturgy is the *raison d'être* of the hierarchical priesthood. Priests are made for it, and it is the exercise of their ministerial functions which sustains them in their priestly identity.

The liturgy is the heart of the Church. The worship of Christ, emanates from his heart, the the 'holy temple of God' and the 'tabernacle of the Most High'. On earth as in heaven, Christ, our High Priest, offers his Father the only acceptable worship. In the heart of Jesus, the earthly liturgy forms one perfect hymn of praise with the heavenly liturgy. There is found the throne of divine mercy; there the altar and the place of the sacrifice of the Redeemer.

It is so that they may distribute the Blood of our redemption and the infinite riches of the pierced heart of Jesus that our priests, members of this sacerdotal hierarchy, have been marked with the character and filled with the grace of ordination.

Our primary function is, therefore, one of worship, and it is through worship, thus through the merits of Christ alone, that man is sanctified. This was taught by the last Council: the liturgy is the 'source and summit of Christian life'. It is through the worship of Christ, in the administration of the Sacraments, that the faithful receive the priesthood of baptism, and cross over into Christian life. Christ prays in them, they are made acceptable to the justice of the Father and are made recipients of the goodness of his Spirit of love, through their humble union with the unique sacrifice of the Word.

It is fitting then that Christ's faithful should drink at the pure source of Catholic liturgy. This was clearly understood by Pius XI, at a time which was already troubled by the evils of indifference and threatened by the odious de-Christianization of society, when he instituted the liturgical feast of the kingship of Christ. Indeed, the Pope declared in his encyclical *Quas Primas:*

> It is important to understand as fully as possible the doctrine of the royal dignity of our Saviour. Thus, no means seems more able to achieve this result than the institution of a specific and special feast in honour of Christ the King, since to instil into the people the truths of faith and thereby to elevate them to the joys of interior life, annual solemnities of liturgical feasts are far more effective than all the documents, however important, of the Church's magisterium.

The latter usually only reach a small number and the most cultivated people, the former touch and instruct all the faithful. One, if one can put it thus, speaks only once, whereas the other speaks every year in perpetuity. And if these last address above all the intelligence, then the former spread their saving influence over the mind and the heart, therefore to the whole being!'

In the light of this it falls to us, priests of Jesus Christ, to bring Christ's faithful to love the sacred liturgy, to instruct them in its teaching and to draw them into its mystery: the mystery of the worship of Christ. How remote, then, will become that false, mediocre and sinful conception which debases the liturgy to the self-centred celebration of an ill-defined assembly.

Let us take care, dear confreres, to conserve carefully the precious treasure which has been entrusted to us, in the condition in which it has been handed down over the centuries by the constant and living tradition of the Church. May we be delivered from the desire to subjugate the liturgical tradition to ephemeral pastoral trends. May we not, above all, reduce this treasure we love to the prey of futile arguments.

It is the pure richness and the noble beauty of Catholic worship which we should set against the false mysteries of a world bereft. Our world, this world of which perhaps we do not see enough, seemingly protected as we are, is sinking into anarchy and chaos. Thus, I do not hesitate to remind you of one of the greatest French bishops of the last century, Cardinal Pie, teaching with authority in the face of a world intoxicated by its own importance: the problems of society will be resolved by the public worship of God.

Truly, the loving submission of the creature before his Lord is manifested effectively in the sacred liturgy. This submission before God is the basis of

Ordination, of interior order, but also of external, and therefore social, order: perfect harmony, the order above all of that pre-eminence from which temporal order receives its laws and by which it is sanctified.

We always come back to the same point, in spite of many different arguments: there will only be true peace in human society within the reign of Christ. To achieve this, I have the temerity, with Cardinal Pie, to wish for a new flourishing of Catholic worship, and of its extension through all the earth. By the sacred actions, in which supernatural justice and charity operate, Christianity was founded. Only by the same means will it be renewed. Only through public religious observance, the participation in the perfect Sacrifice of the Saviour, will the Christianity of tomorrow be sanctified, and thus confirmed and consolidated.

This looking forward full of hope towards the Christianity of tomorrow invites us to conclude with a fervent prayer to Our Lady of the Rosary, Our Lady of Victory. We know that this feast was instituted by Saint Pius V following the great battle of Lepanto, a Christian victory which delivered the West from the Turkish threat. This victory, in which people had almost given up hope, was attributed by all contemporaries to the intercession of the Most Holy Virgin and to the prayers of Pope Saint Pius V. I believe that the double patronage of the most majestic Mother of God, bastion of the Catholic Faith, and of Saint Pius V, the pope who codified the Roman Mass to which we are indefectibly attached, is a very good augur for the battle in which we are engaged. Let us ask them for their zeal for the house of God. May they bear our humble prayer to the Throne of Grace, in these words of the Byzantine liturgy:

O Lord, thou who blessest those who bless thee, and sanctifiest those who sanctify thee; sanctify those who love the splendour of thy mansion. Grant them glory by thy divine power, and never abandon us who hope in thee.

Amen.

THE ACTIVE PARTICIPATION OF THE FAITHFUL ACCORDING TO THE RECENT MAGISTERIUM

Martin Edwards

Fr Martin Edwards is a Master of Arts (University of St Andrews) and, based at the Venerable English College in Rome, he obtained a Licentiate in Theology at the Pontifical Gregorian University. A parish priest in the Archdiocese of Southwark, Fr Edwards is currently also President of the Priestly Association of St John Fisher.

INTRODUCTION

I AM grateful to the organizers of this conference for limiting our discussion of this important subject to the relatively concise period covered by the recent magisterium, which has been interpreted here to mean from the post-war papacy of Pius XII to the introduction of the *Novus Ordo Missæ*. This is a period of some twenty years; a negligible time-span in the broad sweep of Church history, but also a period in which the concept of the active participation of the laity in the liturgy was much discussed, and, indeed, developed. This delimitation has obvious advantages, but disadvantages too; in this short period we cannot appeal to the objectivity of rites and buildings, since these, which have undergone, in this time, a process of rapid and drastic change, have done so artificially and deliberately, following and embodying liturgical theory, rather than, as in ages past, providing the empirical data on which these theories were later built. Cardinal Ratzinger has a germane observation:

> J. A. Jungmann, one of the truly great liturgists of our century, defined the liturgy of his time, such as it could be understood in the light of historical research, as a 'liturgy which is the fruit of development'.... What happened after the Council was something else entirely: in the place of liturgy as the fruit of development came fabricated liturgy.[1]

Given this reality, we would waste our time appealing to the ritual and architectural evidence available today: such 'evidence' would tell us more about the experimental theories of contemporary innovators than about the faith of the worshipping community. Consequently, this paper will be concerned almost exclusively with the teaching of the recent Magisterium.

It was Bossuet who wrote that: 'There is no perfection in the Christian life or practice aside from participation in the eucharistic banquet',[2] yet this perfection, this participation in the Mass, is often claimed as a modern discovery, coming from the era of colour television and the Beatles. Bernard Botte was following as well as directing this trend when he entitled his study of the modern liturgical renewal From Silence to Participation.[3] This idea that a new dawn of glorious participation has succeeded the sad night of silence and neglect is far from uncommon these days.

We shall see in this paper that such a simplification is very far from the truth. Indeed, Pope Benedict XIV, who is credited with inventing the papal encyclical, urged the faithful to participate in the Mass in the encyclical *Certiores effecti* which was published on November 13, 1742. Pope Saint Pius X spoke of 'active participation' in *Tra le sollecitudini* at the start of the century; a term taken up and employed by Pius XI. These documents fall outside the scope of this paper which is concerned only with the teaching of the recent magisterium, but they are mentioned here to show that the teaching of the recent magisterium follows in a great tradition which goes back at least as far as the first papal encyclicals.

THE RECENT MAGISTERIUM

• *The Encyclical* Mediator Dei

We begin with an examination of the teaching of Pius XII's great liturgical encyclical *Mediator Dei*. Here the concept of participation is introduced in the context of an understanding of the liturgy that is radically Christological, and, to use the Pope's own term 'theocentric'. Participation is seen, first and foremost, as participation in the drama of redemption. Through our fallen humanity, through sin, we are, by our very nature, participants in the liturgy of grace and redemption. Pope Pius XII reminds us that it was God's gracious and merciful design to restore the relationship between God and man that had been destroyed by sin, and this was effected by the sacrifice of his only-begotten Son.[4]

The Pope then makes the point, which was so central to his theological vision as well as our subject, that the sacrifice that Christ offered in his mortal body should continue without intermission down in the ages in his mystical body, that is, the Church. Thus is the liturgy established within the grandest and most thrilling perspective: an infinity from the rubrical niceties that have come to characterize our understanding of participation in recent years.

Having established the theological methodology that will direct and colour his teaching on the sacred liturgy, the Pope quickly addresses the idea of participation in the concrete and narrower sense in which we commonly understand it, noting that participation of the faithful in the liturgy is one of the fruits of 'the scholarly interest in the sacred liturgy (which) took place towards the end of the last century and has continued through the early years of this one'. [5] He goes so far as to say that this participation is a duty (*officium*) for all the faithful, according to their station. This concept of participation as a duty was quickly taken up and developed by liturgists.

The Pope notes that the very nature of man means that worship must be exterior as well as interior. He is made up of body and soul: a composition mirrored in the exterior and interior aspects of worship. Man is a social being, and hence worship, which comes to us through and in the Church, necessarily has a social and communal aspect. However, the Pope is clear in stating, that 'the chief element of divine worship must be interior'. [6]

This necessity of interior worship is portrayed as an antidote to the formalism with which we have recently become so familiar. The Pope recalls, in words that sound like prophecies fifty years later, that Christ himself expels from the Temple

> people who pretend to honour God with nothing but neat and well-turned phrases, like actors in a theatre, and think themselves perfectly capable of working out their eternal salvation without plucking their inveterate vices from their hearts. [7]

Worship must be, first and foremost interior, if the faithful are to join in that great *per ipsum* which is the sacred drama of the liturgy, if they are to 'give themselves to Him completely', [8] if they are to appropriate to themselves the graces of redemption and justification offered in Christ through the liturgy. [9] As L. Della Torre notes, commenting on this section of the encyclical:

> To participate actively in the liturgy it is not enough to have faith which recognises the mystery and assents to it; a whole complex of interior attitudes which derive from faith, a truly Christian orientation and tonality, is required. [10]

This treatment of the nature of worship is extremely relevant for our understanding of authentic participation, for, it will be seen that if we locate the chief element of divine worship in the interior dispositions of the worshipper, in his openness to the graces offered in the Mass, then authentic participation will itself, of necessity, reflect this focus on the internal and spiritual, without prejudice to external manifestations of liturgical involvement. Without this willingness to dispose oneself to grace, to seek God sincerely in his sacraments, then the liturgy, although it objectively contains these sacramental graces, becomes an empty and pointless show—a hose-pipe running life-giving water into an arid desert, sounding brass or a tinkling cymbal, [11] 'a stream of vital energy that flows from Head to members' as the Pope later calls it, [12] flowing to no effect.

This crucial openness to the effects of the sacred liturgy, the religious attitude which enables the faithful to appropriate the treasures of grace contained in the liturgy is called 'piety' in *Mediator Dei;* a term which has somewhat negative connotations in English. Piety (*pietas*) is a crucial word in our comprehension of this encyclical; it means, of course, far more than is implied by the English translation. Piety is both the meaning of true participation, and also the end to which this participation tends. Guéranger, a century earlier, has spoken in similar terms of the crucial place of '*onction*' in true worship. [13] The whole of the second part of the encyclical *Mediator Dei* is devoted to a detailed instruction on the participation of the faithful in the Eucharistic Sacrifice. [14] The Pope begins by echoing a theme already somewhat expounded in the introduction; that is, the duty of the faithful to participate in the Mass:

> It is therefore desirable, Venerable Brethren, that all the faithful should be aware that to participate in the Eucharistic Sacrifice is their chief duty and supreme dignity, and that not in an inert and negligent fashion, giving way to distractions and daydreaming, but with such earnestness and concentration that they may be united as closely as possible with the High Priest... And together with him and through him let them make their oblation, and in union with him let them offer up themselves. [15]

It is notable that the Pope once more speaks of a duty on the part of the laity to participate in the Mass; an idea that will be taken up and expanded in later magisterial documents. This participation, the duty and dignity of all the faithful, is essentially interior and Christocentric: it

> requires that all Christians should possess, as far as humanly possible, the same dispositions as those which the divine Redeemer has when he offered himself in sacrifice. [16]

Thus, to participate in the Mass is to identify oneself with Christ in his role of priest and victim. This is an understanding of participation that springs from the very nature of the liturgical action: practical consequences flow from this perception, but the emphasis, as ever, is on the profound meaning and significance of the sacred rites, and only secondarily on the rubrical and external activities with which the drama is surrounded. This identification with the divine Victim is not only to be practised when the faithful 'stand before the altar'; but, rather, this self-oblation, refined and perfected in the sacred liturgy, should inform the whole of one's life, so 'that each one's faith ought to become more ready to work through charity, his piety more real and fervent...' [17] The faithful, participating in Mass in this spirit will be living the great boast of the Apostle of the Gentiles: 'With Christ I am nailed to the Cross. I live, now not I, but Christ liveth in me'. [18]

It is a sublime and elevated view of the sacred rites, and one which the Pope is at pains to emphasize in the face of a certain tendency to trivialize the Mass which was already evident in those days: 'let the faithful, therefore, consider to what a high dignity they are raised by the Sacrament of Baptism'. [19] This lofty and 'theocentric' vision does not preclude the practicalities of participation (the Pope mentions the offertory, the 'dialogue' Mass etc.); these are mentioned, as it were in passing, not because the Pope thinks them unimportant or mistaken, but because they are seen as means to an end: and that end is to 'promote the people's piety and intimate union with Christ'. [20] Thus, the Pope warns that the value of the methods of external participation should not be exaggerated: for this union with Christ can be achieved in other less liturgical ways, and not all the faithful are capable or willing to join in this sort of participation.

This awareness of, and sensitivity to, the needs of the individual Christian would imply that heavy-handed methods of participation which swamped the piety of 'unliturgical' Christians are to be avoided. The Pope here evinces a pastoral concern in his understanding of participation that has often been lacking in the concrete implementation of many recent liturgical reforms.

• *From* Mediator Dei *to Vatican II: participation in practice*

We have spent so long considering the teaching of *Mediator Dei,* because this encyclical not only represents the high point of Pope Pius XII's teaching on the liturgy, but is, arguably, the most significant magisterial document on the liturgy produced in this century. The encyclical had, of course, a great influence on the pastoral implementation of the liturgical movement, but was by no means the Pope's final word on the subject. In various allocutions and decrees of the sacred congregations, the problems and challenges of the unfolding liturgical movement were addressed. These were years marked by significant liturgical changes, beginning with the new Holy Week services of 1951. It is notable that the Decree of the Sacred Congregation of Rites of February 9, 1951, while granting approval for the new rite, lists the participation of the faithful as one of the reasons for restoring the Easter Vigil. [21]

In 1953 the Apostolic Constitution *Christus Dominus* [22] was intended to facilitate the full participation in the liturgy achieved through sacramental communion, as was the later *Motu Proprio, Sacram Communionem.* [23] In 1955 the Sacred Congregation for Rites issued *Maxima Redemptionis,* [24] once more justifying the change in the times of celebration of the various Holy Week services by a double appeal to ancient tradition and pastoral necessity: i.e., to enable the faithful to participate more easily. 1955 saw the appearance of Pope Pius XII's last liturgical encyclical, *Musicæ Sacræ Disciplina.* As the title suggests, the main subject of this encyclical is sacred music, but it is not lacking in teaching on participation. In words that recalled *Tra le sollecitudini* and looked forward to *Sacrosanctum Concilium,* the Pope accords pride of place to Gregorian chant, without, however, disdaining polyphony. Music, the Pope notes, is a wonderful means of achieving the participation of the faithful in the sacred services: 'It should make the liturgical prayers of the Christian community more alive and fervent so that everyone can praise and beseech the Triune

God more powerfully, more intently and more effectively...' [25]

Musicæ Sacræ was his last liturgical encyclical, but Pope Pius XII never ceased to urge the faithful to draw near to the founts of grace in the sacred liturgy, and to participate fully and actively in the sacred rites. The Apostolic Constitution *Primo exacto sæculo* expresses sentiments found in very many less formal documents and addresses:

> The Eucharist, in fact, may be called the centre and principal reason for the Christian life, for truly it is from the Eucharist that strength from on high and divine graces flow most abundantly into our souls... It is for this reason that they demand an active, efficacious love from us, a love, we say, that sustains and forms our wills, our way of acting, the whole course of our lives. [26]

In the very last days of the pontificate of Pius XII, the Sacred Congregation of Rites published an Instruction entitled *De Musica Sacra,* on sacred music and the liturgy. This instruction devotes several paragraphs to a discussion of the participation of the faithful in the sacred liturgy, largely a resumé of the teaching of *Mediator Dei,* and then the following comment is made:

> It is this harmonious participation that the pontifical documents have in mind when they speak of 'active participation', of which the foremost example is the celebrant and sacred ministers who assist at the altar with the desired interior piety by observing exactly the rubrics and the rite. [27]

So here we have a mention of 'active participation', attributed somewhat vaguely to 'the pontifical documents'. *De Musica Sacra* gives as a reference for 'active participation' pp. 530 - 537 from the AAS version of *Mediator Dei:* but, in fact, the phrase is not found in this section of the encyclical. Indeed, it would seem that the Pope, if anything, was careful to avoid using it, since in this section of the work he explains the paramount place of interior dispositions and the dangers of an exaggeration of the notion of 'objective piety'. The adverb *actuose* is found twice in this section of *Mediator Dei,* the adjective *actuosus* once, but not in the context of active participation. (Interestingly each time the word appears here it cannot be translated as meaning simply 'active': it seems that only when the word is appended to participation that it inevitably takes on this meaning). Perhaps Pope Pius XII had realized the ambiguity inherent in the now classic phrase *actuosa participatio:* an ambiguity that would be exploited fully by progressive liturgists in the years that followed.

• *The Second Vatican Council and* actuosa participatio

The Constitution on the Sacred Liturgy of Vatican II, *Sacrosanctum Concilium,* turns, almost immediately, to the question of the participation of the faithful in the liturgy. The relevant teaching is to be found in paragraphs 11 and 14. The first instance recalls much of the magisterial teaching we have already considered, and could, in fact, be considered the recapitulation of many of the previous pronouncements:

> Pastors of souls must, therefore, realise that, when the liturgy is celebrated, something more is required than the laws governing valid and lawful celebration. It is their duty also to ensure that the faithful take part fully aware of what they are doing, actively (*actuose*) engaged in the rite and enriched by it. [28]

The second mention of participation is somewhat different, and appears to constitute a certain development of doctrine:

> Mother Church earnestly desires that all the faithful should be led to that full, conscious, and active participation in liturgical celebrations which is demanded by the very nature of the liturgy, and to which the Christian people, 'a chosen race, a royal priesthood, a holy nation, a redeemed people' (I Pet. 2:9, 4-5) have a right and obligation by reason of their baptism. In the restoration and promotion of the sacred liturgy the full and active participation (*plena et actuosa participatio*) by all the people is the aim to be considered before all else... [29]

Bugnini, who was certainly in a position to know, has asserted that no article in *Sacrosanctum Concilium* is unaffected by this desire to promote participation before all else; it is a thought recurring over and over again, affecting all that the Fathers say on the various aspects of liturgy: 'Everything is presented with an eye on the conscious and devout participation that should result from the properly organized instruction of the faithful'. [30]

The term *actuosa participatio* used by the council is not new: Pope Pius X had used it nearly sixty years before in the Motu Proprio *Tra le sollecitudini:*

> We deem it necessary to provide before everything else for the sanctity and dignity of the temple, in which the faithful assemble for the object of acquiring this spirit from its foremost and indispensable fount, which is the active participation in the holy mysteries and in the public and solemn prayer of the Church. [31]

Pius XI also used the term in the Apostolic Constitution Divini Cultus:

> In order that the faithful may more actively participate in the divine worship (*Quo autem actuosius fideles divinum cultum participent*) let them be made once more to sing the Gregorian Chant, so far as it belongs to them to take part in it'. [32]

Thus the term *actuosa participatio* was well established in magisterial documents, but the emphasis on 'active participation of the faithful...before all else' found in *Sacrosanctum Concilium* is novel, and appears, in fact, to be hard to reconcile with previous teaching: Vorgrimler considers that 'This summons to 'active participation' necessarily results from the renewed understanding of the Church.' [33] Pope Pius X, as we have just seen, considered that it was the sanctity and dignity of the temple which had to be considered before all else, and Pius XII, it will be recalled, was careful to emphasize that active participation, although important, was not, literally, essential, and that the faithful have the right to assist at Mass in the manner suited to their dispositions and that the importance of active participation should not be exaggerated. [34]

The elevation of 'active participation' into the guiding principle and supreme norm of liturgical reform was to have very profound and far-reaching consequences. If the active participation of the faithful is the aim to be considered before all else, then much of great importance in the liturgy may, legitimately, be sacrificed. Michæl Davies calls this phrase a 'time bomb' and points out that it placed virtually unlimited power 'in the hands of those invested with the power to implement in practice the details of a reform which the council authorized but did not spell out in detail.' [35] Davis [36] claims that an illustration of this would be the near-total disappearance of Gregorian Chant from our churches, despite the council's teaching that 'other things being equal', Gregorian Chant should be given pride of place in liturgical services.[37] Hence, liturgical experts could, and did, claim that since Gregorian Chant impeded the active participation of the faithful (since most of the faithful are incapable of actively joining in the singing of the proper of the Mass), it should be replaced by music which promotes active participation, that is, by hymns and popular songs. The same reasoning explains much else in the post-conciliar reforms: the eclipse of sacred polyphonic music, a musical style which Pius XII had stoutly defended, could be justified, as polyphony, almost by definition, does not permit the active participation of the whole congregation. This emphasis on active participation before all else led quickly to the substitution of vernacular tongues for Latin, notwithstanding the teaching of John XXIII, and indeed of the council which had stated that 'The use of the Latin language, with due respect to particular law, is to be preserved in the Latin rites'.[38] And, finally, this insistence on active participation of the faithful before all else as the guiding principle in liturgical reform was eventually to entail the virtual abolition of the traditional rites. Baumstark and Jungmann were not the only great liturgical scholars to foresee and (in some sense) direct this process, for both saw that, once the liturgy is celebrated in the vernacular

> only then would we come face to face with the much deeper problem of how to make palatable to modern man the religious modes of thought and manners of speech which were crystallized 1500 years ago. [39]

Jungmann saw the solution to this problem would lie, in part, in 'a certain amount of clarification and enlivening of liturgical form'.[40]

These developments would seem to justify Davies' dramatic description of the demand for the consideration of active participation before all else as a 'time-bomb'. Certainly, it was a pregnant passage, which, we shall shortly see, was to bear abundant fruit. However, it is far from certain that this is what the Council Fathers intended or even said in the relevant citations from *Sacrosanctum Concilium.* In both quotations the Latin words *actuose* (no. 11) and *actuosa* (no. 14) are habitually translated as 'actively' and 'active' respectively. Hence the famous phrase *actuosa participatio* which has commonly been translated as 'active participation'. This translation, although widely accepted, is far from obvious. In fact, there is a Latin word for 'active' (*activus*), yet *Sacrosanctum Concilium* uses, as we have seen, *actuosus*, which has a broader and more nuanced meaning. Lewis and Short's *Latin Dictionary* defines *actuosus* as 'full of activity, very active, with the accessory idea of zeal and subjective impulse; different from *industrius,* which refers more to the means by which an object is attained'.

Hence the translation of *actuosa participatio* as active participation is by no means obvious or sufficient. There is perhaps no single English word which fully translates *actuosa,* but to interpret it simply as meaning 'active', when another Latin adjective exists for this term, and so interpret *actuosa participatio* as referring principally to activity, is surely a distortion, or, as Cardinal Ratzinger has said, a 'fatal narrowing' of the meaning of the word and of the important teaching contained in these paragraphs of *Sacrosanctum Concilium:*

> The council also correctly reminded us that the liturgy also means *actio*, action, and insisted that the faithful be accorded an *actuosa participatio*... Certainly, it is a correct concept, but one which, in post-conciliar interpretations, has suffered a fatal narrowing. The impression has been given that active participation only exists where there are tangible signs of exterior activity: talks, words, chants, homilies, readings, hand-shaking... But it has been forgotten that the Council also included in its understanding of *actuosa participatio* silence, which aids a truly deep, personal participation, permitting us to listen in our hearts to the Word of the Lord. Hence, in some rites, there is no trace left of this silence.[41]

This debate about the meaning and significance of *actuosa participatio* is more than a mere pedantic semantic quibble, but is relevant not only to our understanding of the nature of the liturgy but also to our assessment of recent liturgical changes. If *actuosa participatio* is interpreted as Ratzinger suggests, as a profound and personal sharing in the liturgy, then it is clearly in conformity with previous magisterial pronouncements on the participation of the laity in the sacred liturgy. However, if *actuosa participatio* is simply translated as active participation, and so taken to mean simply activity in the liturgy, then this marks an abrupt change of emphasis relative to previous papal teaching and provides the justification for the radical break with liturgical tradition that Cardinal Ratzinger, among many others, has identified in many post-conciliar reforms. If this phrase is used, to avoid the pedantry of continual Latin quotations, it must be borne in mind that we mean by it something more than external activity, a participation that springs from a true, interior and personal sharing in the liturgy. Such an understanding of *actuosa participatio* is in keeping not only with previous teaching, but with other pronouncements of the Second Vatican Council. The Dogmatic Decree *Lumen Gentium* recalls *Mediator Dei* when it identifies participation with the self-offering of the faithful in union with the Divine Victim which finds its fulfilment in Communion:

> Taking part in the eucharistic sacrifice, the source and summit of the Christian life, they offer the divine victim to God and themselves along with it. And so it is that, both in the offering and in Holy Communion, each in his own way, though not of course indiscriminately, has his own part to play in the liturgical action. [42]

Indeed Pope Paul himself frequently interpreted *actuosa participatio* in this broader sense: that is, 'a full, heartfelt participation as opposed to a passive, negligent one'.[43]

It has been seen in the above that the term *actuosa participatio* has usually been translated as 'active participation', and, it will be shown below that this active participation has been understood, by the architects and implementors of the post-conciliar reforms, to mean activity: words and movement, exterior involvement. However, it has also been established that another, more nuanced interpretation is possible: that actuosa participatio has been taken to mean a living and real involvement in the liturgy, and that this understanding of the term not only existed before the council, but, in the teaching of Pope Paul VI, survived the conciliar use of the term. In view of this, it would, perhaps, be safe to conclude that the council's use of the term *actuosa*, as the dictionary definition would also suggest, must mean something more profound than activity, and that the narrowing of the term has been the cause of many partial and one-sided interpretations of *Sacrosanctum Concilium.*

• *From Vatican II to the* Novus Ordo Missæ

This period, it will be remembered, was marked by a bewildering profusion of documents on the liturgy, many of them applying the guiding principle of *actuosa participatio* to the practical reform and modification of the liturgy. *Inter Œcumenici* (September 26, 1964) was the first document from the Sacred Congregation of Rites on the implementation of the conciliar constitution *Sacrosanctum Concilium.* It is unnecessary here to review in detail the changes and modifications it introduced: simplification of ritual, permission for the vernacular, the setting up of diocesan liturgical commissions, services of the word in the absence of a priest etc. What is relevant to note is that the justification for these changes is given as the pressing need for active participation before all else:

> The reason for deciding to put these things into practice now is that the

liturgy may ever more fully satisfy the conciliar intent on promoting active participation. [44]

Inter Oecumenici appeared before the closing of the second Vatican Council; and, even before the council ended, concerns about the implementation of the liturgical reform and the errors concerning the Mass and the Eucharist that were starting to plague the Church had reached the highest levels of the Church. In the encyclical *Mysterium Fidei* (Sept. 3, 1965) Pope Paul VI condemns some of the errors concerning the Eucharist that were then causing 'serious pastoral concern and anxiety'[45] and then proceeds to a magnificent presentation of the Church's unchanging faith in the Blessed Sacrament. During the course of this exposition, the subject of *actuosa participatio* is not neglected. Pope Paul understands this active participation in the sense in which it was expounded in *Mediator Dei* which he quotes with approval, along with the passage from Lumen Gentium cited above:

> To shed fuller light on the mystery of the Church, it helps to realise that it is nothing less than the whole Church which, in union with Christ in His role as Priest and Victim, offers the Sacrifice of the Mass and is offered in it. The Fathers of the Church taught this wondrous doctrine. A few years ago our predecessor of happy memory, Pius XII, explained it, and only recently the Second Vatican Council enunciated it in its treatise on the People of God as formulated in its Constitution on the Church. [46]

Tres Abhinc Annos appeared, as the name suggests, three years after *Inter Œcumenici.* This time, the list of changes and innovations is even longer: the *Ordo Missæ* is altered once more, with suppression of genuflections, signs of the cross, modifications to the communion rite etc. The instruction also allowed, *inter alia,* the use of the liturgical colour purple for funerals, and ordered that the maniple was no longer obligatory. These, and many other changes, (including the extension of permission for the vernacular to be used even in the Canon of the Mass) were made in order to aid active participation. Referring to previous post-conciliar reforms the Instruction notes:

> Their rich yield is becoming quite clear from the many reports of bishops, which attest to an increased, more aware, and intense participation of the faithful everywhere in the liturgy, especially in the holy sacrifice of the Mass. To increase this participation even more and to make the liturgical rites, especially the Mass clearer and better understood, the same bishops have proposed certain other adaptations... [47]

These documents, a small selection from the wealth of material available, all clearly illustrate that the post-conciliar liturgical reforms were motivated, to a great extent, by the desire to increase participation, and that participation is interpreted in a distinctly more prosaic and narrow fashion than had been hitherto the case. Hence, Bugnini was by no means exaggerating when he claimed that 'the full and active participation of all the people... has been the basic motive at work in the modern liturgical renewal'. [48] The rites produced by this liturgical renewal are eloquent testimony to the sort of participation envisaged here.

CONCLUSION

The preoccupation with *actuosa participatio* has dominated more than the post-conciliar liturgical reform. Active participation was, as we have seen, from the time of Pope St Pius X onwards, the slogan of the Liturgical Movement, then a *leitmotif* of Vatican II's *Constitution on the Sacred Liturgy, Sacrosanctum Concilium*, and then the guiding principle of the subsequent liturgical reforms. There now exists in the Church an *Ordo Missæ* fashioned with active participation in mind; drawn up and approved by men who regarded the participation of the faithful in the Sacred Liturgy as more important than anything else. It might not be out of place to conclude by asking, has it worked? Has this dedicated adherence to the concept of participation borne fruit? Is active participation happening? Is the 'rich yield', the 'more intense participation of the faithful everywhere in the liturgy' reported by the bishops to the Sacred Congregation of Rites and cited in *Tres Abhinc Annos* still so evident and universal?

Quantitatively, participation has certainly declined, at least in the ancient churches of the West. In England and Wales the official annual Catholic Directory reported a Mass attendance figure of 2,111,219 for the year 1964; this had declined to 1,111,077 by 1996; a virtual halving of Mass attendance during a period in which the Catholic population has continued to increase. England's experience is by no means unique: these stark statistics tell us of millions who are not participating in the Mass at all, and leave us with a lingering doubt as to whether the fact that this decline has mirrored and kept pace with the increased emphasis on participation is more than a coincidence.

And what of that which we might call qualitative participation, the experience of those who still come to Mass, and assist at the rites designed with participation in mind? This, of course, is more difficult to assess: in the final analysis, even after our brief overview of the magisterial teaching, our answer to this will be largely based on anecdotal evidence and our own experience. But are we wrong in concluding that the experience of recent liturgical reforms tells us that the multiplication of words can sometimes drown out the Word; that a proliferation of actions can sometimes obscure the action; that participation expressed in activity can sometimes be an obstacle between us and participation in the holy mysteries?

That this has happened should come as no surprise to those who have read Dom Guéranger's comments on the 'anti liturgical heresy' in the *Institutions Liturgiques*. There he points out that if once the sacred language of Latin is removed from the Mass, if everything is reduced to the level of the immediately comprehensible, then:

Exposed to profane gaze, like a virgin who has been violated, from that moment on the liturgy has lost much of its sacred character, and very soon people find that it is not worthwhile putting aside one's work or pleasure in order to go and listen to what is being said in the way one speaks in the marketplace... [49]

The answers to the questions posed above are beyond the scope of this paper but they do at least illustrate the paradox that many learned and distinguished authorities since Guéranger have noted, that, perversely, over-emphasis on participation can smother the very effect it wishes to produce, or, more precisely, that the *actuosa participatio* called for by the recent Magisterium has been seriously misinterpreted when it has been viewed almost exclusively in terms of activity, and that an over-emphasis on activity can destroy participation. This was noted shortly after the introduction of the *Novus Ordo Missæ* by the Benedictine scholar Dom Bernard McElligott, and the years since have witnessed no great reversal of the situation he describes. In fact, the challenge he identifies at the end of this quotation could be considered the liturgical imperative of our day:

It seems to me that the right balance between personal interior and public external worship—in which the interior personal worship is the fundamental religious thing—is being lost or forgotten, and that we are in some danger of our religion becoming chiefly a matter of externalism. This corresponds to what the Catholic psychologist Karl Stern has noted as a disease or abnormality of our age, namely an 'activism', opposed to the values of wisdom and insight summed up in Our Lady. But if this externalism is happening, then we must do something about setting it right. [50]

NOTES

1. From Cardinal Ratzinger's preface to Mgr Klaus Gamber, *The Reform of the Roman Liturgy: Its Problems and Background,* Una Voce Press, San Juan Capistrano, 1993.

2. Quoted by HH Pope John XXIII during his installation at St. John Lateran, Nov. 23, 1958.

3. Or, rather, allowed the English translation of *Le mouvement liturgique: Témoignage et souvenirs,* Desclée et Cie, Paris, 1973, to be so titled.

4. *Mediator Dei* no. 1 (Vatican Library Translation, St. Paul Books and Media, Boston) .

5. *ibid.,* no. 4

6. *ibid.,* no. 24

7. *ibid.* Cf. Mark, 7:6 and Is., 29:13.

8. *ibid.*

9. A little later the Pope adds: 'Emphatically, therefore, the work of Redemption, which in itself is independent of our will, requires a serious effort on our part if we are to achieve eternal salvation'. *ibid.* para 31.

10. L. Della Torre, *Understanding the Liturgy,* St. Paul Publications, Langley, 1967, p. 21.

11. I Cor., 13:1.

12. *Mediator Dei,* no.31.

13. Dom P. Guéranger, *Institutions Liturgiques,* extraits, Editions de Chiré, 1977, p. 109Ff.

14. *Mediator Dei,* nos. 80-111.

15. *ibid.,* no. 80.

16. *ibid.,* no. 81.

17. *ibid.,* no. 99.

18. Gal., 2:19-29.

19. *Mediator Dei,* no.104.

20. *ibid.,* no.106.

21. Decree of the Sacred Congregation of Rites, February 9, 1951, cited in Papal Teachings: *The Liturgy, Selected and Arranged by the Benedictine Monks of Solesmes,* St. Paul (English) Edition, 1962, p. 417.

22. Jan. 6, 1953 cited *ibid.,* pp. 422 - 427.

23. Decree of the Sacred Congregation of Rites, March 19, 1957, cited *ibid.,* pp. 519 - 520.

24. Nov. 16, 1955, cited *ibid.,* pp. 468 - 470.

25. *Musicæ sacræ,* nos. 31 & 34

26. Nov. 1, 1957, cited in *Papal Teachings,* op. cit., p. 523.

27. AAS, 50, (1958) p. 638.

28. *Sacrosanctum Concilium,* no.11.

29. *ibid.,* no. 14.

30. Mgr. A. Bugnini, *The Reform of the Liturgy 1948 - 1975,* The Liturgical Press, Collegeville, Minnesota, 1990. p. 41.

31. *Motu Proprio given in Official Catholic Teachings: Worship and Liturgy,* ed. James J. Megivern, McGrath, Wilmington, 1978.

32. AAS, 21, (1929), p. 39.

33. *Commentary on the Documents of Vatican II,* ed. Herbert Vorgrimler, Burns and Oates, London, 1967; Vol I, p. 17.

34. *Mediator Dei,* no.115

35. Michæl Davies, *Pope John's Council,* Kansas City, 1992, p. 239.

36. Cardinal Ratzinger has made the same points more learnedly and less succinctly in *Un Chant Nouveau Pour Le Seigneur,* Desclée, Paris, 1995, pp. 150- 169.

37. *Sacrosanctum Concilium,* no.116.

38. *ibid.,* no. 36 (1). The Instruction *Tres Abhinc Annos* of the SCR of May 4 1967 extended permission for the vernacular for the whole Mass by appealing to this need for participation before all else (AAS, 59 (1967) p. 442).

39. J.A. Jungmann, S.J., *Pastoral Liturgy,* Challoner Publications, London 1962, p. 98. (Originally published in German under the title *Liturgisches Erbe und Pastorale Gegenwart,* by Tyrolia-Verlag, Innsbruck.

40. *ibid.,*

41. Cardinal Ratzinger, *Entretien sur la foi,* cited in *La Liturgie Traditionnelle, Pourquoi?,* p. 25, supplement to *La Lettre D'Oremus: Le concile nous a justement rappelé que la liturgie signife aussi actio, action, et a demandé qu'on assure aux fidèles une actuosa participatio... Certes, c'est un concept correct, mais qui, dans les interprétations post-conciliaires, a subi une restriction fatale. Il en est ressorti l'impression qu'on n'avait une participation active que s'il y avait activité extérieure tangible: discours, paroles, chants, homelies, lectures, poignées de mains ... Mais on a oublié que le concile place aussi dans l'actuosa participatio le silence qui favorise une participation vraiment profonde, personnellle, nous permettant d'écouter intérieurement la parole du Seigneur. Or, de ce silence, il n'y a plus trace dans certains rites.*

42. *Lumen Gentium,* no. 11. Some years previously Father Congar had written, in a chapter devoted to the participation of the laity in the Mass: 'Communion crowns all... If the faithful participate in the eucharistic oblation as has been said, it is obvious that their final act of participation will be to unite themselves with the Victim in whom all the other offerings are hallowed and accepted, uniting them-

selves in such a way as to form but one body with him. He who truly offers sacrifice should also partake of it'. (Y. Congar, O.P., *Lay People in the Church,* Geoffrey Chapman, London, 1962; originally published in French by Les Editions du Cerf under the title *Jalons pour une théologie laicat*).

43. Cf. sermons and allocutions in *Documents on the Liturgy,* 1963 - 1979, ICEL, Liturgical Press, Collegeville, pp. 125 - 126.

44. AAS, 56, (1964), p. 878.

45. *Mysterium Fidei,* AAS 57 (1965) p. 753.

46. *ibid.,*p.761.

47. AAS, 59 (1967), p. 442.

48. Mgr A. Bugnini, *The Reform of the Liturgy 1948 - 1975,* The Liturgical Press, Collegeville, Minnesota, 1990. p. 41.

49. Dom Guéranger, *Liturgical Institutions,* Vol. I, Chapter VI (first published 1840).

50. From the text of an address given to the Association for Latin Liturgy at Campion Hall, Oxford, June 16, 1970, and printed in *The Remnant,* Vol. 4, No. 21, November 15, 1971.

THE CONCEPT OF PARTICIPATION
ENVISAGED IN THE PREPARATORY
SCHEMA ON THE LITURGY OF THE
SECOND VATICAN COUNCIL

Ignacio Barreiro

Fr Barreiro, born in 1947 in Montevideo, holds two doctorates from the University of his native capital, one in Law and one in Social Science. Between 1975 and 1983, Fr Barreiro was a member of the Uruguayan Ministry of Foreign Affairs. Having studied for the priesthood in the archdiocese of New York, Fr Barreiro was ordained in 1987 and obtained a Doctorate in Theology at the Pontifical University of the Holy Cross in Rome on his thesis 'The Experience of God and the Faith in God according to St Thomas Aquinas'. *Fr Barreiro exercises his ministry in Rome and is also Chaplain to the* Institute Dietrich von Hildebrand.

IN this paper I wish to study the concept of lay participation in the preparatory works for the schema on the liturgy of the Second Vatican Council. The contemporary reality which leads us to focus on this question, is what Klaus Gamber describes as 'too much emphasis which is being given to the congregation actively participating in the liturgy and doing away with many of the essential elements of liturgical cult and ceremony'. Also part of the current problem is the way in which the phrase *actuosa participatio* has been translated as 'active participation', in which the reality that is brought to mind tends to be more an external activity. As Dom Bernard McElligot has pointed out by translating the word *actuosa* for active in the post-conciliar period,

> the Church's intention has been misunderstood, and generally, if perhaps unconsciously, taken to mean bodily activity; whereas what the Church really asks for is full, sincere, mental activity, expressed externally by the body.

To understand better the debate in the Central Preparatory Commission(CPC) of the council, it is useful to dwell first on the background of the question. The Church through her history has always had a concern for the effective participation of the faithful in the sacred liturgy. This concern pervades the Bull

Transiturus of Urban IV, of August 11th 1264. In this magnificent document Urban IV decrees the celebration of the Feast of *Corpus Christi* throughout the entire Church. St. Thomas Aquinas clearly teaches that the spiritual benefits that a person receives from his participation in the liturgy are proportional to the measure of his devotion and fervour. St Pius X in his *Motu Proprio, Tra le Sollecitudini,* of November 22nd 1903, teaches that the active participation of the faithful in the liturgy is the foremost and indispensable fount of the true Christian spirit. Pius XI in the Apostolic Constitution *Divini cultus,* with the object of achieving a more active participation of the faithful in divine worship, requested that those parts of the Gregorian chant that belong to the people should be sung by the people.

Since the turn of the century, and in many cases before, some very notable advances had been made in the liturgical awareness of the faithful. A growing percentage of them were able to follow the Mass with the assistance of bilingual hand-missals. As Fr. Conlon points out, 'What cannot be doubted of this form of participation is that although it was not always audible or vocal, it was prayerful.' This manner of following the Mass fulfilled the most vital element of a rightly understood lay participation in the holy Sacrifice which is internal participation; this is something that we cannot readily affirm of many more audible and visible forms of contemporary participation.

A fundamental element towards interpreting the Schema on the Liturgy, placed for the consideration of the CPC, was the Encyclical Letter *Mediator Dei* of Pope Pius XII, of November 20th 1947. Pope John XXIII in his allocution to the members of the CPC of April 3rd 1962 made an express commendation of the importance of this document. In his presentation of the 'Schema' on the Liturgy, Cardinal Larraona, President of the Preparatory Liturgical Commission (PLC), underlined that *Mediator Dei* constituted a true *Summa Theologica* and a legal and pastoral compendium of all the liturgy. This encyclical with regard to true participation in the liturgy underlines that 'the chief element of divine Worship must be interior'. Later the Servant of God adds;

> It should be clear to all, then, that God cannot be honoured worthily unless the mind and heart turn to him in quest of the perfect life, and that the worship rendered to God by the Church in union with her divine Head is the most efficacious means of achieving sanctity.

With regards to the participation of the faithful in the eucharistic Sacrifice the Pope states that, 'it is their chief duty and supreme dignity', and then he adds

> with such earnestness and concentration that they might be united as closely as possible with the High Priest, according to the Apostle: 'Let this mind be in you which was also in Christ Jesus'. And together with him and through him let them make their oblation, and in union with him let them offer up themselves.

With regard to the use of the Latin language the venerable pontiff teaches that, 'The use of the Latin language, customary in a considerable portion of the Church, is a manifest and beautiful sign of unity, as well as an effective antidote for any corruption of doctrinal truth'. Dom Cipriano Vagaggini, OSB, one of the most influential members of the PLC, recognized the importance of the teachings of this encyclical with regard to the participation of the laity in the liturgy.

An important antecedent of the preparatory process for the Schema on the Liturgy was also the work of the Pontifical Commission for the Liturgical Reform. This Commission was initially presided over by the Cardinal Clemente Micara, Prefect of the Sacred Congregation of Rites, until January of 1954 when Cardinal Gætano Cicognani as the new Prefect of the SCR assumed the presidency. This commission met from June of 1948 to July 1960. A fundamental input for its work was the *Memorandum on the Liturgical Reform,* drafted by Frs Löw and Antonelli. The recent publication of the minutes of this commission allows us to explore better the history of the preparatory process on the Schema on the Liturgy. The scope of this commission was to study a general reform of the liturgy, because in the view of the members of this commission, the liturgy is an organic whole which does not admit partial reforms. In its detailed consideration of the reform of the rites of Holy Week, this commission underlined the need for a more active participation of the faithful. Within this concern it was agreed that the renewal of the baptismal promises at the Paschal Vigil could be made in the vernacular, but the proposal to have some of the lessons of this vigil read in the vernacular was rejected in the session of November 13th 1951. In the discussions that led to this decision Fr Albareda, after strongly defending the moral value which Latin has as the only language for the official liturgy of the Church, objected to the granting of permission for the use of the vernacular in the reading of the prophetic lessons of the Pascal Vigil because it would constitute a grave precedent to renounce the use of Latin in such a solemn rite. What Fr. Albareda had in mind, was that the permission to use some vernacular in the Paschal Vigil would contribute to the abandonment of Latin in the official liturgy of the Church. Later on February 20th 1959, at the petition of the German episcopate, the commission reversed its decision and allowed the reading of the Passion in the vernacular and the four readings of the Pascal Vigil.

In the Encyclical Letter *Musicæ Sacra Disciplina,* of December 25th 1955, Pope Pius XII, to underline the note of the universality of the Roman Liturgy and so that Catholics everywhere might experience the comfort of the unity of the Church, insisted that Gregorian Chant should always be connected with the Latin words of the liturgy. At the same time the Pope allowed in non-solemn Mass the singing of hymns in the vernacular so that the faithful could participate in the Holy Sacrifice, accompanying the sacred action with the mind and the voice, uniting their devotion with the prayers of the priest, obviously with the understanding that those hymns would be appropriate to the different parts of the Sacrifice. Pius XII in his address of September 22nd 1956 to the participants of the First International Congress of Pastoral Liturgy, underlined that the serious concern of the Church for the active and conscious participation of the faithful in the liturgical actions should not lead to the abandonment of Latin.

There are two other very important documents which came out on the eve of the council, which should be considered. The Apostolic Letter *Iucunda laudatio,* of John XXIII dated December 7th 1961 was addressed to Mgr H. Anglés, Rector of the Pontifical Institute for Sacred Music, for the fiftieth anniversary of the Institute. In this letter the Pope praised the Institute for the cultivation and defence of Latin in the liturgy. On February 22nd 1962 John XXIII signed the Apostolic Constitution, *Veterum Sapientia* on the study of Latin. In this document Latin is depicted as the universal and immutable vehicle that the Church has to communicate her teachings, and re-affirmed the need of preserving Latin in the sacred rites. These two documents have to be seen in the light of the pressures that had been growing since the early fifties in favour of the use of the vernacular in the liturgy and in particular against the initiatives presented in the PLC in favour of the use of the vernacular in the liturgy.

The PLC, which was chaired by Cardinal Gætano Cicognani, and had Annibale Bugnini as its secretary, was largely dominated by members of the liturgical movement. At the death of Cardinal Cicognani his position was taken by Cardinal Arcadio Larraona. The work of this commission was subdivided into thirteen sub-commissions. For the scope of this work the most relevant for us are the sub-commissions on the 'Participation of the Faithful in the Sacred Liturgy', and 'Use of Latin and Sacred Music'. The main point of contention in the sub-commission on the Participation of the Faithful was if this participation should be based on the common priesthood of the faithful or on the ecclesial nature of the liturgy. The sub-commission on the 'Use of Latin' had a tormented history due to controversies that were caused by the proposals to increase the use of vernacular in the liturgy. In the end, the proposal which was included in the schema presented to the CPC, established the general principle that 'The use of Latin in the Western Liturgy is absolutely to be preserved.' At the same time this general principle was very much restricted by the statement that in many places the use of the vernacular was of great usefulness to the people and the possibility that Episcopal Conferences could introduce the vernacular with the permission of the Holy See.

Even if the Oriental Churches have different traditions and customs with regard to the participation of the laity in the liturgy and in the use of liturgical languages, nevertheless it is of interest to consider the debate in the CPC on the question of the use of vernacular languages in the celebration of oriental liturgies. It was generally felt at that time that the linguistic practices of the Oriental Churches could have an influence in the current debate on the introduction of the vernacular into the Latin liturgy. Cardinal Ernesto Ruffini pointed out that this matter should be carefully considered because it not only involves the participation of the people but principally it is a question of the preservation of the integrity of the faith. He also underlined that the multiplication of liturgical languages will lead to divisions and the growth of nationalism. Cardinal A. Jullien urged caution, because of the probable impact of this provision for the Oriental Churches upon the question of the use of Latin in the Latin Church: 'Lest the Latins say,' remarked Cardinal Jullien, 'if these and those, why not we also?' . Fr. Michæl Browne, Master General of the Dominicans, expressed his concerns that if in the 'Schema on the Oriental Churches' the differences within the Oriental Church were praised, this would lead to the approval also of differences within the Latin Church, which was a way of alluding to the proposal of introducing different vernacular languages within the Latin Church. Cardinal Paolo Marrella, supported the position of Cardinal Ruffini and underlined the fact that he did not see any use in translating the liturgical books of the Latin Church into the vernacular. Several other members of this commission, like Cardinals Siri, Godfrey, Richaud, and Roberti, and Bishops Lefebvre, Bazin and Ngô-Dinh-Thûc and Rev. Gut supported the concerns of Cardinal Jullien. Finally it should be noticed, against those who considered that in the Oriental Churches languages should not be mixed, that His Beatitude, Paul II, Chiekho, Babylonian Patriarch of Baghdad, underlined that the essential parts of the Mass like the words of consecration in the Holy Sacrifice of the Mass, should be said in the liturgical language. This should also be the case for the prayers that the celebrant says in low voice.

In his presentation of the guiding criteria used by the PLC in its work Cardinal Larraona indicated that the members of the clergy should be imbued with a growing liturgical spirit in such a way that they would be able to transmit this spirit and knowledge to the faithful. The faithful should participate more in the liturgy based on two principles: first, preserving the hierarchical nature of the liturgy as it was taught in *Mediator Dei:* second, showing the pastoral character of the liturgy in such a way that the People of God would grow in their participation in the living source of the Christian spirit and piety. In his explanation of the Schema, the Cardinal underlined the necessary interior dispositions that the faithful should have, if they were going to attain to the sources of grace opened by the liturgy. In the celebrations of the liturgical year the faithful have to respond internally to what they do externally, because this is the only way to receive fully the fruits of the liturgy. He noted that one of the main objectives of the schema was to increase the active and conscious participation of the faithful in the sacred rites. For this reason one of the main duties of the pastors was to make the liturgy as comprehensible as possible for the faithful and, as a consequence, all the things that are obscure for the faithful in the liturgy should be avoided. Taking into account the communal and hierarchical nature of the liturgy it is important to highlight the dynamic participation that all should have in the liturgy to avoid anyone being a mute and inert spectator, so that all should enter actively into the sacred action with their spirit, heart and body. Very much connected with the concern of the participation of the faithful was the search for inculturation of the liturgy and thus the cardinal notes that the schema seeks to introduce in the liturgy whatever is noble and dignified in a given culture and that it is not necessarily connected with superstitions and does not favour errors. These adaptations should be introduced only with due permission from the Holy See. As we have seen above, the text on the use of Latin had its limitations, but it should be noted that in making comments on this text of the schema, Cardinal Larraona indicated that the teachings of Veterum Sapientia, should be confirmed and sanctioned, and in particular the injunction of the Pope against those who attacked the use of Latin. Cardinal Larraona in his presentation of the second chapter of the schema which dealt with the Most Sacred Mystery of the Eucharist, stated that it was the desire of the Church that the faithful should understand better the Holy Sacrifice of the Mass and should participate in the liturgy in a more active and conscious fashion. He noted how recent studies and liturgical congresses had shown the communal aspect of the Mass. In the celebration of the Eucharist the whole family of God is called to gather round the altar. In his explanation of the inclusion of the 'Common Prayer' or 'Prayer of the Faithful' he noted that this prayer would strengthen the spirit of communal participation of all those who assisted at the Mass. He proposed that the 'common prayer', the lessons, and the hymns should be in the vernacular. In his presentation of the third chapter of the schema on the other sacraments and sacramentals, Cardinal Larraona, said that the objective of the proposed changes was truly pastoral, seeking a more conscious and active participation of the faithful.

In many of his interventions Cardinal Francis Spellman emphasized the need for a stronger and more fruitful liturgical life for the faithful; he insisted, however, that great care must be given to this issue and that great circumspection and prudence must accompany the efforts to achieve this desirable objective. He stated that the faithful should not be mere spectators but that they should participate in the Sacrifice of the Mass with a good understanding, in an active and conscious fashion. He insisted that the fundamental participation of the faithful in the liturgy should be internal. Cardinal Spellman warned that the level of internal participation, 'in spirit and in truth', may often be far from what the externals might indicate. Internal participation, he explained, ought to be achieved through 'appropriate liturgical education of the clergy and the faithful which would lead to a more intense and profound participation; otherwise, the liturgy may even lose its more mystic and arcane character'. He also warned that experiments with the liturgy would cause shock, confusion and damage to the faithful. He underlined how these experiments instead of assisting in a better participation of the faithful, could cause scandal to the simpler faithful when they would see the change of the rites of the Church. Basing his comments on his experience as Military Vicar, he observed that American servicemen travelling abroad always admired and benefited from the unity of rite and language in the Church. He called for the preservation of Latin in the Mass, citing several important passages of John XXIII's recent apostolic constitution *Veterum*

Sapientia. Cardinal Spellman complained about those who wanted to reduce the expressions of reverence in the Mass - the signs of the Cross, the kissing of the altar, genuflections and inclinations - and wondered whether these innovations would be to the advantage of the faithful. He warned that the simplification of the formula used for the distribution of the Holy Eucharist could diminish reverence for the Eucharist. Spellman also noted that the proposal of adding more scriptural readings to the Mass could not be controverted in principle; but he warned that this could decrease the time available for the homily and make the Mass longer and more burdensome, jeopardising, as a consequence, the daily participation of working people.

Cardinal Giuseppe Siri underlined that nothing should be changed in the liturgy save with great caution and with evident reasons. He warned that if changes were introduced in the liturgy, the faithful would not understand, and that these would produce a negative effect.

Cardinal Ernesto Ruffini in his comments on the first chapter of the schema underlined that too much liberty was being granted to the bishops conferences in relation to inculturation, liturgical language and universal prayer. In his view this liberty could create confusion and grave discrimination that would shock the faithful. With regard to the proposals of the 'Schema on the Most Sacred Mystery of the Eucharist' he expressed his strong disagreement with the proposals for reducing the prayers at the foot of the altar, for the reception of the Eucharist under two species and for concelebration, and underlined that all those proposed changes were going to scandalize the faithful. Cardinal G. T. Heard expressed similar concerns.

Cardinal Paul Léger expressed his concern for the internal participation of the faithful in the liturgy by proposing an emendation that would underline the importance of this concept in the schema. With regards to liturgical language he welcomed the introduction of the vernacular and he proposed that the norm of the schema on the use of Latin should be drafted in a less rigid form. He insisted that the parts of the Mass destined for the instruction of the faithful and the prayers that belong to the faithful, should be in vernacular.

Cardinal Julius Döpfner expressed his support for the use of vernacular languages within certain and well-determined limits to foster a more fruitful participation of the faithful in the liturgy. At the same time he maintained the need to preserve Latin, taking into account the multi-secular traditions of the Western Church. So he proposed that as the fundamental principle, Latin should be preserved as the primary liturgical language and that the vernacular should be used where the salvation of souls and the active participation of the people would require it. He would limit the use of the vernacular to the scriptural readings, the prayers made by the faithful and hymns. He noted that the unity of the Latin Church could be protected through a vital and active participation of the faithful. With regard to the changes in the rites of the Mass, he stated that they should lead to a better understanding of the liturgy and increase more active participation. He noted also that the reception of the Eucharist under two species by the laity would increase their active participation in the liturgy and increase their devotion to the Precious Blood, but he also warned that in this innovation, caution was needed.

Cardinal Bernard Alfrink praised the draft of the PLC on the use of the vernacular in the liturgy. He expressed the need to introduce the vernacular languages in the liturgy, in particular for the lessons, the monitions, and in some prayers and hymns. He also defended the bishops who would like to introduce the vernacular in the liturgy: clearly implying criticism of *Veterum Sapientia.*

Cardinal Alfredo Ottaviani strongly objected to the second chapter of the schema on the Most Sacred Mystery of the Eucharist and voted against it. He noted that the proposals were of a revolutionary nature that would shock the faithful. The cardinal underlined that the liturgy is for the people and not for the learned. With regard to the introduction of the vernacular he could accept that it could be used in the pedagogical parts of the Mass but Latin should be used from the Offertory to the Communion. Cardinals Micara, Spellman, Copello, Ruffini, Heard, and Archbishops Antezana y Rojas, Beras, Lefebvre, Rakotomalala, expressed support for these opinions.

Cardinal Achille Liénart defended the changes in the liturgy which came from bishops who advocated them, not for the love of change, but for the spiritual welfare of their flocks. He underlined that it is not sufficient to say: 'Educate your faithful well and surely they will like the liturgy'. Experience shows that the more instructed the faithful are on the liturgy, the more they aspire to have an active participation in the liturgical ceremonies. In his view the bishops that have taken care of a renewal of the 'liturgical sense' in their dioceses can testify to an increase of the theological life in the laity, an increase of the community spirit and of zeal for the apostolate.

Cardinal Carlo Confalonieri after noting that the guiding principle should be the pastoral good of the faithful, pointed out that the people should be introduced anew to the liturgy. If, on one hand, the Latin language should be retained as much as possible, on the other the people should pray with knowledge of what they are praying and be able to truly participate in the sacred actions.

Archbishop F. Seper supported the principle that Latin should be retained as the liturgical language of the Western Church. In this regard he noted that it is one of the signs of the unity of the faith. He also mentioned the problems that modern languages had with their constant evolution. At the same time he showed himself in favour of the use of the vernacular for the scriptural readings, the collect and the post-communion and the hymns that the faithful might sing.

Cardinal Giuseppe Pizzardo, in his brief intervention, stated that the possibility of using the vernacular in the liturgy should not be unrestricted and should not conflict with the principle that Latin should be preserved as the liturgical language of the Western Church. He admitted that exceptions to this principle could be granted by the Holy See. Cardinal McGuigan underlined the importance of preserving the Latin language and in this regard, to avoid confusion, he objected to the concession to Episcopal Conferences of any faculties. Cardinal William Godfrey seconded the comment that Cardinals Spellman, Ruffini and Ottaviani had made on the first chapter of the schema. He used strong terms in support of the preservation of Latin in the liturgy and condemned those who wanted to suppress Latin from the Western liturgy. Cardinal J. D'Alton underlined the importance of the principle that 'the visible unity of the Catholic Church is chiefly manifested by the visible uniformity of its worship.' He indicated that two values should be carefully preserved: the richness of the local culture and the visible unity of the universal Church. As a consequence all the ritual adaptations in the Holy Sacrifice of the Mass and other acts of the Eucharistic worship should be strictly reserved to the Holy See. He also proposed that the council should solemnly forbid the use of the vernacular in the Offertory, Preface and Canon of the Mass and in the form of the Sacraments. Cardinal Fernando Quiroga y Palacios underlined the need to preserve the use of the Latin language. He also noted that when it was useful for some dioceses to use the vernacular, this should be done always with the involvement of the Holy See to preserve the unity of the Church.

Cardinal Giovanni Battista Montini strongly defended the use of the vernacular language and inserted in the *Acta* a study that upheld this position. In this document he underlined the pastoral urgency for the use of the vernacular in the liturgy, so that the faithful could duly participate and be instructed in the ceremonies. Cardinal Montini stated that a language is not of the essence of religion, but at the same time he noted that a single language is a sign of unity and an efficacious instrument to present the truth in an accurate way. He proposed, then, that the Introit, Collect, Epistle, Gospel, Creed, Offertory antiphon, and the Our Father, should be said in the vernacular. At the same time he agreed that from the Preface to the Communion, Latin should be used. He also proposed that the vernacular should be used in the sacraments and sacramentals.

Cardinal Franziskus Köning noted that the schema developed that which had been contained in a seminal form in the encyclical *Mediator Dei*. He stated how the schema was aiming at an increase of an effective participation, the decrease of ignorance, the custody of the purity of the faith and maintaining the unity of the Latin Church without affecting the principle of preserving the Latin language.

Several members of the commission who supported the introduction of the vernacular languages in the liturgy, underlined the value that this change would have in missionary countries. But in this regard it is useful to mention the intervention of Archbishop T. B. Cooray of Colombo who highlighted the problem affecting missionary countries with a multiplicity of languages, resulting in the difficulty of having to select a particular language to the exclusion of others used in the same region. He also noted that in certain languages it is difficult to find the appropriate expressions for the form of the sacraments and sacramentals. He suggested that many difficulties could be avoided if the sacred ministers would have the faculty to explain in the vernacular the ceremonies. With regards to the sacrificial parts of the Mass he insisted that only Latin should be used. With regards to inculturation, the Archbishop of Saigon, Ngô-Dinh-Thûc, criticized the presumption of the periti who were ready to indicate that certain architecture and music would favour conversions. He indicated that a given music and architecture was only associated with the cult of idols.

CONCLUSIONS

• Conscious Participation

A caricature of the liturgy as it was celebrated before Vatican II has been made, describing it as 'celebrations for large passive congregations in which the faithful 'attended' mainly as spectators'. The fact is, as we have seen above, that the Church has never accepted that description as a valid option. The Church has always proposed that the faithful should participate in the Holy Sacrifice of the Mass with piety and devotion, elevating their minds and hearts in adoration to the Real Presence of Christ in the Eucharist. Most of the speakers in the CPC underlined the fundamental importance of the internal participation of the faithful in the liturgy. To attain a better internal participation several members of the commission insisted on the need of a better understanding of the liturgy which would lead to more active and conscious participation. To improve the level of participation three means were suggested: 1. changes in the liturgy to foster participation. 2. the use of the vernacular. 3. an improved liturgical education of the clergy and the faithful.

• Changes in the liturgy to foster participation

The main reason which was alleged to justify the proposed reforms in the liturgy was to increase the intelligibility of the liturgy to foster, as a consequence, a better participation of the faithful in the liturgy. But more than one member of the commission questioned if the proposed changes would truly be for the spiritual advantage of the faithful. Also the concern was expressed that the changes proposed in the schema would lead to confusion, shock and scandal for the faithful. Here two types of scenario were envisaged: first the shock that the changes in themselves might cause; second, the confusion that the faithful would suffer as they would see the Mass and the other sacred rites being celebrated in diverse ways in different countries, taking into account the freedom that was offered to the episcopal conferences.

In the schema it was proposed that the different episcopal conferences could introduce adaptations in the liturgy to incorporate elements of a given national culture. With regard to this proposal several members pointed out that the uniformity of the liturgy is a sign of the unity and universality of the Church.

• *The language of the liturgy*

The introduction of the vernacular in the liturgy was seen by several members of the CPC as a means of increasing the conscious participation of the faithful. But the first thing that should be noticed here, is that not a single member of the commission proposed the abolition of Latin in the liturgy. Even those who strongly defended the introduction of the vernacular would limit it to the didactic parts of the Mass, the hymns and the common prayer, and only a few proposed its use for the prayers of the Mass. Also, with regard to the use of vernacular, it was pointed out that dogma is expressed in linguistic formulations, and that this always leads to difficulties with translation.

• *An improved liturgical education of the clergy and the faithful.*

This improved liturgical education of the clergy and the faithful would lead, in the opinion of some members of the commission, to a more active external participation in the liturgy which in turn would lead to an increased internal participation. The question is, as one of the members of the commission pointed out, that a more active external participation does not provide any guarantee that this external active participation is truly representative of an increased internal participation.

THE LITURGICAL ROLE
OF THE CHOIR

Dom Emmanuel de Butler

Dom Emmanuel de Butler OSB is a monk at the Benedictine abbey of Barroux in France, where he has been Master of Ceremonies for fifteen years and teaching liturgy to the novitiate for over a decade. He has contributed to various magazines and other publications, especially as author of a series of articles on the Roman liturgy in La Nef.

IN order to treat this subject in the time allotted, I have chosen to limit my study to the following question: may we speak of a true liturgical function for the choir (I will use indiscriminately this term and that of schola (cantorum)) in the celebration of the Solemn Mass, in the same sense as we do for the ministers of the altar, for example? I will treat this question from the point of view of the history of the liturgy.

Firstly, a definition of terms: in this study we will use the term 'Roman Mass' to mean the Romano-Frankish Mass rite born of the Carolingian reform, which rapidly imposed itself on the whole of Europe before being fixed in various regions or religious orders with some variations in its details. Thus, the term 'Roman Mass' will cover the Mass rites of the Dominicans and Cistercians, of Lyons etc., which, overall, reveal differences of only secondary importance from the Mass of the Roman Curia during the same period.

The oldest document to come down to us giving a relatively detailed description of the solemn celebration of the Roman Mass is the *Ordo Romanus Primus,* generally attributed to the seventh century. We read therein:

> as soon (as the entrance procession begins) the first cantor of the schola intones the antiphon at the introit. ... The schola intones the *Kyrie eleison*...when the antiphon is finished.... When they (the members of the schola) have finished, the Pontiff begins the Gloria in excelsis Deo,... and he does not sit until the response 'Amen' has been made to the first oration. ... The subdeacon who is to do the first reading (the epistle)

goes up to the ambo as soon as he sees the bishops and priests sit down after the Pontiff, and reads it. Thereafter another goes up with the chant book and performs the responsory. Then another performs the 'Alleluia'.'

There follows the chanting of the Gospel by a deacon, then the celebrant and ministers receive the gifts, while the schola sings the Offertory. It would seem to be the 'regional' subdeacons who intone the Sanctus, and when it has been sung the celebrant begins the Canon. The schola sings the *Agnus Dei,* which accompanies the rite of the fraction, at a sign from the archdeacon. We read thereafter: 'as soon as the Pontiff begins to distribute Communion in the Senatorium (where the lay dignitaries are placed) the schola begins the Communion antiphon, and sings it until all the people have communicated'. [1]

As far as the sung liturgical texts are concerned, we should make several points:

1) These chants differ first of all as regards their performers. There are:
  • those proper to the celebrant: the intonation of the *Gloria,* the singing of the Collect, Secret and Postcommunion, the Canon [2] and the *Pater Noster.*
  • those belonging to certain ministers and particular to them: the Epistle, the responsory or Gradual, the Alleluia and the Gospel.
  • those belonging to the schola or the assembly: the Introit, the *Kyrie,* the *Gloria* (there is no *Credo* in the Mass at this period), the Offertory, S*anctus, Agnus Dei* and Communion antiphon.

We may remark that at this period the schola (and indeed the congregation) perform a true liturgical ministry in the same sense as the deacon or lector. Its role is not to beautify the liturgical action by the gratuitous addition of this or that piece of singing, but to perform the chants which are an integral part of the liturgy.

2) Next we may note that the different chants do not all serve the same purpose:

  • those which are proper to the celebrant are truly priestly actions: nobody can perform them in his stead.
  • others are meant to accompany other actions.
  • the Introit accompanies the entrance procession of celebrant (and ministers) and the prayers at the foot of the altar, the Offertory, the procession with the offerings of the faithful, the Communion antiphon—as its name implies—the procession at Communion. In the same way, the *Agnus Dei* is destined to accompany the fraction of the Hosts for Communion.
  • others stand in their own right; no liturgical action takes place during them: thus the *Kyrie, Gloria,* and *Sanctus.*
  • still others are meant to be listened to attentively. They are performed by soloists while celebrant, ministers and congregation listen: this is the case for the Epistle, Gradual, Alleluia and Gospel.

Thus, for the celebration of solemn Mass in the High Middle Ages, the liturgical functions appear separated quite distinctly: cantors sing the Introit and *Kyrie* (which are not recited privately by the celebrant); the celebrant intones the Gloria and remains standing throughout the chant (a clear sign that he sings it with everyone, or that he attaches such an importance to its singing by choir and congregation that he does not feel able to sit during it). The readings are performed by their respective ministers, everybody else listens. There is one chant which, it is insisted, is to be sung in common by everyone: celebrant, ministers and faithful; this is the *Sanctus*. 'Let the priest himself, with the holy angels and the people of God, sing with one voice: *Sanctus, Sanctus, Sanctus...,*' [3] Herard of Tours (858) makes the same point. 'Let the priests not begin the Canon before the *Sanctus* is finished, but let them sing the *Sanctus* with the people'. [4]

This custom of priest and people singing the *Sanctus* in common was to disappear under pressure of circumstances, with the arrival of very ornate (and, indeed, polyphonic) melodies which prevented its singing in unison, which is nevertheless the ancient tradition of the Church.

The *Ordines* after the *Ordo Romanus Primus* all follow this same principle of distributing the liturgical functions according to the specific roles of the various 'actors' [5] in the liturgy. A systematic study of the documents which describe the liturgy of the Roman Mass shows that this principle is observed everywhere until the end of the eleventh century.

This structure, fundamentally communitarian, in the positive sense of the word, of the liturgy of the Mass, is confirmed by St Thomas Aquinas who deals with the following objection in the *Summa Theologica:*

'It is the priest who, as we have said, is the minister of this sacrament. Therefore everything that is said in this sacrament ought to be said by the priest, and not certain words by the ministers, and others by the choir'. Here is his reply:

> In this sacrament, as has been said, we touch upon realities which concern the whole Church. And that is why certain words are said by the choir, because they concern the whole people. Some are said by the choir from beginning to end, because they are given by inspiration to the people as a whole. Others are continued by the people only after being intoned by the priest who takes the place of God, to signify that these things come to the people by divine inspiration alone, such as faith and heavenly glory. And this is why the priest intones the Symbol of Faith and the *Gloria in Excelsis Deo.* Other are said by the ministers, such as the teachings from the Old and New Testaments, to make clear that these teachings were made known to the people through ministers sent by God. Others are said by the priest alone from beginning to end; these are those which belong properly to his office of priest, to whom it belongs, according to the Epistle to the Hebrews, 'to offer gifts and prayers on behalf of the people'. [6]

But a question comes to mind: if the celebrant is alone to accomplish these different roles (as in the case of the 'private' Mass) what is he to do? The solution was simple, and would emerge gradually, the celebrant would himself replace these absent ministers and read these readings and chants in place of the other 'actors'. So doing, he adds to his own, strictly priestly office a ministry of supplying for other roles.

This custom, whose timid appearance we may trace to the eighth century, was to appear with an extraordinary vigour in the tenth to eleventh centuries in the guise of the 'apologies'. By this term are meant the private devotional prayers which the celebrant began to recite during the long moments when he had 'nothing to do' (e.g. while he waited for a chant to finish) or 'nothing to say' (e.g. while he puts on his vestments), or while he performed a particularly meaningful action (e.g. when he kissed the altar as he went up to it or left it). Dom Edmond Martène, the great scholar of the eighteenth century, quotes a very great number of these apologies- the famous *Missa Illyrica,* [7] and also at St Denys, [8] Troyes, [9] St Martin of Tours, [10] etc. Some of these prayers indeed were to find their official place in the *Ordo Missæ.*

The circumstances which led to the apologies falling almost all into disuse are rather complex, and we cannot go deeply into the question here. But the facts are plain; the celebrant begins to read more and more in place of the apologies the texts read by choir and ministers. There is no doubt that there occurs a transposition to the solemn Mass of that which is done at the 'private' Mass. Mgr Gromier indeed speaks of '...the introduction of the low Mass into the pontifical Mass'. [11] Here he is but echoing numerous other liturgists. We might quote in particular Le Brun des Marettes, who betrays a rather biting sense of humour:

> The priest in those days recited not the Epistle and Gospel at the Altar, which were chanted by the subdeacon and the deacon, neither aught which was sung by the choir. He did but listen. Thus did each one fulfil his office. But since such time as low Masses became so frequent, the low Mass has been fitted into the high, and the priest has had to say it all. As well might he have to sing it all, and thus we had no need of deacon and subdeacon. Whereas I recall that I once read in Navarre, *Præstat Sacerdotem missam solemniter celebrantem Epistolam & Evangelium audire, quam interim legere.* (It is preferable for the priest who celebrates a solemn Mass to listen to the Epistle and Gospel, rather than meanwhile to read them). What should we say to a man who would read a sermon while a preacher did preach? Doubtless we should say to him, why do you not listen *etc.* [12]

The apologies and the 'doubling' of the liturgical texts were destined, moreover, to coexist quite happily; in the *Ordo* of the Dominican conventual Mass edited by Legg from a manuscript of the thirteenth century (given as document 'i' below in the list of documents cited) we find that the celebrant and all the ministers 'double' all the chants, but not the Epistle and Gospel. With regard to the Epistle, we read: 'having finished the Collects, the priest goes and sits down, the acolyte gives him the book, so that he may, if he wishes, look at the office beforehand and recite the prayer *Summa Sacerdos*'. [13] We have purposely underlined the word 'all', for, at least as far as the Dominicans are concerned, this includes the acolytes; the recitation of these texts in a low voice is not therefore to be considered as a priestly prerogative, but as a manner for all those who cannot be in the stalls with the community because they are busy at the service of the altar, to unite themselves to the singing. At Citeaux [14] and in the Benedictine Congregation of Bursfeld [15] it is suggested that the deacon and subdeacon go and sing with the choir between the Epistle and Gospel.

From the twelfth century onwards, the liturgical books were generally to sanction the custom of 'doubling' and give it the force of law. Certain particular rites, however, adopted it only with timidity: even after the Council of Trent we never find the use of 'doubling' by the Carthusians for the *Gloria,* the Gospel and the *Credo;* as for the Epistle, the celebrant is left free. '...the celebrant (at his seat) listens to it attentively, or reads it, the same for the responsory (Gradual) and the Alleluia or Tract...' [16] In the sixteenth century, Paride Grassi wrote, still, that the bishop celebrating pontifically was not to double Epistle and Gospel. [17]

The table overleaf, limited to the documents which may be consulted in the meagre library of a young monastery [le Barroux], and in spite of the lack of precision of certain old documents (which are more *aides-memoires* than systematic *exposés*), gives us nonetheless a sufficiently clear idea of the different stages of this evolution.

	Introit	Kyrie	Gloria	Epistle	Gradual/Alleluia	Gospel	Credo	Offertory	Sanctus	Agnus Dei	Communion
Ordines Romani (7th-9th c)[a]											
Jean d'Avranches (1060)[b]											
Cluny:Udalric (1080)[c]											
Cluny: Hirshau (end of 11c)[d]											
Monte Cassino (end of 11c)[e]									c		
Latran (11c)[f]	c	?	cdsp	c			cdsp		cds	cd	
Cîteaux (1191)[g]			apologies						cd	c	
Bayeux (13c)[h]	cds	cds							cds	cds	
Dominican (13c)[i]	cdsa	cdsa	cdsa / apologies /cdsa	cdsa			cdsa	cdsa	cdsa	cdsa	cdsa
Dominican (1869)[j]	cdsa	cdsa	cdsa	c	cd	c	cdsa	cdsa	cdsa	cdsa	cdsa
Indutus Planeta (1243)[k]	cds	cds	?	cd	cd	?		c?	cds	c?	c?
Pontifical of Durandus (13c)[l]	cds	cds	cds				cds	cds	?	?	?
Sarum (1320)[m]											
Sarum (1489)[n]	cds	cds	cds				.		cds		cds
Subiaco (14c)[o]	cds	cds	cds	cd	cds		cds	cds	cds	cds	cds
Bursfeld (1474)[p]	cds	cds	c					c	c	[c]	?
Chezal-Benoît (1531)[q]	cds	cds	cds				cds		cds	cds	
Carthusian (1259)[r]	c.*ad lib.*		c.*ad lib.*								
Carthusian (1932)[s]	c	c		c.*ad lib.*	c.*ad lib.*			c	c	c	c

• *Abbreviations:*

    ad lib. ad libitum (at choice)

      a: acolytes

      c: celebrant

      d: deacon

      s: subdeacon

• *Documents used:*

a: M. Andrieu *op. cit. passim,*

b: Joannis Abrincensis 'Liber de Officiis Ecclesiasticis', (J.P. Migne, *Patrologiæ cursus completus,* Paris-Montrouge, 1844-1864, 221 vol. (abbreviated to PL). The first number indicates the volume, the second the column) 147, 33 sq.

c: 'Antiquiores Consuetudines Cluniacensis Monasterii collectore Udalrico Monacho Benedictino' (PL 149, 716 sq.)

d: Sancti Willhelmi Consuetudines Hirsaugienses (PL 150, 1010 sq.)

e: Ordinarium (Monasterii Cassinensis), tempore Oderisti abbatis, in E, Martene, *De Antiquis Monachorum Ritibus* (henceforth abbreviated as AMR), Lib. II, Cap. IV, §1, n. VII.

f: Bernhardi Cardinalis et Lateranensis Ecclesiæ Prioris *Ordo Officiorum Ecclesiæ Lateranensis.* München, Datterer, 1916 (Historische Forschungen und Quellen, 2-3) pp. 80-85.

g: Consuetudines, Cap. Llll, in P. Guignard, *Les Monuments Primitifs de la règle Cistercienne,* Dijon 1878, pp. 142-149.

h: ex ms. 'Ordinario insignis ecclesiæ Bajoccensis', in E. Martene, *ÆR,* Lib. I, Cap. IV, Art XII. (Ordo XXIV) The thirteenth century ms. is at Bayeux, Bibliothèque du Chapitre, ms. 121.

i: Directions for the celebration of high Mass by the Dominican friars from a thirteenth century manuscript, in *Tracts on the Mass,* edited by J. Wickham Legg, Henry Bradshaw Society, vol. 27, London 1904, pp. 75 seq.

j: *Cæremoniale juxta Ritum S. Ordinis Prædicatorum Revmi Patris Fr. Alexandri Vincentii Jandel ejusdem Ordinis Generalis Magistri jussu Editum.* Mechlinæ, H. Dessain, 1869, pp. 290-321, 371-376. This ceremonial keeps open the possibility for the celebrant to recite the apologies when he is not occupied (p.372).

k: Haymon of Faversham, *Indutus planeta,* in J.W. Legg, *op. cit.,* p. 179 seq. This work, fundamental for the origin of the *Ritus Servandus* of the Missal of 1570, concerns above all the 'private' Mass, and the indications it gives for the solemn Mass are rather imprecise.

l: M. Andrieu, *Le Pontifical Romain au moyen âge,* vol. III, *Le Pontifical de Guillaume Durand,* Città del Vaticano, Biblioteca Apostolica Vaticana, 1940, Studi è Testi 88, pp. 631-641.

m: 'Sarum Ordinary of the Fourteenth Century', in J.W. Legg, op. cit. p. 1 seq. This compilation, though very laconic, does not, however, seem to suppose that the celebrant 'doubles' what is sung by the choir.

n: *Missale ad usum Sarum,* 1489, by Michæl Wenssler, Basle (cited in E. Martene, ÆR Lib. 1, Cap. IV, Art. XII. (Ordo XXXV)). Introit, *Kyrie* and *Gloria* are 'doubled', but for the rest of the Mass we do not know whether there is any 'doubling'.

o: *Consuetudines et Cæremoniale Regularis Observantiæ Monasterii Sublacensis (...) in Lucem Editæ per D. Leonem Allodi monachum ejusdem monasterii.* Sublaci, typis Protocoenobii, MCMII, pp. 37-41.

p: *Ordinarius Divinorum de Observantia Bursfeldensi,* 1474, Cap. XLIII-XLV, consulted and cited by E. Martene, AMR; for our study, see Lib. 2, Cap. IV.

q: *Cæremoniale et Statute Congregationis Casalis Benedicti* (B.N. Lat. 13322, c. 15, ff 69r-71v) consulted and cited by E. Martene, AMR, Lib. 2, Cap, IV, § 1, nn. 14, 17.

r: *Antiqua Statuta* (Statutes of Dom Riffier, 1259) *in Statuta et Privilegia Ordinis Cartusiensis,* Basiliæ, apud J. Amorbach, 1510, parte 1 cap. 4, (cited in E. Martene, ÆR, Lib. 1, Cap. IV, Art. XII. (Ordo XXV) and many times in AMR).

s: *Ordinarium cartusiense,* Parkminster, 1932, pp. 144, 147, 153.

The Ritus Servandus in Celebratione Missæ of the Roman Missal of St. Pius V in 1570, was to prescribe the 'doubling' of all the texts (including Epistle and Gospel) but distinguishing those of the proper (doubled by the celebrant alone) from those of the ordinary (doubled by the celebrant accompanied by the deacon and subdeacon). It would be erroneous, however, to attribute to this doubling any other significance than of being a private reading done for the celebrant's personal devotion. Mgr Gromier (and we know with what knowledge and conviction he defended the Tridentine liturgy) writes in his *Commentaire du Cæremoniale Episcoporum:* '... the [celebrating] bishop reads the texts [of the proper] for himself, simply in order to be aware of them'.[18] The *Cæremoniale Episcoporum* still seems to give more importance to the texts read by the bishop than to the texts sung by the choir, which would be contrary to the natural order of things.[19] It would be astonishing if the bishop (when assisting pontifically), having recited his Sanctus, even with the canons, should continue without taking into account the true Sanctus being sung by the choir'[20] Mgr Gromier here, recalls two fundamental principles:

• The singing of the choir is a true liturgical action in the proper sense, more important than the reading done by the celebrant in private; and

• The celebrant should base his actions on those of the choir or congregation in order to respect the normal ordering of the Mass; this principle has been neglected for several centuries, but was formerly universally respected. Among the numerous examples, we take one from the Cistercian Mass (remembering that this is but a particular form of the Roman Mass):

> the celebrant was not obliged to recite in a low voice those parts of the Mass sung by the choir or the ministers, he should never make the choir wait needlessly. Thus, as soon as the Kyrie was finished he had to intone the Gloria or sing Dominus vobiscum, keeping the completion of whatever he had not the time to recite for the singing, of the Gloria or Epistle.[21]

The reform of the Easter Vigil promulgated by Pope Pius XII in 1951, initiated a return to the traditional usage by prescribing that, for the readings and chants of the first part, 'the celebrant and ministers, clergy and people listen seated'. The missal of 1962 would extend notably this restoration of the ancient practice: 'at the sung Mass, everything which the deacon, subdeacon or lector sing or read in fulfilling their proper function is omitted by the celebrant'.[22] Let us look closely at this rubric, which gives us our guiding principle: 'Each one should not exceed his own ministry'. It would not seem that the *Constitution on the Liturgy* departs from this principle when it declared less than two years later (December 1963):

> In liturgical celebration each one, priest or layperson, will perform, while executing his function, all and only that which is proper to him in virtue of the nature of the action and the liturgical norms. Even the servers, readers, commentators and those belonging to the Schola Cantorum perform a true liturgical ministry.[23]

The Instruction *Inter Œcumenici* of 26 September 1964 was to make a concrete application of this principle:

the texts of the proper (Introit, Gradual, Alleluia, Tract, Offertory, and Communion) which are sung or recited by the schola or the people, are not to be recited by the priest in private. The celebrant may sing or recite with the people or the schola the parts of the Ordinary (Kyrie, Gloria, Credo, Sanctus, Agnus).

This small amendment of the rite of Mass, separating properly the roles of celebrant and schola, was, in general, well received. Let us quote the example of a certain French bishop:

> Should we conclude nonetheless from these dissensions (the liturgical disorders which were beginning to appear) that everything should have been left unchanged? The council responded in the negative, with balance and prudence. Some things had to be reformed and restored. It is clear that the first part of the Mass, made for the instruction of the faithful and for making them express their faith, needed to fulfil these purposes more clearly and in a certain way more comprehensibly. In my humble opinion two such reforms seemed useful; firstly the rites of this first part of the Mass with some translation into the vernacular. To arrange things so that the priest comes nearer to the faithful, enters into communication with them, prays and sings with them; let him stand then at the ambo, say the Collect, the Epistle and the Gospel in their own language; let the priest sing the *Kyrie,* the *Gloria* and the *Credo* with the faithful according to their divine, traditional melodies. These are salutary reforms which make this first part of the Mass attain its true purpose. [25]

These remarks, so full of sound common sense, were made by Mgr Marcel Lefebvre.

Should we end by expressing some desires? Let our attachment to the traditional liturgy be rooted ever more deeply in a profound knowledge of its essence and structure, so that we avoid the ever present danger of an excessive preoccupation with the rubrics, considered purely externally, which might be to the detriment of the principal laws of liturgical celebration. Let a true renaissance of Gregorian Chant, especially in the churches where the traditional liturgy is celebrated, allow the schola and the congregation to be given their full place as actors in the liturgy. Experience shows that this is possible; our friends present here from *Una Voce* and the *Schola Saint Grégoire* can witness to that. Let priests set themselves the goal of permitting Christians from their earliest years to savour the beauty and the depth of the liturgical texts and melodies, and the marvellous teaching which they contain. Then without doubt, we will see the rebirth of that true 'active participation in the sacred mysteries and the public and solemn prayer of the Church', desired by Pope St. Pius X with all his heart, and wherein he saw 'the first and indispensable source of the true Christian spirit'. [26]

NOTES

1. M. Andrieu, *Les Ordines Romani du haut moyen âge.* 6 volumes, Louvain 1931 et seq. OR I, 44-117.

2. But this is already said in a low voice as early as before the year 900: OR V, 58 (M. Andrieu, *op. cit.*)

3. *Admonitio Generalis* of Charlemagne (789). n.70 in *Capitularia regum Francorum (Monumenta Germaniæ historica* ...) Hanover, Hahn and Berlin. Weidman, 1826 *et seq.*, vol. 1 page 59.

4. Herard of Tours *Capitula* n. 16 (PL 121, col. 765).

5. M. Andrieu *op. cit. passim.*

6. ST IIIa QLXXXIII Art.4 ad 6um.

7. *De Antiquis Ecclesiæ Ritibus* (henceforth abridged as ÆR) edition known as that of Antwerp (1736-1738), four volumes reprinted from 1967 to 1969 by Georg Holms, Hildesheim. Lib. I. Cap. IV, Art XII, Ordo VII.

8. ÆR, Lib. I, Cap. IV, Art XII, Ordo V.

9. ÆR, Lib 1. Cap. IV, Art XII, Ordo VI.

10. ÆR, Lib. 1, Cap. IV, Art MI. Ordo VII.

11. L. GROMIER, *Commentaire du Cæremoniale Episcoporum,* La Colombe, 1959, p. 185.

12. J-B Le Brun des Marettes, *Voyage Liturgique en France, ou recherches faites dans diverses villes du Royaume,* published in 1718 under the pseudonym of the Sieur de Moleon, p. 256.

13. p. 76.

14. *Consuetudines,* Cap. LIII, in P. Guignard. *Les monuments primitifs de la règle cistercienne,* Dijon 1878, pp. 143.

15. *Ordinarius Divinorum de Observantia Bursfeldensi,* 1474. Cap. XLIII.

16. *Ordinarium Cartusiense,* Parkminster, 1932, pp. 152

17. L. Gromier, *op. cit.,* p. 184.

18. L. Gromier, *op. cit.* p. 301.

19. *ibid.* p. 378.

20. *ibid.* p. 371.

21. F. Schneider, O.C.R., *L'ancienne Messe Cistercienne,* Abbey of Our Lady of Konigshoeven, Tilbourg, 1929, p. 134.

22. *Codex Rubricorum,* n. 473

23. nn.28-29 (my underlining).

24. nn.48 a&b.

25. M. Lefebvre in *Itinéraires,* July August 1965, n. 95, pp. 78-79.

26. *Tra le sollecitudini,* 22 November 1903.

MINISTERIAL AND COMMON PRIESTHOOD IN THE NEW TESTAMENT

Don Reto Nay

Dr Nay, born in 1962, is a priest of the dio-cese of Coire. He studied theology in Coire and in Jerusalem. Having obtained a Licenti-ate at the Pontifical Biblical Institute in Rome where he subsequently became Doctor of Holy Scripture on a thesis on the prophet Ezechiel, Dr Nay now teaches at the International Theo-logical Institute at Gaming in Austria.

We must respect the silence of the New Testament which never says of a Christian that he is a priest. Of only one person, that of Jesus Christ, the Letter to the Hebrews, alone, affirms this salvific function. For it is indeed a question of function. Moreover, the discretion of scripture—apart from the Letter to the Hebrews—on the priesthood of Jesus him-self is pregnant with meaning. Faith does not automatically grasp this aspect which belongs to a greater whole.

THIS is one of the conclusions drawn by the Canadian Dominican Jean-Marie-R. Tillard in his article 'Priesthood' published in the *Dictionary of Spirituality* (1990). It reflects a widely held position in the teaching of Catholic theology. At present it may even be considered to be a moderate voice in the chorus of opinions within the Church of today. In the long term, if it proved to be exact, it would lead to major changes in the doctrine and prac-tice of the Church as regards the ministerial priesthood. Indeed one can already see the first signs of this on the horizon. It must therefore be our first task to cast an eye on this challenge to the priesthood.

THE CHALLENGE TO THE PRIESTHOOD

In the course of my studies at the major seminary in Chur, a seminarian who had just spent a year studying in Lyons explained to me that the New Testa-ment did not justify a ministerial priesthood. In this context he quoted Hebrews 7:27 according to which Christ offered up his sacrifice 'once for all'. The min-isterial priesthood of the Church would be a consequence of her inculturation in the Hellenistic world. This thesis has been defended recently by Herbert Haag, a priest of the diocese of Basle and retired professor of Old Testament at Tubingen. According to Haag, at the beginning of the Church, the Eucharist was not celebrated by a priest but led by a president (male or female). What looks spectacularly like the neo-Marxist ecclesiology of a certain modern heterodoxy, was, so Haag says, as things stood in the early Church. As it happens it is difficult not to think of the German philosopher and romantic poet, Frederick von Schlegel, who wrote about a certain type of historiography: 'One has always discovered among one's ancestors one's own desires and wishes and above all oneself'.

Haag reaches his conclusions in avoiding the truths of the faith by an ideological use of critical historiography. He makes use of his own reconstruction of the past in order to weaken the faith of the Church in the present. The aim of this historical revisionism is the relativist interpretation of doctrine. But the attempt to understand the whole of the faith owned by the Church of today by historical and partial hypotheses is bound to fail. Faith is not a historical hypothesis but a living reality in the Church. One cannot seize it through the remains of the past. Outside the living body of the Church there is no science of faith, at best an ideological critique defined by the personal prejudices of each writer.

There can only be life in a living body. *Mutatis mutandis,* faith can only be revealed in the believing body of the Church who possesses faith in the '*nunc*' of the Holy Spirit. For the believers, faith is only perceptible through the work of the head, the heart and the hands of the Church. The attempt to discover faith by returning to the historical and theoretical sources is an approach which leads to all heresies. Historiography only sees the witnesses of the past in the clarity of its own epoch. The light with which the historian illumines the past is his: it depends on his personal point of view. The historical study of faith is thus only pertinent if faith, witnessed in the historical documents, is perceived in the light of the Church of today. Neither the Church, nor theology, live on a historical regression, but on the faith contained in the liturgy, the holy Scriptures, the Fathers and the doctrinal decisions of the Magisterium.

Intellectual archæologism found in Haag and others does not refer apparently only to the past. A profoundly dishonest feature is proper to it. It pretends the existence of another world and of another Church, whose historian is the pastor and high priest. But there is, of course, only one Church, that which exists today. One sees the past, not in the past but in the present. It is in the present that it is rebuilt by the human mind. Yesterday no longer exists and it will never revive. The traces that it may have left behind only exist in the present. One can thus say that history deals with the present and that escaping back into history often helps to conceal an ideological design for the present.

To sum up: the modern challenge to the ministerial priesthood results from a historical and ideological reading of the biblical texts concerning the priesthood. These writings cannot be understood within a historical-ideological framework, but within the context and in the light of the faith of the living Church of today.

Having shed some light on this problem we are now going to tackle the question of the priesthood of Christ which is at the root of the ministerial priesthood.

Was Christ a priest?

The ministerial priest is a priest in as much as Christ is a priest. The discourse on the ministerial priesthood must therefore begin with the priesthood of Christ.

Regarding the vocabulary: a priest is a minister who offers sacrifices. No priest without sacrifices and no sacrifices without a priest. The priest may deal with many things, but only through the sacrifice does he become a priest. Why does the priest offer sacrifices? To atone for sins. Three key notions thus come into play: priest, sacrifice, atonement.

Where does one find the priesthood of Christ in the Gospels? The answer may surprise us—if we recall Fr Tillard: it is true that Christ, in the Gospels, never introduces himself as a priest. He links his mission with the King-Messiah, the Son of Man, the Servant of Yahweh and the Prophet. The only priests recognized by Jesus are those in the Temple, although his relations with them have been tense. Even the early community does not seem to have developed a priestly conscience. Their members offer their sacrifices in the Temple, witness Acts 21:26:

> Then Paul took the men, and the next day he purified himself with them
> and went into the Temple, to give notice when the days of purification
> would be fulfilled and the offering presented for every one of them.

Jesus who belonged to the tribe of Judah did not have the right to offer sacrifices personally. In an environment where only the Levitical priesthood was known he could not present himself as a priest without being misunderstood. Besides, it is only at the end of his earthly life that his priesthood becomes visible and understandable. Nevertheless Jesus never competes with the Levitical priesthood. Witness Acts 6:14: the trial of St Stephen denies that Jesus was preparing to upset the cult and order received by Moses.

There i,s therefore, a reason why the Gospels are not very explicit with regard to the priesthood of Christ, for Jesus had not yet offered his sacrifice when he was preaching to the Jews. However, the Gospel is full of allusions to what is about to come. To the tree of the Gospels are already grafted the buds ready to bloom at the appropriate time. The fruits will be reaped by the Letter to the Hebrews.

Let us look briefly at some of these buds. The first is found in St John's Gospel at the end of the Messianic Week which opens the public ministry of Jesus. It is the cleansing of the Temple, of which Jesus refers to its destruction and rebuilding (John 2:19-21):

> Destroy this Temple, and in three days I will raise it up. The Jews then said: It has taken forty-six years to build this Temple, and will you raise it up in three days? But he spoke of the Temple of his body.

Christ unites both: the Temple, the place of the Levitical sacrifice, and the temple of his body, the place of the new sacrifice. Some commentators understand this text only in relation to the King-Messiah who will build a house and establish the throne of his kingdom for ever (2 Samuel 7:13). This interpretation avoids any priestly overtone. As King-Messiah Jesus would simply rebuild the Temple. But in St John, Jesus does not talk about the King-Messiah but about his body. It is his body which in the near future will need a 'reconstruction', not the Temple which is working perfectly at the time Jesus is speaking. The body of Christ, called to become the new Temple, gives to Christ an eminent priestly quality. No wonder that the death of Jesus had consequences for the Temple: 'and behold; the curtain of the Temple was torn in two, from top to bottom' (Mt 27:51). The curtain of the Temple hid the central part of the sanctuary, where the tables of the law were kept. These had disappeared after the Temple had been destroyed by Nebuchadnezzar. When the Israelites had returned from the Babylonian captivity and rebuilt the Temple the Holy of Holies had remained empty. [1] This vacuum in the old temple is brought to light by the sacrifice of Jesus on the cross. The death of Christ shows that a new Temple and a new priesthood had become necessary.

Another Gospel bud regarding the priesthood and sacrifice of Christ is found in John 1:29. St John the Baptist calls Jesus the Lamb of God who takes away the sins of the world. The lamb is the animal of sacrifice for the feast of Passover and the Baptist, by calling Jesus thus, points him out as the new paschal lamb.

A theological working out of the sacrifice of Jesus will be found finally in the Letter to the Romans, 3:21-26. This is a key-passage in the whole letter. St Paul first introduces the position of the pagans and the Jews towards God. The assessment is terrifying: the pagans and the Jews are guilty before God. The Mosaic Law has been nothing more than a catalyst helping to increase sin. Is there a solution? Romans 3:22-25 gives the answer:

> [...] there is no distinction; since all have sinned and fall short of the glory of God, they are justified by his grace as a gift, through the redemption which is in Christ Jesus, whom God put forward as an expiation by his blood, to be received by faith.

Some exegetes have suggested that this means God sacrifices Jesus as victim. But let us look at the central affirmation in verse 25 which refers to Christ as 'an expiation by his blood'. Expiation is the translation of the Greek ὑλαστηριον 'hylasterion'. Hylasterion—in Hebrew, כפרת 'capporet',—is the table which covered the Ark of the Covenant. According to Leviticus 16, once a year on the Day of Atonement, this table would receive the blood of a bull which the high priest would sprinkle on the Ark to atone for his own sins and those of the people. According to Romans 3:25 Jesus is the new expiation by his own blood. What does this mean? First, 'by his own blood' means, not by the blood of a bull. If Christ bleeding is the expiation, then the table no longer needs blood from outside. It gives its own blood. Christ is therefore simultaneously the priest who sprinkles the blood and the victim who gives the blood. This does not cancel the Levitical sacrifice but fulfils it. However, the priesthood of Christ is quite different from that which was practised in the Temple.

The result of our analysis is thus twofold. It is true that in the Gospels and the Acts of the Apostles we cannot find explicit references to the priesthood of Christ. However, the preaching of Jesus paves the way for understanding his death as a sacrificial act accomplished by the high priest Jesus Christ. So, was Christ a priest? The only answer is 'yes'. It is now time to make clear the nature of this priesthood.

WHAT IS THE PRIESTHOOD OF CHRIST?

The priesthood of Christ is not some kind of purified and renewed Levitical priesthood. We must not forget that the Temple, especially during the major festivals, looked more like a slaughterhouse than a place of worship. The first chapter of the book of Leviticus gives some idea of the course of this sacrificial activity in offering a holocaust. First a bull without blemish had his throat slit. Then it was cut into pieces and the sons of Aaron offered the blood by shedding it around the altar. Next they lit a fire on the altar and placed the pieces of meat with the head and the fat on top. The entrails and the feet of the bull were washed and burnt on the altar.

According to the Letter to the Hebrews Jesus Christ is not a priest according to the order of Levi or Aaron, but a high priest according to the order of Melchizedek. In comparison with the places mentioned above this is a step forward. The sketch is thus completed. The third chapter of the Letter to the Romans speaks of the new way whereby Christ has fulfilled the law. The Letter to the Hebrews makes clear this new way at the end of the sixth and in the seventh chapter. Before we go into details, let us first give an overview of the Letter to the Hebrews. The thirteen chapters can be subdivided in three parts:

- 1-2   Jesus is higher than the angels

- 3-10   Jesus is the high priest

- 10-13   Exhortation

It is enough to know that the letter to the Hebrews deals mainly with the priesthood of Christ. The end of the sixth chapter explains how the old priesthood is replaced by the new priesthood (Hebrews 6:19ff):

> We have this as a sure and steadfast anchor of the soul, a hope that enters into the inner shrine behind the curtain, where Jesus has gone as a forerunner on our behalf, having become a high priest for ever after the order of Melchizedek.

God still receives reparation for sins. The novelty consists in the fact that Jesus presents himself to God not so much as a Levitical high priest, but as priest according to the order of Melchizedek. Hebrews 7 explains this change and shows that the priesthood of Melchizedek is more perfect than that of Aaron.

The contents of the letter are as follows. The letter first speaks of the purification of sins, effected by Christ. How does Christ purify sins? By atoning for them. How is atonement effected? By sacrifice. Who offers sacrifice? The priest. Consequently: Jesus, who atones for sins, must be a priest. Apart from the final point this reasoning is perfectly obvious to a believing Israelite. The difficulty resides in the fact that Jesus, who does not belong to the tribe of Levi, cannot be a priest according to the Law of Moses. For the Letter to the Hebrews this is not a problem: Jesus Christ is not a Levitical priest, but a priest according to the order of Melchizedek. Is this the correct conclusion?

This is an easy question to answer. In the Old Testament there is a messianic text which establishes a connection between the Messiah and the priesthood of Melchizedek. This text is in psalm 109 (110):4: *'Tu es sacerdos in æternum secundum ordinem Melchisedech.'* The Letter to the Hebrews quotes this text in the fifth chapter (5:6). Two things flow from it: Jesus is a) a priest and b) he is a priest after the order of Melchizedek. What is the difference between these two priestly orders? Hebrews 7 gives us the answer which starts with the mysterious meeting between Abraham and Melchizedek. It is a short story in Genesis 14 (17-20) and the only time when Melchizedek appears personally in the bible. The meeting takes place after Lot has been freed. Let us read the text (18 - 20):

> And Melchizedek king of Salem brought out bread and wine, he was priest of God Most High. And he blessed him and said, 'Blessed be Abram by God Most High, maker of heaven and earth; and blessed be God Most High, who has delivered your enemies into your hand'. And Abram gave him a tenth of everything.

That is all. Basing itself on this story and on Psalm 109:7, Hebrews 7 explains the priesthood of Christ. Five aspects are brought out:

• The priesthood of Melchizedek is for ever. This comes as a result of Psalm 109 and of the fact that Genesis 14 ignores the family and ancestry of Melchizedek. He is without father, without mother and does not have a family tree. His days know no beginning nor end. This is true also of Christ.

• The priesthood of Melchizedek is more perfect than that of Abraham, because Melchizedek blesses Abraham. He who blesses is higher than he who is blessed. Melchizedek is therefore greater than Abraham and his descendants of whom the Levitical priests are part.

• The priesthood of Melchizedek establishes a new law. For in replacing the Levitical priesthood which had failed the law, which depended on it, had to be replaced.

• The priesthood of Melchizedek is strong because it is founded on imperishable life, not on the law of the flesh. This is shown by the resurrection of Christ.

• The priesthood of Melchizedek is formed by an oath of God. That is why Jesus is the guarantor of a better covenant.

Let us sum up. Christ, a priest after the order of Melchizedek, is different from the Levitical high priest. His priesthood is, firstly, eternal. It therefore does not need to be supplied because the effect of its sacrifice could weaken. Secondly, it goes beyond the religion of the Temple. Thirdly, it introduces a new Law. Fourthly, it is powerful because of the resurrection of Christ, no longer having to fear death. Fifthly, it is guaranteed by the irrevocable word of' God. In one sentence: the sacrifice is no longer offered by men but by God himself.

The old rite was an effort to draw oneself by one's hair out of the swamp of sins. One offers to God a sacrifice and God offers reconciliation. This system could not work because God is not interested in goats and bulls. Besides, God has no price. He does not need animals for they belong to him already. The sacrifices do not add anything to his honour. That is why God says in Psalm 51:

> I will accept no bull from your house, nor he-goat from your folds. For every beast of the forest is mine, the cattle on a thousand hills. I know all the birds of the air, and all that moves in the field is mine. If I were hungry, I would not tell you; for the world and all that is in it is mine. Do I eat the flesh of bulls, or drink the blood of goats? Offer to God a sacrifice of thanksgiving. (Ps 50:9-14).

God is not interested in beefsteak. He wants the heart of man and his consent. Worship is what God awaits. Everything belongs already to God except the 'yes' of man to whom he has given freedom. He wants to draw him to himself, not with his all-powerfulness but with his love. This 'yes' which means the offering of oneself, God has been waiting for it for a long time. This offering was the sacrifice which he desired and which has been offered by Jesus Christ. The sacrifice then has not been abolished, but the sacrificial gift has been replaced. Before God no one can be substituted by a bull. On the cross Jesus has offered to God this 'yes' that mankind could not give him.

It was not of course a splendid liturgy in alb and chasuble with impressive fanfares, sublime choirs, outstanding singing and Handel's *Halleluiah Chorus.* It was an execution. And yet the death of Jesus on the cross is the only true liturgy in history, a cosmic liturgy unfolding not within the restrictive domain of the Temple but before the whole world. Jesus appears before the face of God. He enters the true Temple not to present there the blood of animals but to offer himself. Christ has thus gone beyond the liturgical play of the temple and has placed himself on the altar. Instead of the blood of animals he has given his blood. He has accomplished what the whole of mankind could not do.

Yet, could not the Levitical high priest have gone ahead of Christ by placing himself on the altar in order to bleed for mankind? Definitely not. The cult requires an immaculate offering. The animal of sacrifice must be perfect. But among all men a perfect lamb without blemish could not be found. This was going back to the story of Sodom and Gomorrah: there was not a just man to save the city. Time was passing by and no just man could be found. Century was following century and no just man appeared. And eventually, there was Bethlehem. It is hardly surprising that the huge empire of injustice in place was trying to get rid of the child of Bethlehem. It finally succeeded. Yet this most abominable crime in human history had a most felicitous ending. For the first time someone who had not deserved to die by his own sins died. He gave his life which was truly his own. God accepted his life as an expiation for the whole of mankind.

FROM THE PRIESTHOOD OF CHRIST TO THE MINISTERIAL PRIESTHOOD OF THE CHURCH

The death of Christ was the only cult that restored justice for ever. Why then has the Church still need of ministerial priests? To this question Martin Luther replied that the Gospel, in order to be proclaimed, has no need of a special ministry. Has he thus done away with the priesthood? Quite the contrary! According to Luther everyone who has crawled out of baptism can boast to be priest, bishop and pope (WA 6,408). The Protestant ministry is concerned solely with the smooth running and practical organization of the Church. Priestly ordination coincides with baptism. This opinion is a complete break with tradition. We will restrict ourselves to showing that it is also a break with the New Testament.

Our starting point is John 20:19-21. We are on the evening of Easter Day. The apostles are gathered together behind closed doors. They are afraid of the Jews. Suddenly, Jesus appears and stands in their midst, saying : 'Peace be with you!' He shows them his hands and his side and the disciples are glad when they see the Lord. Jesus says to them again: 'Peace be with you!' And he continues: 'As the Father has sent me, even so I send you'. There is therefore a profound link between the mission of Christ and that of the apostles. That is why their mandate must be understood in conformity with the mission of Christ. Christ seals his words by breathing on the apostles and sending them the Holy Spirit (v. 22). Against Luther it must be said that this action means far more than the transfer of a function imposed by pragmatic reasons. The apostles share truly - in the Spirit - in the mission of Christ and therefore in his priesthood. The priest, holding the ministerial priesthood, is therefore a priest as he shares in the priesthood of Christ. The sacrifice of the priest is the sacrifice of Christ which consists in the offering of oneself. It is anyway the reason for the celibacy of Jesus and of the ministerial priest.

John 20:21 is the key-passage which moreover remains surrounded by a number of biblical witnesses which explain the priestly mission of the apostles and of those who carry on the mission of Christ. Here follow some examples: [2] Christ commands the apostles to proclaim the Gospel throughout the whole world (Matthew 28:19; Mark 16:15). He grants them his authority (Luke 10: 16; Matthew 10:40). He gives them power to bind and to loose (Matthew 18:18) as well as to baptize (Matthew 28:19), to celebrate Mass (Luke 22:19) and to forgive sins (John 20:23).

The mission of the apostles, bound to that of Christ, is also founded in the letters of St Paul. According to St Paul the apostles have received from Christ 'grace and apostleship to bring about the obedience of faith for the sake of his name among all the nations' (Romans 1:5). They are the 'servants of Christ and stewards of the mysteries of God' (1 Corinthians 4: 1). They are 'ambassadors for Christ, God making his appeal through us' (2 Corinthians 5:20), entrusting to them 'the message of reconciliation' and giving them 'the ministry of reconciliation'(2 Corinthians 5:18ff).

The New Testament is also witness to the use of the powers which have been bestowed upon them. They preach everywhere (Mark 16:20) and give laws and orders to the faithful (Acts 15:28ff, 1 Corinthians 11:34). They judge in the tribunal and pass sentence (1 Corinthians 4:21; 5:3-5). They baptize (Acts 2:41; 1 Corinthians 1:14), celebrate Mass (Acts 2:42,46; 20:7) and pass on Church duties by the laying on of hands (Acts 6:6; 14:22; 1 Timothy 4:14; 2 Timothy 1:6; Titus 1:5). Alongside the apostles, one finds in the early Church presbyters (Acts 20:17,28; 1 Peter 5:1-2; Titus 1:5-7) and deacons who have functions in the Church. Philip the deacon preaches and baptizes (Acts 8:5,38). The presbyters of Jerusalem decide together with the apostles on the role of the old law (Acts 15:22ff). The presbyters of the community administer extreme unction to the sick and forgive sins (James 5:14ff). The associates of the apostles do not receive their ministry and power from the community but from the apostles (Acts 6:6; 14:22). In apostolic times the charismatics play an important part in the building up of the Church (1 Corinthians 12114), however they are not part of the hierarchy, they do not have a Church ministry. St Paul asks that charism be subordinate to apostolic ministry (1 Corinthians 14:26ff).

To sum up: the ministerial priesthood of the Church is the priesthood of Christ, passed on to the apostles by Our Lord on the evening of Easter Day. The consequences of this mandate are documented in the New Testament.

THE ROYAL PRIESTHOOD OF ALL BELIEVERS

It remains for us to clarify the passage from the ministerial priesthood, entrusted to the apostles and passed on by the laying on of hands, to the royal priesthood of all baptized believers. The *locus classicus,* where it is mentioned, is the First Letter of St Peter. This short text is rather difficult to understand (2:4-5):

> Come to him, to that living stone, rejected by men but in God's sight chosen and precious; and like living stones be yourselves built into a spiritual house, to be a holy priesthood, to offer spiritual sacrifices acceptable to God through Jesus Christ.

The reading of this text will enable us to understand the priesthood of all the baptized.

The text contains two directives: 1) Come to Christ, the living stone! and 2) Like living stones be yourselves built up! Let us look at the second: 'Be built up!' What is being built up? The letter answers: a spiritual house to be a holy priesthood. How is it built up? With 'living stones'. Why the image of the stone? The letter uses it in the context of building a house. In a house built of stones each stone has a place and a function. It is the entirety of the stones which decides whether each individual stone is part of a bridge, a dam, a monument or the outline of a road. On the other hand there can be no whole without individual stones. There is interaction: the whole made up of individual stones and the character of individual stones made up by the whole.

This is also true of the spiritual house, the Church. Every Christian is part of the walls. The image of the stone helps to understand the ability of each baptized person to take his place among and in relation with the other baptized. It is true that today one finds too often an excessively 'communist' view of the Church. Life and death cannot be delegated to a community. Nevertheless, communion remains an important aspect of Christianity. The royal priesthood is the most mature expression of it. Indeed, the royal priesthood, as opposed to the ministerial priesthood, is not exercised by a single individual, but by all the living stones, built into a spiritual house. It is precisely the image of the stone which expresses the community character of the royal priesthood.

The word 'stone' recalls the ability of Christians to enter into communion with each other. This ability is essential for the exercise of the royal priesthood. But St Peter does not write 'come as stones' but 'come as living stones'. 'Living' and 'stone' are opposite terms. Either one is a stone or one is living. Nothing is more dead than a stone, inanimate matter *par excellence*. One could say some beautiful things about the ability of stones for communion. But in the end, no one would like to spend one's life as a stone, not even as a stone on the bewitching side of a pyramid.

The term 'living' adds then to the word 'stone' a meaning which radically alters the image of the stone and eliminates any fantasy according to which the royal priesthood would be some kind of workers' paradise built on the corpses of previous generations. For the Christian is not a stone of the walls of an earthly citadel, but a living stone in a spiritual house which unites in itself death, the essence of all that has been created, with life which is stronger than death. It is the image of the resurrection which St Paul associates with the sinner redeemed by grace. He who was dead and is alive now in Christ. As sinners we are lifeless stones. Through the atonement of Christ we become living stones. Let us be careful though! The life received is not ours but Christ's. In the words of St Paul: 'It is no longer I who live, but Christ who lives in me' (Galatians 2:20). This is possible because, from now on, through baptism, we become part of the body of Christ, living stones of the spiritual house.

To recap: 'stone' means the dead sinner, 'living', life redeemed for him; 'living stone' indicates the Christian in so far as he is incorporated in the new Temple which is Christ.

The living stones are the origin of the spiritual house for the formation of a holy priesthood. How is the spiritual house of living stones built? The Letter of St Peter answers: in gathering the living stones around the cornerstone. Here is the arrangement in the letter

- The faithful are living stones.

- The living stones are arranged in relation to the cornerstone.

- A spiritual house for a holy priesthood is formed.

- This priesthood offers spiritual sacrifices acceptable to God.

The royal priesthood is achieved according to this order. The first two points are united between them. It all begins with the transformation of the faithful into living stones through baptism and confirmation. These sacraments are not some kind of inoculation administered by mouth, but an incorporation into the body of Christ.

The second point explains the connection between the living stones and Christ. The image of the stone is retained. For the faithful Christ is the cornerstone, for the unbelievers he is the stumbling block, an obstacle that must be eliminated. That explains Christ's death.

Let us examine once more the place of the living stones in relation to the cornerstone. There can be no house without a right arrangement of the stones. Two things follow from this; from what a Christian does, who is a part of the spiritual house of which St Peter's first Letter speaks. As living stone the Christian is 1) in line with Christ and 2) supported by the same Christ. The cornerstone gives direction and support. The living stones make up a building which is standing thanks to Christ. In so far as they are related to him the living stones are part of the spiritual house.

We then reach the third point. Those who are bound to Christ become a spiritual house for a holy priesthood. What does it mean? 'House' relates to the dwelling and therefore to being, whereas 'priesthood' refers to doing. 'For a holy priesthood' means that the genesis of a new being in Christ helps to unfold a new activity. Originally there is the spiritual house, the body of Christ. The risen sinner has been incorporated into Christ, who becomes his new dwelling. The latter is quite different from the image of a flat. The occupant and his flat are truly distinct, whereas he who dwells in Christ participates of him. Christ's life becomes his life. This unity of living implies unity of doing.

The doing of Christ becomes the doing of the Christian and the doing of the Christian becomes the doing of Christ. Or to be more precise: the body of the Christian becomes the body of Christ, the temple from which, according to St John, the Spirit proceeds. As one participates in this Temple the doing is transformed by it. The action of the Christian becomes a part of the activity of the body of Christ. If then, according to the Letter to the Hebrews, Christ is priest for ever, therefore the Christian, as part of the body of Christ, participates in the doing and the priestly being of Christ. This is the royal priesthood of all the believers, a common priesthood bound to the body of Christ in which every Christian participates. That is why the first Letter of St Peter does not say that we are royal priests but that we form a royal priesthood.

The fourth point explains the effectiveness of this priesthood by the offering of spiritual sacrifices which are presented 'through Jesus Christ'. It is he who offers the sacrifice of my life. The organ depends on the executive power of the head. Nobody would say that it is not Christ but only his hands which offer the sacrifice. His wounds have bled, but it was Christ who suffered. One cannot say that during his passion the back has suffered first, then the head crowned with thorns and so on. The suffering of the part is the sacrifice of the whole. This is equally true for the royal sacrifice of all the faithful. It is not achieved by me or by you, but by him, Jesus Christ. In this way the personal suffering of the Christian becomes a powerful source of salvation.

We will not ask why the sacrifices offered by Christ are acceptable to God. The reason is that they are of a spiritual nature. 'Spiritual' is the opposite of 'carnal' and here it means that it is not to do with a championship of sufferings or a tournament of good works. The sacrifice is acceptable to God through the working of the spirit in which it is offered. 'Spiritual' can be understood in a weak sense as something which exists more within an abstract theory than in reality. Obviously this is not correct. The Spirit is the love between the Father and the Son. The sacrifices are spiritual when they are offered in love. Jesus gave up his life for love (Ephesians 5:2). Love is worth more than suffering. A little suffering with a lot of love is worth more than a lot of suffering with a little love.

To sum up, the baptized are integrated as living stones in a holy house to offer spiritual sacrifices. A house where sacrifices are offered is a temple. Christ is this house, the New Temple of the New Covenant. By participating in the Temple as a living stone the Christian participates in the sacrifice of Christ: *Agere sequitur esse.* The sacrifice of the royal priesthood consists in all the activities of individual Christians in so far as they are in conformity with Christ.

To conclude let us look at the royal priesthood as a community action and particularly at the epithet 'royal'.

It can be said that Christians form a royal priesthood, but not that every Christian is a royal priest. If you touch a house with your hand you are only in contact with a small part of it, with a single stone. This stone is the house in as much as it is a part of it. We are a spiritual house for the holy priesthood as we participate in a much greater whole that does not belong to us and is not even visible to our eyes. As it cannot see the whole the living stone must believe in the existence of an imperceptible entity. That is why St Peter talks of trust in verse 6. We will not be confounded if we put our trust in the cornerstone. The royal priesthood is exercised in the trust of faith. The house in which we participate is spiritual, that is, invisible. The living stones do not perceive the whole. They are living in the believing, not in the seeing. They are like the stones of a building, joined together by a cornerstone which they cannot perceive. It is only because the house remains standing that this enables them to deduce from it that it exists. In the same way the organs of the body depend on the heart, enclosed in the chest, invisible, in complete darkness. Here too it is only the living body that enables it to deduce its existence. The organs of the body 'trust' in the heart, which they cannot see, just as the stones of a house depend on the cornerstone which they also cannot see. It is the night of faith. For one who does not believe sacrifice and love seem to be sown in the wind. Why? Because as he is not in line with Christ he does not know it. Likewise the living stones are blind. But they know that without the cornerstone they would not be where they are.

Let us end by asking ourselves why the priesthood of the baptized is called a royal priesthood. Obviously, because the priesthood of Christ is the priesthood of a king. This kingship is revealed during the passion, especially in St Matthew's Gospel, at the moment when the cornerstone is rejected by the builders and sacrificed for our sins. In Matthew Jesus presents himself before Pilate as king of the Jews. Then he 'receives the crown of thorns, a royal emblem'. Along the same line of thought, he is enthroned on the cross. Even the passersby who scoff confirm Christ's royal status. Christ is the king who reigns by himself suffering, not by making others suffer. The royal priesthood is a priesthood that suffers and does not make suffering. It is only in the eyes of the world that the royal priesthood is a career upside down. From God's point of view suffering accepted with supernatural love transforms the one who suffers: he becomes a king. This suffering is stronger than the powerful of this world because it has no need of them.

We finish with a summary of our paper. Firstly, we have dealt with the challenge to the priesthood. Is there a priesthood in the New Covenant? Yes is the answer, if one reads the texts within their ecclesial context, not within a historical-ideological context. Secondly we asked the question whether Christ was a priest, and by saying yes we have seen how Christ, in His preaching, has prepared the understanding of His priesthood. Thirdly, we have explained the priesthood of Christ as a priesthood after the order of Melchizedek: priesthood for ever, higher than the Levitical priesthood, bound to the new law, stronger than death and guaranteed by an oath of God. Fourthly, we have shown with the help of John 20 and other New Testament passages that the ministerial priesthood of the priest comes from the priesthood of Christ. Fifthly, the royal priesthood has been presented as an incorporation of the being and action of the baptized, living stones, in the holy house which gathers together all suffering into the sacrifice and the New Temple of Christ.

NOTES

1. cf. Pompey (63 B.C.) in Flavius Josephus chapter 7 of the first book of the *Jewish Wars*: 'Among the disasters of that time nothing sent such a shudder through the nation as the exposure by aliens of the Holy Place, hitherto screened from all eyes. Pompey and his staff went into the sanctuary, which no one was permitted to enter but the high priest, and saw what it contained: the lampstand and the lamps, the table, the libation cups and censers, all of solid gold, and a great heap of spices and sacred money totalling two thousand talents'.

2. For a complete list cf. Ludwig Ott, *Grundriss der katholischen Dogmatik* 335s.

Translator's Note: all biblical quotations are from the Revised Standard Version *of the Bible.*

THE CHOIRMASTER AND HIS LITURGICAL ROLE

Marcel Pérès

M Marcel Pérès, born in 1956, is director of the ensemble Organum, *which he founded in 1982 and with which he has made some thirty recordings devoted to the various repertoires of the Latin liturgy. His research covers a wide spectrum, including Roman and Carolingian chants, as well as the neo-Gallican repertoire of the 17th and 18th centuries. M Pérès has been the director of the* Centre Européen pour la Recherche sur l'Interpretation des Musiques Médiévales *(CERIMM) since 1984.*

A S this century draws to a close, it is surprising to find that what we understand by the term 'Sacred Music' - a term which applies equally to ancient forms of Christian music as to those of other religions - has brought into existence hundreds of festivals and made possible the sale of millions of CDs.

Notwithstanding, contemporary Catholic music has no place in this movement. Among Westerners there is a growing interest in religious music from outside Europe, whereas one would seek in vain any concert programmes made up of liturgical items chosen by our pastoral liturgy committees, which might arouse the slightest enthusiasm among audiences of Iranians, Tibetans or the inhabitants of Western Africa.

Yet this century was ushered in by a Pope, St Pius X, who declared that the People of God were to pray with beauty. His declaration was to crown those major efforts of Catholic musicians, liturgists and musicologists who had been doing their utmost, since the middle of the nineteenth century, to endow the liturgy with music of value, worthy of its purpose. One is forced to conclude, as the century draws to a close, that these efforts have not produced the results expected of them. One can naturally lay the blame for this at the door of the cultural revolution which followed the Second Vatican Council, or one can find sociological arguments to offer as an explanation. One can accuse the massive de-Christianization of whole populations, or changing tastes and a different attitude towards the sacred. All these points need to be taken into consideration, but in the context of this short study we would like to re-examine what actually took place during the last century from a slightly different angle from the one usually chosen, in order to throw new light on the present disappearance of the reform desired by Pius X and declared in his *Moto Proprio* of 1903.[1] From the musical point of view, there were numerous fundamental changes at that time which transformed the nature of the sung liturgy, everything that is, that constitutes the æsthetic side of liturgical celebration. The most radical of these transformations was the progressive suppression of the cantors and therefore of all that they represented.

At the present time the role of the cantor has completely disappeared from liturgical thinking. For over a century every effort has been aimed at eliminating his role in order to replace it by the parish choir, and subsequently, after the council, by the ideology of the 'song of the People of God'. The cantors have been consigned to the attic, or condemned to the underground prison cells of history. Very few Catholics even know they ever existed and that some continued to flourish, in a few country parishes, right up to the middle of the twentieth century. From now on people are more likely to talk of the 'animator' to describe any willing soul whose principal function is to lead the congregational singing.

And yet cantors used always to have an essential part to play in any liturgical celebration. From earliest times these men, known as 'Psalmists', or 'Lectors', were responsible for proclaiming in song the words of the collective prayer. The prime role of a cantor was to keep alive a memory, the memory of the chant, of the sound of the prayer of those who had gone before. It fell to them to breathe life into the celebration of an action ancient beyond memory. The cantors were the guardians of far more than a repertoire: they were the keepers and witnesses of the whole way of enacting the liturgy.[2]

In this paper we propose to set out a number of markers to help us to understand how it is that the Church has detached herself from these liturgical performers, and, in particular, what she has lost in causing their disappearance. The present malaise discernible in the liturgy might perhaps begin to disperse if today's reflection were to include a different way of looking at our liturgical past.

A brief glance at the bibliography of nineteenth century plainchant is enough to reveal the nature of the problem. If there are hundreds of articles and studies on the subject of the restoration of Gregorian chant, we can on the other hand, hardly find any to tell us about the traditions of the chant as used by Catholics of that period. Of recent studies on the subject of cantors there is only the unpublished thesis by Jacques Cheyronnaud (1984). It consists of an ethnographical study of the last cantors in the north-west of France, entitled *The Village Church Lectern and its Cantors (19th -20th century) An Introduction to a Public Service in Music.*[3] Jean-Yves Hameline has written a few articles which make mention of the topic, but it is clearly a subject of little interest to the general public.[4]

For the majority of nineteenth century commentators any mention of cantors is invariably derogatory, as if these men were, so to speak, the incarnation of everything the Church was trying to discard. They poured ridicule on their style of singing, expressing themselves filled with indignation at the very sound of it. They often compared them to bellowing, howling animals. They accused them of heavily hammering out the chant and choosing a pitch that is too low and inaccessible to the average member of the congregation. To put it in a nutshell, they reproach them for lacking any artistic sense. This explains why a favourite theme of the period is to prove that plainchant, once reformed, can become something musical in its own right, worthy of a place among the arts, according to Dom Mocquereau in his first lecture to the *Institut Catholique* in 1896. [5]

The writings of the nineteenth century reformers need to be replaced in their original contexts. Without discernment, we today can no longer uphold their rejection of cantorial traditions then still a living reality, even if these traditions reflected little more than a faint glimmer of past splendours and only too often showed signs of decadence.

The language of the nineteenth century writers serves as a vehicle for ideas that go far beyond a simple historical reflection on æsthetics. Fundamental principles were at stake, for it was essential for the Church to avoid missing any opportunities to restructure and keep pace with an evolving society. It seemed as if she would have to do away with any æsthetic practices that leant too far in the direction of the seventeenth and eighteenth centuries. For, in order to survive, the Church would have to adopt a new way of thinking, making it impossible for her in future to be identified with socio-cultural paradigms which events had rendered obsolete. It became necessary to define an art which was 'Catholic', to launch consciences into times ahead that differed from those that had been harmful to the Church : the eighteenth century, which had seen the end of a society with its ecclesiastical structures incapable of adaptation in order to survive, and the seventeenth century—too much linked in people's minds with Gallicanism, especially in France, in opposition to Ultramontanism which was gaining the ascendancy. In order to construct a new ecclesial environment, Catholics chose to take as their model two emblematic figures capable of being dissociated from the recent past from which they were distancing themselves. These figures were Palestrina and St Gregory the Great.

Palestrina, who had reached the height of his career just after the Council of Trent, could be taken as the model of a Roman musician of the time of the Counter-Reformation. His polyphony, made accessible through modern editions, offered three advantages:

• In the first place, his style was completely different from the traditions of 'fauxbourdon' and similar improvisatory techniques still actively practised by the cantors.

• Secondly, this music, which was allied to the Renaissance, made it possible to efface the last vestiges of the learned polyphonic compositions of the Baroque era;

• Finally, it was fundamentally different from the music of contemporary opera, with which many Catholics were loath to identify themselves, because of its worldliness.

St Gregory the Great was promoted, because the chant that bore his name and whose original flavour of antiquity they were endeavouring to rediscover, enabled them to explore new ways of performing the chant that broke with living traditions. This so-called 'Gregorian' chant led their minds back to a time qualified as the Golden Age of the chant, thus turning their attention away from the true mediæval plainchant, the chant to be found in the manuscripts and in the writings of the theoreticians from the twelfth to the sixteenth century, a period that was peremptorily dismissed as decadent.

Today, unfortunately, as a result of these choices, 150 years after the first research was undertaken into the archæology of the chant of the Latin churches, we still have no true history of plainchant that takes into account all the facts of every century.

Yet how many treasures are contained within those repertoires of monophonic and polyphonic music, and over the centuries how many different kinds of performance practice! They go to make up an unbroken chain where one can perceive the work of a truly Catholic tradition. Let us understand by the word 'tradition' not a hard and fast reiteration of musical and liturgical formulæ, but a continuous flux through which every new element arising from the genius of a particular period never appears as a rupture with the heritage from the past, but rather as a re-evaluation, or, to express it in the way the Greeks would, as an explanation of tradition.

These repertoires were not only thought of as a collection of melodies, but in the first place, as a sound, as a way of using the voice in accordance with the sacred function. That was the tradition from which the Catholics were severed as a result of the twentieth century reforms. That is why it seems to us that all contemporary reflection on the liturgy and its music should be firmly based upon a new approach to the history of liturgical chant, so as to be better placed to rediscover the riches of the past and the link with the whole of tradition.

At the present time, many of the parameters for our appreciation of the facts of history have evolved. Contemporary reflection upon the æsthetics of liturgy should take into account new avenues of thought that have opened up during the past few decades about art in general, and in particular about the history of the art of music.

The growing interest in ancient music and in music beyond the confines of Europe has profoundly modified our perception of the æsthetics of the past.

Even if the general public has drawn little benefit as yet from the openings offered by this movement, a fundamental evolution has clearly taken place. For the first time, men are attempting objectively to cross the frontiers of cultures other than those that prevail in their own ethnic groups. Works of the past are no longer thought of as expressions of bygone days: they appear as objects capable of opening the mind of modern man to other perceptions, which have disappeared with time, or suffered a considerable diminution of their former intensity. This new approach is based on a meticulous study of every detail of a particular style: the choice of materials, the manner in which they are prepared, learning techniques. Little by little the work comes to be seen, no longer as an object in its own right, but as a tool which allows those who use it to live through an experience accessible to people of today. Both the arts and the sciences gain through it a supplement of humanity. For these ancient styles teach us how to see things in a new light, to hear afresh, to live in time and space. To the realities that spring from our modern societies, other realities are superimposed: they come and graft themselves on to the former, like counterpoints or marginalia.

As for the liturgy, the practice of past centuries in all its depth and intensity should not be considered a dead letter. Today's Catholics have much to learn from former liturgical practices. In order to do so they must know what they are, and to get to know them they must move on to putting them into practice.

To understand more clearly the context of what I am proposing, may I be allowed to recall briefly how I myself was drawn progressively to make the observations I am about to relate?

With our *Ensemble Organum* we have had since 1982 the opportunity to explore a great many liturgical repertoires. Our concerts have enabled us to breathe new life into the music by recreating the links which were those of the liturgy. Wherever possible it has been equally precious to reconstruct the liturgical enactment, by which I mean the position of the singers in the church and their orientation, the materials required for the readings, and the number of singers. Sometimes paying attention to particular living liturgical traditions can be profoundly beneficial. The study of Corsican sacred chant preserved by oral tradition is precious, since it represents one of the best-preserved vestiges of post-Tridentine Catholic cantorial practice. Similarly, and in a most fruitful manner, Byzantine chant can throw light on questions of voice production, of vocal ornamentation hinted at by the early Roman notations, and referred to by a number of mediæval theoreticians. So it is possible to gain some idea of the performance styles suggested by these types of chant, and then to find out what constitutes their particular characteristics ; among them we shall single out the five following points which seem to us to be essential:

• Chanting and vocal processes

• Proclaiming the liturgical text

- The materials necessary for reading the music : books and the lectern

- Places where the chant is sung

- The role of the organ

These five points would appear to have been essential to the celebration of the liturgy for very long periods at a time. At present they are largely ignored by those who give any thought to liturgy.

Yet these technical details were the essential lines of transmission for ensuring the perpetuity of traditions as well as of the knowledge they carried. Ignorance of such liturgical knowledge is the reason why our present celebrations have gone off course when compared with those of the Church of earlier centuries, whereas they would gain in depth and intensity if they took on board the heritage which each generation of Catholics has patiently handed down to the next.

CHANTING AND VOCAL PROCESSES

The sacred chant cannot be considered merely as an association of text and melody. The act of liturgical chanting is first and foremost a vocal process, in other words, a particular way of using one's voice, an entering into the sound and a particular way of living in the space and time of the celebration. The contours of the melody are merely the result of this attitude. To have forgotten this fundamental distinction can be the cause of many misunderstandings, such as those suffered by Catholics since the last century.

The all-encompassing reform of Pius X has given its seal of approval to the type of chant and manner of its performance recommended by the Benedictines of Solesmes; but in so doing it has excluded other traditions of Catholic chant which had been less and less understood as the nineteenth century progressed.

Singers used to sing in a low range—let us remember that the pitch for church music was a tone lower than at present—and with a strong, rich vocal quality, using all the resources of the art of embellishment. The Solesmes ideal is very different. To their way of thinking the perfect voice is characterized by its high range—implying an angelic sound—its sweetness, its absence of vibrato and exclusion of any kind of embellishment, which they would consider futile and superfluous.

PROCLAIMING THE LITURGICAL TEXT

The meaning of the text is not the main reason for its being sung. We should remember that the original sense of the Latin word *oratio* refers back to a well-established art of speech. Indeed, the orator's skill consists in displaying the architecture of discourse correctly, so that the principal articulations of the text, by their arrangement in a harmonious form during the time of their emission, guide the listener to an understanding of the meaning. But this structure depends, in the first place, upon the word, the Latin word, whose scansion is characterized by the alternation of syllables, long, breve and semibreve.

On this precise point Catholics, at the beginning of the twentieth century, experienced a second cultural revolution. On the one hand they abandoned their various national pronunciations of Latin, with the result that the phonetic, and consequently the genetic link between Latin and their native tongue—especially in the case of the Romance languages—was lost. But what was more serious, they completely changed their manner of scanning the Latin. For several centuries the tonic accent has corresponded to a long syllable, as, with rare exceptions, in all the Romance languages. In liturgical chant the syllables fall naturally into three possible durations, corresponding to longs, breves and semibreves. On the pretext of returning to an imaginary antiquity at some ill-defined period hard to determine, the Solesmes reformers substituted a form of Latin scansion in which all syllables are of more or less equal duration. This biased opinion enabled them to justify, in their interpretation of the chant, their theory of a basic indivisible unit of time, the standard length of which was to be the measure of a single syllable. Thus a time-honoured tradition of the scansion of the sacred texts was sacrificed in order to give credence to a hypothetical interpretation of Gregorian chant.

THE MATERIALS NECESSARY FOR READING THE MUSIC: BOOKS AND THE LECTERN

Another reform dating from the beginning of the twentieth century had a disastrous effect on the chant of the Church: the modification of the materials for reading the music, the service books and the removal of the furniture on which they were placed, the lecterns.

Ever since the end of the twelfth century, Catholics, who formerly had sung everything by heart, got into the habit of singing from books, usually very big ones, so that several singers could sing from the same text. These books would be placed upon a lectern, which very soon became an essential piece of the liturgical furniture and occupied a recognized place in the church. The practice continued for over seven centuries. I shall not here go into the major reasons which brought about the appearance of the lectern: they are linked with a global evolution in our societies during the thirteenth century of the status of the book and of reading.

These large books were replaced at the beginning of the twentieth century by smaller volumes, which were highly practical, but which led the cantors to adopt an entirely different posture when singing. The enormous books placed on the lectern forced the singers to raise their heads and thus to stand upright and open their lungs. In this way they could project their voices upwards with a vigorous breath. The wearing of copes during the celebration of the most solemn liturgies reinforced this attitude.

On the other hand, the small volume encourages the choristers to lower their heads in order to read the minute notation, their round shoulders completely closing the rib cage, their voices directed downwards as a result of constraint in breathing. This posture could only end in the generalization, towards the middle of the twentieth century, of recourse to some kind of mechanical amplification of the voice, which utterly disfigures contemporary liturgy. I mean the use of microphones, without which few priests and few liturgical animators are able today to fulfil their duties. [6]

Furthermore, they invented a new form of square notation similar to the notations of the Middle Ages but actually very different. It served to support the theories of Dom Mocquereau but had no real rhythmic significance. It was used for the Vatican Edition of the Gregorian melodies and imposed on all Catholics at the start of the twentieth century. This square notation, still in use at the present day, even in the *Graduale Triplex,* actually makes it impossible for performers to have access to the various rhythmic interpretations practised in former centuries.

PLACES WHERE THE CHANT IS SUNG

The positioning of the singers is never fortuitous; whether it be in the stalls, around the lectern or in other specified areas, it is always determined by the requirements of the liturgy. I shall only touch lightly on this particular point, since to understand the relevance of these liturgical areas, themselves linked to a living conception of ecclesial space, one would have to go into the whole meaning of space and movement in liturgy, and the importance of light; whether sunlight or the light from candelabras, graduated according to the solemnity and the spirit of the celebration. Finally, mention should be made of the importance of certain places because of their acoustics, which can vary according to the period or the architecture, a point which our ancestors considered to be of fundamental importance. It will be enough to recall that the chants of the Proper were normally sung facing the altar. All of this would be material for a specific study.

THE ROLE OF THE ORGAN

Many organists are wondering how the organ should be used in our liturgies of today, but few of them try to understand the traditional way in which the organ was used by Catholics for nearly nine centuries. Today one often hears it said that the organ must be at the service of the liturgy. But the congregation is required to sing. Therefore, they say, the organ must be used to accompany and sustain the chant. This line of reasoning, which at present prevails, is unfortunate. When the organ accompanies it does not sustain anything; in fact it does quite the contrary: it prevents people from getting fully involved in the chant. There is a belief that the organ helps to keep the pitch: this is completely untrue. The majority of organs today are badly tuned and a tone higher than the pitch traditionally used for the liturgy (which placed A around 390 cycles per second instead of the modern 440). The clergy often opt for equal temperament so that the organist can accompany in any key. But with equal temperament every interval is out of tune with the exception of the octave. It has never been used by Catholics before the end of the nineteenth century. The temperament traditionally used by Catholics from the fifteenth century to the nineteenth, for playing in alternation with plainchant, is mean-tone temperament, made up of eight pure major thirds.

In the Catholic tradition the organ was never intended to accompany the chant. It was only during the second half of the nineteenth century that plainchant began to be accompanied. Ever since the organ was introduced into the liturgy, round about the year 1000, its function has always been to alternate with the choir at well-defined moments : it was strictly reserved for major feasts, that is to say roughly twenty times in the year, and only at two points in the liturgical day, at Mass and Vespers. At Mass the organ alternates in the chants of the Ordinary (*Kyrie, Gloria, Sanctus, Agnus, Ite missa est*). At Vespers it alternates in the same way, at every other verse of the hymn and the Magnificat. The organ plays one verse, the choir sings the next and so on. This leaves time for the organ to display all its resources and the choir to express itself freely, without being drowned by the sound of the organ.

Each proudly fulfils its appointed role. The *Kyrie* or the *Gloria* interpreted in this way might take up to twenty minutes or half-an-hour. Our civilization has lost the sense of how much time one should devote to different things. Liturgy should be allowed its essential share of it.

WHAT OF THE FUTURE?

The state of affairs I have been describing might seem to be very negative, so far removed from the ancient cantorial traditions is the present situation and all that has been adopted over the past century. There are, however, some possible signs of hope that all has not been lost. It seems to me that it is important not to seek the creation of mass movements. The way forward cannot at first be the work of more than a small number. It can only be from the time when this appropriation of ancient traditions becomes perfectly natural within a small group that its influence might be spread further afield.

The phenomenon of the renaissance of those lay confraternities in Corsica with whom we have been working actively for several years, might serve as a model for starting up a revival of traditional liturgical chant. These confraternities try to revive their liturgical traditions which managed to escape the reforms carried forward by Pius X. Relations with the ecclesiastical authorities are not easy, but we help the confraternities to put into practice a liturgical charter enabling them to order harmoniously the duty of the members to preserve their liturgical patrimony, not ignoring episcopal preoccupations with bringing them into line with post-conciliar pastoral concerns.

As for other places, it is possible for interesting experiments to be attempted in certain parishes, but the Church being an eminently hierarchical organization, any renewal has to be approved by the liturgical head, that is to say, by the cathedral. In order to move things on, the good will of the bishop is necessary, to provide a structure for this renaissance. A group of lay people and religious, working together in the cathedral with the bishop, under the artistic guidance of a professional liturgist, might perform regularly a traditional liturgical use. From this centre, religious and cantors would go out into the parishes, taking with them the cathedral model. The existing confraternities, or if it were deemed necessary, newly-created ones, could be the carriers of this diffusion.

These practices, however, will only develop successfully when children, from the beginning of their religious instruction, are taught what one might call a 'liturgical catechism'. Catechesis and liturgical initiation should be one and the same thing. It is only possible to transmit the great principles of the faith if the liturgy remains the centre of the spiritual life and of the æsthetic experience.

NOTES

1.   *Moto proprio: Tra le sollicitudine,* 1903.

2.   On the early cantors, consult the *Dictionnaire d Archeologie Chrétienne* for the sources, described by Dom Leclercq in his article entitled : 'Chantres'. See also Michel Andrieu, 'Les ordres mineurs dans l'ancien rite romain', in *Revue des Sciences religieuses,* 1925; Solange Corbin, *L 'Eglise à la conquête de sa musique,* 1960.

3.   Jacques Cheyronnaud, *Le lutrin d'église et ses chantres au village (XIXeme-XXème siècles) - Approche d'un service public musical.* Thèse de doctorat de Troisième Cycle en Ethnologie; 1984. Ecole des Hautes Etudes en Sciences Sociales - Centre d'Ethnologie Française.

4.   Hameline (J.Y.), 'Le son de l'histoire. Chant et musique dans la restauration catholique', *La Maison-Dieu,* 131, 1977, 5-47.

5.   'Transversalité', *Revue de l'Institut Catholique de Paris,* 63, July -September 1997, 183 - 226.

6.   The quality of voice production was extremely important Remember the three kinds of enunciation required of the officiant, called the ceremonials tones, or inflexions of the voice

(i)   The *voce intelligibili,* when the priest chants aloud so as to be heard by all the congregation.

(ii)   The *voce mediocri,* to be used in order to be heard by those nearest to him, but always in a quieter voice than what is recited aloud.

(iii) The *voce secreto,* for what has to be whispered. He says it to himself but not so as to be heard by those around him. c.f. Vavasseur, le R.P. le, *Cérémonial selon le Rite Romain,* Paris, T. i., p.264

HOMILY
AT THE SECOND SOLEMN MASS

Bishop Juan Rodolfo Laise

Bishop Laise, a Capuchin Friar, was born in 1926 in Buenos Aires, ordained priest in 1949, and raised to the episcopate in 1971, since when he has been bishop of the diocese of San Luis in the Argentine. He is the author of numerous catechetical, spiritual, and theological works.

Dear friends of CIEL,

BELIEVE me, it has been a pleasure to accept your invitation to celebrate the pontifical Mass during your annual conference. I am impressed to see how many of you there are, so interested in the sacred liturgy. As we all know, despite the fact that the second Vatican Council began its deliberations with the liturgy, thus showing its fundamental importance, we have in fact witnessed the liturgy disintegrating, almost everywhere, and seen a general lack of interest in liturgical studies. I must therefore congratulate the organisers of this timely conference.

Liturgy takes the first place in our religion, for religion means the reconciliation of man with God, and it is the liturgy which defines the relationship, and demonstrates how man is dependent upon God. The Church, as mother and teacher of the nations, has the vocation to instruct these nations and to lead them to their final goal, the City of Heaven. In Latin America we have experienced how modern liturgy has infected the people with the depressing 'Theology of Liberation', whereas for you in Europe the secularization of the liturgy has helped to secularize human life. See how little human life is worth, with your legalization of abortion, and soon of euthanasia! In contrast, it seems that the traditional Roman liturgy stands as a bastion against heresy. It is my hope that your meetings, and your scholarly research, will encourage a return to a more transcendent liturgy, and that the proverb *lex orandi, lex credendi* will be realized in a more striking manner.

May the Blessed Virgin intercede for you, and be close to you in this battle, where the powers of evil are resolved to destroy the Church, the mystical body of her divine Son.

PREACHING DURING THE EUCHARISTIC CELEBRATION

Walter Brandmüller

Born in 1929 and ordained priest in 1953, Mgr Brandmüller is a Doctor of Theology from the University of Munich. Having held the chair in Mediæval and Modern Church History at the University of Augsburg, he became Professor in Ecclesiastical History at the Academy of Dillingen. In 1969 Mgr Brandmüller founded the Societas Internationalis Historiæ Conciliorum Investigandæ *of which he currently is the President. He is also editor of the periodical* Annuarium Historiæ Conciliorum, *which now is in its 24th year. Since 1981, Mgr Brandmüller has been a Member of the Pontifical Committee for Historical Science to which the Holy Father appointed him President in 1998. In the same year he was also made a Canon of St Peter's at the Vatican.*

THE themes 'The diaconate or ordination of women' and 'lay preaching' have one thing in common; in that in both cases we are ultimately dealing with matters concerning the nature of the Church and her sacramental-hierarchical constitution.

This means that we are dealing with the question of whether the Catholic religion—and thus the Church—is the result of human thinking and organizing, or whether it is the foundation and instrument of the human and divine revelation and salvation of world and man by Jesus Christ. According to one opinion, deciding the question of holy orders for women or of allowing lay preaching can be achieved according to sociological, psychological, æsthetic, or human, worldly criteria; which means that if there is a change in the socio-cultural or anthropological context, the decision can be changed and replaced by a more appropriate solution, one which is more likely to meet with acceptance—but then, on the other hand, this may of course be purely and simply impossible. If the Catholic Church is in fact founded by Jesus Christ, God and man, as a means of salvation, then the norms for the Church's existence will, be to a great extent beyond human considerations. The Church's actions and life will be dependent on the will of her Creator and determined by a form established by Jesus Christ once and for all; when deciding such questions as whether lay-people should preach, then this basic principle must be given priority.

In the current, somewhat heated, discussion, many voices are raised which give the impression that the curia and Pope could decide such matters according to their own judgement, using a number of criteria considered to be more or less explicitly pastoral; in other words according to purely practical criteria. There is talk of the shortage of priests and the resultant need for religious services without a priest so as to relieve clergy who are overstretched. In addition, attention is drawn to the greater experience of life gained by lay people who, living in the world, can draw on their personal experiences which give them direct access to the listener when dealing with matters relating to employment, married life, and family matters. Finally they refer to the mission and dignity of the baptized and confirmed Christian who, precisely because of this sacrament is empowered to proclaim the message of salvation. If we then add theological training, what is there to hinder the layman on the way to the pulpit? And, how many laypeople are there today who are not just better trained in theology, but more gifted than their priests in the oratorical arts! Is there not also the question as to how the Church can incorporate so many lay theologians into her ministry?

In view of the shortage of priests, should we not adopt such new methods as preaching by lay people?

So, there are psychological, sociological, and purely pragmatic reasons which, covered in places by a cloak of wretchedly thin theological cloth, are put forward in favour of lay preaching. These are, the advocates of this theory aver, the reasons that Rome should authorize lay preaching, always assuming that these same advocates will actually wait for permission from Rome!

But even this manner of argument requires a deeper examination of the concepts of 'Church' and also of preaching upon which the argument is based. Does not this argumentation imply a concept of 'Church' consisting of a free assembly of people sharing the same religious convictions, whose purpose is to offer a meaning of life, a life-style and approach to life's questions, both for the individual and for the community?

Such a 'church' might—if a so-conceived social structure is deemed worthy of the name 'Church'—be called 'our Church', meaning that one is able to build, form and bring this church into being oneself. We are coming significantly close to such a notion of 'church' when we read something like:

> the parish is not simply a church community to be looked after, but it is a diversified social structure built up by all participants, which, taking into account specific authorized functions, also learns to grasp the effective proclamation of the Word as its own task'.

But can we really describe, in this way, the Church that Jesus Christ built on the rock, Peter, and on the foundation of the apostles and prophets ?

Whenever and wherever we deal with this foundation of Jesus Christ, laws apply that have, as we said, more than a socio-psychological and pragmatic purpose. Here the will of the Founder applies exclusively. We shall seek in vain in scripture for a word of the Lord that commands or forbids lay preaching. The same applies to the question of women-priests. There are many questions which are not answered in the New Testament as they were not asked when the New Testament was written. The Lord, however, sent the Holy Spirit to the Church so as to lead her into all truth. So Jesus' purpose in founding the Church, which can answer the questions of later times, can be found in the authentic tradition of the Church, which includes not only the teaching but her actual life. We see, not infrequently, the traditions of the Church not just in the defined teaching texts or canons, but often in the established conduct of the Church: established, though not written. How are we to understand this? Before the Church started to formulate dogmas, even before there was a New Testament, the Church lived and acted. As the mystical Body of Christ, the Holy Spirit is breathed into her by the Father and Son as her soul, as her innermost principle of life; she is imperishable. She cannot die until her Lord comes again. This means that she cannot lose her identity as the foundation of Jesus Christ. Whenever she preaches authentically or acts sacramentally she fulfils her mission, and hands this mission on to her sacred ministers. She can do no other than to act under the inspiration of the Holy Spirit, even if her members seem to lag behind—sometimes far behind—the moral demands of Jesus Christ.

I

In our case this certainly means that as, for example, during the course of her two-thousand year history the Church, despite the frequent and far-reaching changes in her socio-cultural context, never sacramentally ordained a woman, allowing her to share in the hierarchical-sacramental ministry, this is due to no accident of history. The self-evident and unapologetic attitude of the Church expresses the way in which the Church sees herself and also expresses her sense of the centrally important existence of her hierarchical-sacramental ministries in the act of *repræsentatio Christi capitis*. This is not just the taught tradition, it is also the living, unspoken, tradition which is the Church's norm for her beliefs and actions. For this reason, leaving others to one side, it can be said that women will never be ordained to the priesthood in accordance with the will of Christ, and it is equally unlikely that there will be a womens' diaconate. What is the position if we now apply these criteria to lay preaching?

II.

We often hear it said that primarily historical-social causes brought about the ban on lay preaching in 1234. It may be that this ban was unavoidable for the protection of the Church's beliefs which were being threatened by separatism, sectarianism and heresy, but an impartial examination of the factual background should now be possible and is in many ways required.

It is often said, bluntly, that since a church ban on lay preaching only came into effect in 1234 when there were reasons leading to the ban which were necessary at the time; if these reasons have now lapsed with the passing of time the ban should also be lifted. This assertion, which is the result of gross historical and theological negligence, can, and must, be challenged on each point: and emphatically so.

In fact it should be pointed out that lay preaching was never allowed by the Church, and that, moreover, it was expressly banned at a very early date, and that the reasons for the ban were mainly of a dogmatic nature. It was a recognition of the essential connection between proclaiming the Word and ordination, which formed the basis of the ban and which is evident from all relevant facts and canonical-historical texts available to us. Sufficient material exists from every century for this. To present this matter in its entirety here and now is, however, impossible and for this reason we shall present only a few particularly significant examples.

For our first example we shall take Pope Leo the Great who had reasons to express his views on the question of the preaching licence. He was not only compelled to obtain recognition for the teaching of the Council of Chalcedon against the supporters of Nestorius and Eutyches, but when he began with this, he also had to oppose the unruly monks of the near East who were deeply involved in the christological controversies. In this connection, there exist three letters in which the Pope takes a clear and decisive stance on preaching by monks, that is by lay people. The actual cause of this was a Bishop Thalassius who allowed a monk by the name of Georgius to act as a writer and preacher. Leo the Great expressed his displeasure about this in a letter dated 21st March 453 to Bishop Julian, impressing on him that it was incumbent on his episcopal authority vigorously to prevent the usurping of a bishop's and priest's authority by monks, that is by lay people. It is noteworthy that the Pope described the preaching licence granted by Bishop Thalassius to the monk Georgius as '*prædicandi aliquam contra fidem licentiam*' that is; a licence to preach, against the faith. This means, quite simply, that Leo rejected a preaching licence granted to a monk, who was a layman, on the grounds that it was not only pastorally unsuitable or in contravention to canon law and custom, but that it was an offence against the faith.

Given the close time connection with the aforementioned letter to Bishop Julian, it seems apposite to refer to another letter from Leo the Great dated 2nd

April 453 to Bishop Maximus of Antioch on the same matter of monks preaching *per nefas*. The final paragraph of this letter again takes up the theme of 'preaching by the laity'. It is said that Maximus is to stop anyone, other than priests of the Lord, assuming the right to teach or preach, whether this was a monk or a layman: even if he had a certain amount of theological education. Though it is desirable that all the sons of the Church should be informed about orthodox and sound teaching, it is nonetheless not permissible for anyone who is not a priest to take to himself the function of a preacher, as there must be order in the Church of God so that in the one Body of Christ the leading members should fulfil the duties of their office and lesser members should not oppose superior members. One month later the Pope took the same line when, in the manner of a *ceterum censeo* in a letter to Bishop Theodoret dated 25th June 453, he closed with the remark,

> ....and [I] in particular decree, that with the exception of the priests of the Lord, nobody must dare to preach, whether monk or a layman, even though he may boast of a certain amount of education'.

It is precisely this latter wording that shows that the Pope excludes lay people from preaching, not through lack of education, but through lack of orders.

So, occasioned by the case of the monk Georgius, Pope Leo the Great in three letters over a short period of time, not only forbade preaching by lay people, but rejected it as being contrary to the faith.

Leo worded his ban on lay preaching wholly on principle and with great emphasis. The concluding words of the letter stated '...*quas tamen litteras pro utilitate universalis ecclesiæ...ad omnium volumus pervenire notitiam...*': we wish this letter to be made known to the whole Church for general use...The Pope's words have considerable magisterial weight.

The Trullian Synod of 692 of the Constantinopolitan Church, so named because it was held in the domed hall of the emperor's palace, sums up the teaching of the time on lay preaching. In Canon 64 it was laid down that no layperson could assume teaching authority and publicly teach or dispute on matters of faith. Instead they should obey the order received from the Lord and listen to those who have received the grace of teaching, and let themselves be taught about divine matters by them. The text of the canon closes with a reference to the diversity of the members of the Church and their tasks, as Paul had taught.

Let us now turn to the High Middle Ages

The rapid spread of the phenomenon that can only be inadequately described as the 'poverty movement', where lay people and clerics of all social levels felt drawn to the ideal of the *vita apostolica* in a radical way, so that they gave up their previous way of life and began to live in imitation of Christ as poor itinerant preachers, was, not least, a late consequence of the Gregorian reform. Certainly, reform-minded circles in the Roman curia had been able to win this lay movement for the Gregorian ideals. In the long term, though, it was not possible theologically and ecclesiastically to integrate the clergy-critical trend. At this time and on this matter, Peter Damian mentions in a letter to the Roman city prefect, Cinthius, how they had both spoken on the previous day, the feast of the Epiphany in St Peter's to the people *'prout divina clementia suggerebat...concionaremur ad populum'*. Cinthius had not spoken as city prefect, but as a priest might have spoken. He himself had been hindered by vocal difficulties. The address which Cinthius had given was, according to Peter Damian, an exercise of the common priesthood of the faithful; he quotes the Apocalypse and 1Peter to encourage him *'servata mensura tui ordinis, in ecclesia salutiferæ exhortationis verba depromens':* to speak words of saving instruction in the Church within the bounds of your lay status, serving the people this way as well as in his judicial and administrative activity. He should also conduct ecclesiastical cases *'in quantum tui ordinis facultas suppetit'* to the extent that his lay status allows, so that Rome will find in him a *'pater patriæ'* and the Church a *'defensor'*. The qualification of his talk in St. Peter's as *'exhortationis verba'*, words of instruction, merits attention. They would be used a hundred years later by Innocent III to theologically integrate the Waldensian preaching. The twofold mention of the limits Cinthius' lay status sets on him is equally noteworthy, as it is within these limits that the city prefect makes his *exhortatio*.

The lay movement which was inspired by the Gregorian reform became increasingly independent from the end of the twelfth to the beginning of the thirteenth century and led to the well known and oft researched heretical movements which are only crudely and superficially known as the 'Waldensian' and 'Catharism'. There were numerous individuals and groups who went about preaching repentance and mending one's ways, love of neighbour and enemy, and occasionally heretical and absurd themes, and who often impressed people not just by their preaching, but also by their strongly ascetic lifestyle. Of these movements, the Waldensians, going back to the Lyons merchant, Valdes, was the most important. At the beginning of their development they were thoroughly orthodox and without any anti-hierarchical attitude. In fact their purpose was to oppose the Cathar heresy. They approached Pope Alexander II in a delegation lead by Valdes himself at the Third Lateran Council in March 1179 with a request for approval of their *vita apostolica* and also for a licence to preach, with a dispensation from the canonical prohibition of lay preaching. The regulations from which the Pope was to grant a dispensation can be seen in the *Decretum Gratiani, distinctio* 23 c.29.In their content, they were identical with those of the Synod of Carthage of 398 or the Apostolic Constitutions. The text runs: *'Laicus præsentibus clericis, nisi ipsis probantibus docere (!) non audeat.....Mulier quamvis docta et sancta viros in conventu docere non audeat'* - a layman should not dare to teach in the presence of clerics, except with their agreement, or a woman, even learned and holy, should not dare to teach the assembled community. It would be erroneous to maintain that the mediæval lay preaching movement had found a legal situation where the possibility of lay preaching was, in principle, open. To consider the more or less accidentally-included provision of the *Decretum Gratiani,* with the possible exception of the clause *nisi rogantibus clericis,* to be the only legislative pronouncement on the question, simply cannot be maintained in the light of the foregoing overview of the attitude of the ancient Church to lay preaching. This attitude was wholly negative. In addition, at the point cited in *Dist.* 23c. 29 there is mention of women teaching. We have to agree with Rudolf Zerfass when he states that for Gratian the preaching layman as much as the preaching woman 'were equally beyond all real possibilities'. Thus, his view that Canon Law is fundamentally open to lay preaching, is as incomprehensible as it is contradictory. Moreover Alexander III, who was, incidentally, friendly to the Waldensians and received them with much good will, held firm to the letter of the *Decretum,* by allowing them itinerant preaching under the condition *'nisi rogantibus sacerdotibus',* at the request of the priests, but referred to the local hierarchy for permission or invitation. The examination of the Waldensians by a curial commission, to which Alexander III submitted them, had, as its primary objective, to establish their orthodoxy, and only to a lesser extent their education. This can be seen from the report of the curial official, the Englishman Walter Map, who was entrusted with this examination, when the Waldensians were questioned in succession about the articles of the Apostles' Creed. It is likely that a similar examination of the *Humiliati,* who also appeared, gave a negative impression, for which reason they were refused a preaching licence. In any event the Waldensians in 1180 claimed an orthodox profession of faith whilst Alexander III approved their *propositum*—their religious way of life. The question is, admittedly, whether Alexander III actually meant the same thing as the quoted Council of Carthage. This speaks of *docere,* teaching by a layman which was only allowed in the presence of clerics at their request. There can be no doubt that this meant catechetical instruction by *didaskoloi.* Of preaching in the proper sense, of the word, of authoritative, authentic proclamation, there was no question. In the case of the Waldensians and the *Humiliati* catechetical instruction was not under discussion, but rather the call to repentance and to follow Christ - and this in the form of itinerant preaching. It is to be assumed that Alexander III made a conclusion by analogy, by applying the restriction *nisi rogantibus clericis,* which originally related to the catechism, to the itinerant Waldensian preachers. This was to take into account their religious motivation which the Pope recognized as being sincere. By granting a preaching licence to the Waldensians Alexander III created a new law which was justified by the situation. As the Waldensians, presumably because their requests to preach were rejected by many priests, began to claim authority to preach directly from God, thus bypassing the hierarchy, most of them lapsed into a heretical concept of the Church: heretical because it was spiritualistic, and so they met with rejection from the Church. This, and above all the experience with the Cathars and related groups, led of necessity to the Verona decree of 1184, which anathematized all preaching on private authority, as teaching which departed from the Church's teaching. This is not expressly against lay preaching because it is by lay people, but nonetheless forbids it. This was in connection with the Synod of Verona or the meeting between Pope Lucius III with Barbarossa in order to find a practical solution to the problem of heresy which had become frighteningly apparent.

What Alexander III had only managed to begin—the re-integration into the Church of the itinerant groups of preachers—Innocent III finished with considerable success. His paramount objective was to utilize the Waldensian enthusiasm in the fight against the Cathar heresy. First of all Innocent III succeeded in reconciling the *Humiliati* who had been excommunicated by Lucius III. Innocent III accommodated them by approving, to a great extent, their *propositum* with its emphasis on lay preaching. Here the texts need close examination. They show that in the case of the *Humiliatis'* Sunday meetings these, on being examined, were found to be not in public, but away from the church *in loco idoneo*, in a suitable place. In such a circle and in such a place, brothers of proven faith and religious experience, mighty in word and work, were allowed, with the permission of the diocesan bishop, to give an exhortation based on the Christian life. They were, however, to abstain from discussions on articles of faith and the sacraments. This means, then, that they were not allowed to preach in the sense of an authoritative preaching of the word before the parish, in the church or within the framework of the liturgy. Of particular importance were the reasons given for granting a licence for spiritual exhortation within their own community. 'The Spirit may not be quenched' as the Apostle said, and for this reason the bishop was not entitled to prevent this kind of exhortation. Pope Innocent also motivated the commissioning of the so-called 'Catholic Poor' in the combat against heresy with reference to their simple dress and the burning spirit with which they went to the marginalized. This makes it clear how Innocent theologically classified the exhortations of the *Humiliati* or the activities of the Catholic Poor. As far as he was concerned it was a matter of charismatic, prophetic witness which, although it was most certainly not authentic preaching, was certainly a sign of the spirit and power to awaken and promote spiritual life. In this we can see one of the reasons why Innocent III extended the licence granted for limited preaching within their community to allow a greater number of *Humiliati* within the diocese of Milan to preach in public places and churches.

The Pope acted in the same way with the 'Catholic Poor' of Durandus of Osca who found their way back to the Church from the Waldensians, in the meantime, and had become anti-church and heretical. It should at any rate be noted that this group consisted mainly of educated clerics: something which is mostly overlooked. After all, once doubt about their orthodoxy had been removed, they received corporately, from the hands of the Pope, a licence to preach which was drawn up in such a way that no *missio* was required from the local ordinary. Being obliged to recognize the necessity of a canonical mission to preach, was no longer a problem for them after their return to the Church. Similarly when the *Pauperes reconciliati* of Bernard Prim, who were also mainly clerics, approached Innocent III, the Pope acted in the same way. Like the Waldensians they preached against the Cathars and turned to the protection of the Pope when accused of heresy. Although they had in fact claimed to be able to celebrate the Eucharist without a priest, they now promised to align themselves with the sacramental-hierarchical structure of the Church. On 18th June 1210, their community was recognized by the Church, and they were allowed to preach before clerics and the laity, so that the latter might learn what was necessary for the conversion of the Cathars.

Again we have to agree with Zerfass that if after careful analysis of the relevant text it is established that

> In the perspective of Innocent III there never was any intention at any time of transferring the Church's preaching office to the laity, but to institutionalize new forms of witness to the faith, which until then, had been exclusively practised in private. It was not an old ministry extended to an expanded circle of office-holders, but, so to speak, a new ministry was created within the Church. *Exhortatio,* the pious layman's witness to his faith was upgraded to being an ecclesiastically recognized pastoral resource. The concept of 'lay preaching' is misleading in this context as it suggests an extension of the preaching ministry, in its existing unchanged form, to the laity; as if Innocent III had simply entrusted the ministry of preaching to lay people and only limited its content to the area of ethics. In point of fact he established a new style of preaching, which he wished to be understood and recognized by its derivation from *adhortatio* as a new form of witness to the faith.

Meanwhile not only the reconciled groups and mendicants were to be heard on the streets and town squares with their *exhortatio* but, as before, there were also fanatics and heretics. The provisions of Canon 68 in the synodal statutes of Bishop Odo of Paris (d.1208) state that no person is to be allowed to preach unless he were an *authentica persona* or someone who had the *missio* of the bishop or archdeacon. That this restriction related to clerics and not to lay preachers is suggested by a textual variant which expressly states that no cleric should be allowed to preach who did not meet this requirement. Perhaps Canon 92 of the same statutes refers to 'lay preachers', which strictly prohibits priests to allow strangers to preach whether or not they were educated, no matter where. At the same time priests were to prevent the faithful, on threat of excommunication, from hearing such 'preachers'. The ground for this ban was the danger of spreading heretical teaching.

This created the situation with which the Fourth Lateran Council had to deal. It is noteworthy that lay preaching was not a subject for legislation by the Council but rather it concerned itself with regulating preaching in general. Heretics were to be prevented from propagating false teaching. Firstly, the council banned all preaching not licensed by the Church, on pain of excommunication. Then provisions were made for improving preaching; this referred to a number of synodal statutes from the years before the council in the south of France, where energetic preaching had been successful against the errors that had been flourishing there.

The legislation of Innocent III had been directed formally only against unlicensed heretical preaching. The unofficial or semi-official preaching activities of the various reconciled itinerant preaching groups, to which lay people also belonged, had been included in his pastoral strategy for combatting heresy. This was all changed by his successor, Gregory IX, in the text of a letter which the Pope sent to the Bishop of Milan on 3rd October 1228, the decree *Sicut in Uno Corpore*. The gloss on the scriptural text 'as in one body', concludes that lay people, regardless of their rank or merits, may not exercise the ministry of preaching. To establish this ban, Gregory IX refers to the diversity of charisms in the body of Christ, arguing from the biblical text. The gloss, on the other hand, refers to a notion drawn from social philosophy *'nec universitas alia poterat ratione subsistere nisi huiusmodi magnus eam differentiæ ordo servaret'* —a community can only exist through a well-ordered differentiation of its members, a notion referred to in earlier papal letters, that had been included in the *Decretals of Gratian* (Dist. 89. c7). Though Zerfass has remarked that 'demarcation within the Church was aimed at', this is certainly not to be assumed. Rather, a fundamental principle of the Church's constitution is being expressed here.

Undoubtedly Gregory IX in his letter of 1228 to the Archbishop of Milan and the resultant decree *Sicut in Uno Corpore* restricted non-ministerial preaching, including the lay *exhortatio,* which had been made possible by Innocent III, at least in its public forms. Presumably, the continuing 'clericalization' of the reconciled preaching groups and the Franciscans, begun and continued by Innocent III, had created another situation. Also, the remaining 'lay preachers' had given occasion to tighten anti-heretical legislation: Gregory mentions groups that had appeared in Milan, who probably originally belonged to the *Humiliati,* that had again developed in a heretical direction. After the majority of those reconciled had become clerics, anyone preaching as a lay person was suspected of heresy.

Subsequent synodal legislation supports this interpretation. Thus the 'Statutes of Salisbury' from the years 1238-44 warmly welcome the preachers from the mendicant orders but take a stand decisively against lay preachers. Nobody should allow lay preaching even under the pretext of wishing to serve lepers.

The stance taken by the Council of Trent on the question of the authority to preach has to be interpreted against this background. Already at the seventh session on 3rd March 1547 in which the decrees and canons on the sacraments were promulgated, the council condemned the opinion that all Christians had authority for the ministry of the word and sacrament.

Logically, this theme was also debated in connection with the sacrament of order. In Canon 7 *'De Sacramento Ordinis'* the council condemned the opinion that *'qui nec ab ecclesiastica et canonica potestate rite ordinati (!) nec missi sunt (!), sed aliunde veniunt, legitimos esse verbi et sacramentorum ministros':* that those who are neither properly ordained nor canonically appointed, but come from elsewhere, are lawful ministers of word or sacrament. Positively, then, the council emphasizes that the prerequisite for preaching, as for the administration of sacraments, is ordination and commission.

The council was again occupied with the question of lay preaching when the Bavarian delegate, Augustin Paumgartner, put the question to the council in the name of Duke Albrecht V. In dealing with this question, the council fathers commissioned Charles Borromeo to draft a report for the Pope. The report quoted mainly the evidence of the early Church already mentioned in this paper, and then cited a particularly up-to-date reason against lay preaching: the need to counteract the rejection of the ordained priesthood by the Reformation. That notwithstanding, reform-minded groups raised the matter of religious speaking by laypeople in their meetings. The example of Philip Neri who spoke on religious subjects at meetings of his Oratory is well known. That such things happened in circles inspired by the spirit of Trent shows how little they were seen to be lay preaching. In this connection a decision of the provincial synod of Bordeaux in 1624 should be mentioned, stating that ordination as a deacon was a necessary and minimum requirement for the ministry of preaching.

That this was in accordance with the Church's practice is shown by a remarkable institution, the 'licentiates' in Hungary in the time of the Turkish invasions. Turkish domination, together with a catastrophic shortage of priests, brought the care of souls to a complete standstill in many parishes in Turkish-occupied Hungary. In this acute state of emergency the way out chosen by the bishops was to appoint lay ministers who generally were called 'licentiates', as a licence for the exercise of their ministry was given them by the bishop. They were mostly not academically trained. Young unmarried men were preferred. A not inconsiderable number were former evangelical pastors. Even learned theologians who found their way back to the Church, exercised a fruitful apostolate as licentiates. Did these licentiates preach?

Their tasks were precisely laid down by a number of provincial and diocesan synods. Firstly the Provincial Synod of Pressburg (Bratislava) of 1628 stated that the relevant licence could be only issued for a year, or two years at most. The licentiates were described in the synod decrees as persons to whom the bishops granted a licence to read the word of God and prayers to the people of God because of the shortage of priests. The scope of their duties was to be laid down precisely in the licensing document itself in each case. Although the statutes of the Synod of Tyrnau of 1629 speak of licentiates *sermonem habeant* —they were to preach—there is no mention of preaching in the licensing document found in the documents of the national synod of 1633, but of reading from Holy Scripture and pious books. As there is other evidence of the printing and distribution of sermons in the Hungarian language the instruction *sermonem habeant* clearly refers to reading these sermons. This can be seen in the instruction of Abbot Grasso of Tihany in 1729 in which it is stated that licentiates are to gather the people together on Sunday to hear ecclesiastically approved sermons and pray from ecclesiastically approved prayer books. Only in isolated cases do the sources speak of preaching by a licentiate. Elsewhere there is an express prohibition of licentiate preaching, which very likely refers to previous occasions where the powers of the licentiate had been exceeded. From this material it can be seen that in cases of extreme necessity a number of pastoral duties were entrusted to lay helpers such as baptism, assistance at marriages, burials, the blessing of brides and mothers, religious instruction and prayer services, but not preaching.

An institution similar to the licentiates arose from the needs of the missions particularly in the Far East; the office of catechist. The holders of this office were given the same functions as the licentiates, but more care was expended on their training and employment than with the licentiates. Moreover, the numerous sources we have on their activities, and in particular the synodal or quasi-synodal conditions for their employment, give no hint that they might have preached.

III

If we now draw the theological conclusion from the historical texts and facts, it can be confirmed that the essential link between ordination and preaching is either explicitly or tacitly at the basis of all relevant disciplinary regulations on this matter by the competent ecclesiastical authorities. It is the nature of preaching that makes this connection necessary.

> For preaching is the open addressing of people by the Word of God disclosed in Christ through the ordained and officially commissioned ministers of the Church. ...Insofar as preaching is in accord with divine revelation—which is assured for the Church in general—it not only contains, but is the Word of God. God is the subject of preaching. (Viktor Schurr)

This presumes that the human preacher, as an instrument of Christ's activity—for preaching is God's word in Christ—relates in a unique, ontological way to the Christ who is actually speaking. Preaching is, in fact, a speaking in the person of Christ, *loqui in persona Christi.* Just as for acting in the person of Christ, *agere in persona Christi,* in the Sacrifice of the Mass and in the administering of the sacraments, the sacramental character of ordination, configuration with Christ, *configuratio cum Christo,* is required as a prerequisite, so it is required for speaking in the person of Christ.

The ability to preach authoritatively thus stems from the character impressed on the ordained person.

Accordingly, preaching is distinguished from catechesis, theological teaching, ascetic instruction, witness to faith and prophetic exhortation, precisely because of its sacramentality, and ontological status within the Church. In the above-mentioned types of religious discourse the believer speaks of God and about God. In preaching the preacher speaks not in his own person but in the person of Christ, as likewise he does not baptise, consecrate, absolve, anoint and ordain in his own person but *in persona Christi*. On this alone is founded the saving power of his activities and of his preaching. It is in full accord with this that the Second Vatican Council, following the Council of Trent, names among the chief tasks of a bishop preaching as his outstanding *munus*—office, one for which it is appropriate to possess the fullness of orders and pastoral authority (LG 25).

It is against this background that the most recent regulations on lay preaching in canons 766 and 767 para .1 of the *Codex Iuris Canonici* (1983) and the recent instruction on lay ministries are to be understood. Following the quoted canons, lay people may be allowed to preach in a church or chapel if this should be necessary in particular cases of need, or if under special circumstances it is deemed useful, according to regulations of the Bishops Conference. The homily is pre-eminent among the various forms of preaching. It is part of the liturgy itself and reserved to the priest or deacon (can. 767.1). The liturgy portrays the mysteries of faith and norms for Christian living throughout the Church's year by means of the sacred text. The canon uses almost exactly the words of the *Liturgy Constitution* (para. 52). It is precisely the homily which is obligatory for Sundays and Feast Days in all masses celebrated with the people. Only priests and deacons have the authority for this.

The question is, what can be meant under these circumstances with emergencies and special situations, in which preaching by a layperson in a church or chapel would be possible?

They can, *per definitionem,* only be occasions in which a lay person by preaching gives a personal witness to faith, which may be of great forcefulness and effect, but will never be 'preaching' in the sense of the above definition, namely *locutio in persona Christi.* It is most likely that cases of need or special usefulness will arise at events connected with popular piety.

It is, nevertheless, without doubt contrary to the letter of the law and the nature of preaching, if a bishops conference attempts to retain the lay preaching that has found its way into Sunday Masses, in recent years in spite of the restrictive legislation of the CIC (1983), by considering as 'homily' simply an interpretation of the scripture after the Gospel, and considering a sermon by a lay person in the form of a *statio* before the Mass or before the penitential rite as possible and permissible.

The same trend to reduce the sacramentally-established difference between lay people and priests or deacons is found in the many attempts, on the pretext of a shortage of priests, to make attendance at so-called priestless services obligatory on Sundays and to make them a home for lay preaching.

It is completely absurd that training courses and retreats for lay preachers should be set up, when this is something only for emergencies and exceptional situations. This makes the emergency and the exception into the normal case. All this is an attempt to circumvent the legislation of the Church.

On the positive side it should be emphasized that it is the duty of baptized and confirmed Christians to bear witness to the Gospel to non-believers or to those who have fallen away from the faith. The mission of the layperson is in the world, to the outsiders, not to the community of fellow-believers.

The attempt, where possible, to replace the priest in the pulpit by full-time lay people in Church employment must inevitably lead to error. It should be clear to all those responsible, that what today is widely propagated as lay preaching is founded on the profoundly wrong theological presuppositions mentioned at the beginning of this essay.

These are, to clarify them once again, a false concept of the Church, which, rejecting its sacramental-hierarchical nature describes the Church as a 'Church from below'; a structure made with human hands that can be adequately described with sociological categories. Almost inseparably connected with this is the more or less explicit rejection of the ordained priesthood. This is the thesis, put forward by Luther, that whatever is lifted from the font is already pope, bishop and priest, a misunderstanding that is reinforced by the socialist-egalitarian and totalitarian-democratic trends of our time. Finally, preaching is understood in a way that is not in accord with the character of the Gospel as supernatural, divine revelation but merely as a process of communicative sociology to build or maintain community. This attitude is an inevitable consequence of the way the Bible is no longer seen by many as the revelation of God but simply as a product of ancient near-eastern religious literature. To proclaim this, no supernatural enabling or authority is required. Whoever starts from these presuppositions has not only abandoned the foundations of Catholic faith but those of the Judæo-Christian revelation: even if he is not aware of it himself.

From what has been said it should be abundantly clear that when we are dealing with lay preaching, we are not just skirmishing in a secondary theatre of war with a peripheral problem; we are in the centre of the struggle for the true faith and the true Church. It is clear—and comes from numerous statements in the media—that with the demand for the ordination of women to the diaconate and priesthood, as with the demand for lay preaching, the sacramental hierarchical structure of the Church is to be dismantled and the Church of Jesus Christ is to be recast into a 'democratic-ecumenical' Church for modern man, and this will happen through the well-known and tested march through the institutions.

From what has been said, there is an urgent need for a strict application of the present legislation with prosecution of violations of the laws by lay preachers and priests who tolerate or promote this activity. A bishop who turns a blind eye in the face of such matters makes himself guilty of a grave dereliction of duty.

It should be no surprise that application and observance of laws arising from this new attitude should meet bitter resistance. Without considering the advocates of a certain strongly sociologically oriented pastoral theology, which would be better called 'pastoral anthropology', this resistance can be expected from the not insignificant number of lay theologians who are unsettled or misdirected in their self-image by the lack of a clear professional profile and so feel disappointed by the lack of opportunity for professional advancement, having no future prospects. Their increasing numbers over the last thirty years present considerable potential for social conflict in the heart of the Church, and the question of lay preaching is precisely the point where such a conflict will break out.

Socially wrong developments and tensions within the Church cannot be addressed by abandoning the substance of the faith, but only through a deeper and stronger comprehension of the faith. A difficult and pressing duty awaits fulfillment!

NOTE

The present text is a shortened version of my essay 'Laien auf der Kanzel - Anmerkungen eines Historikers und Theologen zu einem aktuellen Thema' in F. Breid (ed.) *Der Dienst von Priester und Laie,* Steyr, 1991, 133-63. Individual references are in my essay 'Wortverkuendigung und Weihe. Das Problem der Laienpredigt im Licht der Kirchen - insbesondere der Konziliengeschichte' in *Annuarium Historiæ Conciliorum,* 18 (1986) p. 239-71.

THE DOCTRINE OF
THE RITES AND PRAYERS OF
PRIESTLY ORDINATION.

Franck M. Quoëx

Born in 1967 in Upper Savoy, Fr Quoëx was ordained priest at Gricigliano (Florence, Italy) in 1992 by Pietro Cardinal Palazzini. He is a member of the Institute of Christ the King Sovereign Priest, and is Professor of Liturgy and Master of Ceremonies at their seminary at Gricigliano. Fr Quoëx is a Licentiate in Theology from the 'Angelicum' Pontifical University and lives in Rome where he exercises his ministry and is preparing a doctorate on the theology of the liturgy according to St Thomas Aquinas.

INTRODUCTION

THE recent publication of the Roman Instruction *'On Certain Questions Relating to the Collaboration of the Lay Faithful in the Ministry of Priests'* has, for some people, been an occasion of discussion and even argument. For others, such as the organisers of this colloquium, it is above all an invitation to study and to appreciate more deeply the distinction between the hierarchical priesthood and the common priesthood. In this contribution my intention is to assist in this reflection by presenting here the ritual of priestly ordination in the Roman Pontifical. I am not attempting to present a doctoral thesis, but simply, by following the prescriptions of the liturgy, to offer you some historical and doctrinal notes which might help us to understand better the nature and prerogatives of the *Ordo Presbyteratus*.

It is *ad Ordinem Presbyteratus* that the archdeacon summons the young deacon, at the very beginning of our ordination ritual. Now, for a full understanding of what we are going to describe, we must stop and take note of this terminology.[1]

We begin by observing that ever since the time of Tertullian, Christian vocabulary has made use of the term *ordo* in order to designate in a generic way that group of people which makes up the sacred hierarchy. [2] The term was derived from the institutional vocabulary of ancient Rome where *ordo* served to describe particular social colleges and classes. Thus, the Senate was the *ordo amplissimus;* outside the capital of the empire, *ordo* meant those who were in positions of authority in towns. *Ordo* was therefore distinct from *populus* or *plebs.* In the same way, in Christian Latin, the *Sacer Ordo* was distinguished from the *Plebs Sancta* or *Populus Christianus.* The *Ordo Ecclesiasticus* is itself composed of several colleges, among which we distinguish the order of bishops, the order of presbyters and the order of deacons.

The deacon is about to be promoted to the *Ordo Presbyteratus,* which we must carefully translate here with an unfamiliar word: the order of the presbyterate. Although the summons of the archdeacon, in which we read *ad Ordinem Presbyteratus,* does not appear until the end of the thirteenth century, in the Pontifical of William Durandus, Bishop of Mende, it takes us right back to a more ancient vocabulary, that of the *Apostolic Tradition,* attributed to Hippolytus. In the case which we are discussing, that of the ordinary priest, the term *sacerdotium* brings us forward a few centuries. We must firstly take note that there is a development from the word 'presbyter', which denotes a member of the presbyterium, (that college of 'presbyters' or 'elders' by which the bishop is surrounded, rather as Moses was, to help in the direction of the people of God) on to the word *sacerdos* used in the High Middle Ages.

After these semantic preliminaries, we must proceed to define the area to be covered by our investigation. The ceremony which I have in mind is contained in the Roman Pontifical, as edited by Clement VIII in 1595. [3] This was in reality only a new edition, with minimal corrections, deletions and additions, of the *Pontificalis Ordinis Liber* issued by Innocent VIII in 1485. [4] These two books are so dependent on the *Pontifical* of Durandus that the rite which I am going to examine is really no different from that in the book of the Bishop of Mende, putting aside a few minute details. [5] However, there is a gap of more than ten centuries between the formulation of the Roman rite of ordination found in the *Apostolic Tradition* of the third century—the most ancient that has come down to us—and that of Durandus, universally employed in the Roman Church until 1968. [6] The former describes no more than the essential rites of the imposition of hands and the bishop's epiclesis, whereas the rite of the post-Tridentine Pontifical was the result of a long evolution. Moreover, long before the new rite of ordination was composed, a number of liturgists were already engaged in criticism of the so-called Tridentine rite of ordination, regretting that the essential rites had become obscured amongst the abundance of ceremonies which were intended to express in a tangible way the meaning of the sacrament. [7]

This is why it seems to me worthwhile to attempt to understand the form and richness, indeed the sheer complexity, of the rite in the Pontifical of 1595, in order to trace its historical and doctrinal significance. To do this, we must not only investigate the sources, but also discover how to analyse the articulation of these diverse sources in one single rite. I will examine the ordination ceremony as it appears in the Roman Pontifical. This is our scope: without losing sight of the essence of the sacrament, to establish the role and meaning of the different formulæ, gestures and ceremonies which were added to the essential core over the course of the centuries. For, let us not be misled; the Bishop of Mende was the author of only a very few of the prayers in his *Pontifical.* Far from innovating, he merely collected together texts and rubrics. We can identify some very ancient prayers from the Sacramentary of Verona, [8] from the old Gelasian Sacramentary, [9] as well as the eighth-century French Gelasian Sacramentary. [10] The *Ordines Romani* of the High Middle Ages, [11] in both their pure and hybrid forms, offer us the earliest descriptions of the rites which we see developing from the tenth century Romano-Germanic Pontifical,[12] moving on to the Roman pontificals of the twelfth and thirteenth centuries,[13] the immediate ancestors of the book of the Bishop of Mende.

Now, without further delay, let us open the first book of the Roman Pontifical. In the cathedral church, during the course of a pontifical Mass, at precisely distinguished moments of the *Ordinarium Missæ,* the bishop has admitted candidates to the clerical state by giving them the tonsure, has conferred the four minor orders, and then the subdiaconate. These first five ordinations have so far followed a common pattern: an admonition, the *traditio instrumentorum,* and prayers. But after the epistle, for the diaconate, and after the gradual, for the priesthood, we observe a completely different pattern: in these two cases, there is the imposition of hands and a prayer of consecration. The sacramental formulæ and gestures bear witness to an intentional unity, because there is only one priesthood, in which the two different degrees participate.[14]

Let us concentrate our attention now on the unfolding of the rites and on the text of the prayers.

PREPARATORY RITES.

• *The election of the ordinands.*

The ritual of priestly ordination begins with the election of the ordinands. The bishop is seated on the faldstool, in front of the altar, facing towards the choir. The archdeacon (whose function is nowadays performed by the 'Assistant Priest') says: *'accedant qui ordinandi sunt ad Ordinem Presbyteratus'.* The ordinands step forward. Then the archdeacon exchanges a brief dialogue with the bishop, asking him in the name of the whole Church, clergy and people, to ordain these deacons *'ad onus presbyterii'.* He then testifies to their worthiness. This dialogue, derived from the Romano-Germanic Pontifical of the tenth century, found a place in the Roman Pontifical in the twelfth century. It is in effect only a refinement of the presentation of the ordinands which, as far as we can tell from a letter of St. Jerome, was already being done by a deacon in the fourth century. [15]

The bishop next addresses the clergy and people—*annuntiat clero, et populo*—asking the approval of all for this serious act of public concern: the elevation of a man to the duty and dignity of the priesthood. The priesthood is here characterized as *ecclesiastici honoris augmentum.* The surviving text *Quoniam fratres carissimi,* derives from the Sacramentary of Gellone, and is substituted in the *Pontifical* of Durandus for the formula of the old Gelasian Sacramentary *Auxiliante Domino Deo,* which from now on is reserved for the ordination of deacons. However, in the train of the more ancient Roman formula, the text establishes a practice which was already traditional. In contrast with the Gallican usage, which required an acclamation, the bishop only asks for the people's tacit agreement, although he invites those present to speak freely, *pro Deo et propter Deum,* if they know that the candidates are unworthy of the priesthood.

• *The admonition addressed to the ordinands.*

After a brief silence, the bishop then proceeds to exhort the ordinands: *Consecrandi, filii dilectissimi...* We owe this text to Durandus who obviously considered it necessary to compose an admonition, a *sermo* as the rubric puts it, for the use of his confreres in the episcopate. Some of these very elevated formulæ became quite quickly stereotyped. The bishop sums up here the entire content of the various prayers which he is about to say, and explains to those who are on the point of being consecrated the biblical precedents and divine origin of the Christian priesthood, its duties and privileges, as well as the moral and spiritual obligations of the *Presbyteratus Officium.*

Although the text is a product of the thirteenth century, it incorporates a formula which had been in use in various places for the previous century: '*Sacerdotem etenim oportet offere, benedicere, præesse, prædicare, et baptizare'.*[16] As Dom de Puinet has observed,

> the privileges of the priest which are here enumerated may not be properly understood without considering the case of priests appointed to govern parishes, whether urban or rural; this was the situation almost everywhere at the time this text was composed. In the early Church, especially in Rome, it would not have been expressed in quite such a categoric and absolute manner. Originally, all the powers of the ordinary priest were essentially subordinated to those of the bishop.[17]

We shall shortly see this more clearly as we analyse the ancient Roman prayers of institution of the priesthood, and the rites which accompany them.

• *The singing of the Litany.*

Unless they have already been sung at the time of the ordination of the subdeacons, Durandus locates the singing of the litanies at this point. The *Ordo*

Romanus XXXIV (edited at the Lateran about 750, the earliest description of the Roman ritual of ordinations which we possess) already mentions the singing of the litanies. [18] This would seem to be a peculiarity of Roman ordinations, for they are unknown to Gallican sources such as the *Statuta Ecclesiæ Antiqua* of the fifth century and the *Missale Francorum* of the eighth century. The litanies express the solemn and urgent prayer of the whole church, clergy and people, who have just given their assent to the ordination of the candidates. The litanies are sung over the ordinands, who lie prostrate on the ground behind the bishop. The Roman Pontifical of the twelfth century already includes a rubric prescribing the insertion, towards the end of the invocations, *Ut hos electos benedicere et consecrare digneris,* repeated twice.

THE TRANSMISSION OF THE PRIESTHOOD.

• *The* Cheirotonoia.

We have now reached the essence of the rite of priestly ordination. Firstly comes the *cheirotonoia,* the imposition of the hands of the bishop on the ordinands. This rite is repeated by the priests present. Such was already the practice mandated in the *Apostolic Tradition,* which seems to indicate that, at the very beginning, the gesture was accompanied by a prayer of consecration. [19] Subsequently, the imposition of hands was carried out in silence: no doubt the growing number of candidates, as well as the development which the formula quickly underwent—a development to which the *Sacramentary of Verona* is an early witness—made it necessary to separate the gesture and the formula.

We should also note, following the text of the *Apostolic Tradition,* that originally the priests did no more than merely touch the candidate while the bishop said the prayer of consecration. This imposition of hands was probably therefore done by a only a few. The later introduction of an individual imposition of hands on the part of the priests, making contact with the head of the ordinands, would surely also have contributed to the separation. This laying on of hands, performed by the priests present, is clearly mentioned in the *Ordo Romanus XXXV* (a Romano-Gallican ceremonial from the beginning of the tenth century), [20] and is required in the *Pontifical* of Durandus, thence passing on to the *Pontificale Romanum* of 1595. It is specified that there should be at least three of them, vested in chasubles; [21] we must not forget that we are in a cathedral where the chapter attend in vestments, or ritually concelebrate at the high Mass celebrated by the local ordinary. [22] Failing that, some priests, or even all those present, would wear the stole.

After they have laid their hands on the head of the candidate, the bishop and the priests hold their right hand outstretched towards him. Then, with the same formula as in the *Sacramentary of Verona,* the bishop invites the clergy and people to pray that God will grant an abundance of heavenly gifts to those whom he has chosen for the duty of the priesthood, *ad Presbyteri munus,* and that he will grant them the assistance of his grace in the carrying out of the ministry which he has seen fit to confer upon them. There is here, then, a double request: firstly for the freely given grace of the dignity and character suitable to the priesthood, and at the same time a request for the sacramental grace which confers on the chosen ones the ability to carry out the functions of the ministry.

The invitation is now taken up in a confident prayer, introduced by the short dialogue *Flectamus genua, Levate*. This dialogue is often found in the Pontifical, preceding a formula invoking the Holy Spirit, accompanied by a gesture of blessing. Here, before the prayer of consecration, by which the candidates will effectively be elevated to the *munus Presbyteri*, the text asks for the candidates 'the blessing of the Holy Spirit and the virtue of priestly grace', *et super hos famulos tuos benedictionem Sancti Spiritus et gratiæ Sacerdotalis virtutem*. At the same time as asking for the grace of ordination, the prayer also specifies the intention of the Church in this rite: the candidates are presented to God that they might be 'consecrated'. The situation of this prayer, its solemn tone of entreaty, the gesture of blessing which accompanies it, and the force and precision of the words, all enable us to recognise a parallel, in regard to the nature of this prayer, with the prayer *Quam oblationem* from the Eucharistic Sacrifice. Here the Church, immediately before the consecration, asks for the transubstantiation of the Eucharist, and proclaims the intention of the rite.

After this the priests, who until now had been gathered around the bishop, forming a kind of chorus, return to their place in choir. The *flectamus genua* had already interrupted the gesture of holding out the right hand by the bishop and priests, but we might well be surprised that they do not remain by the bishop, in order to keep their hands outstretched with him, and for as long as him, during the consecratory preface which is about to begin At first sight, this would seem to be logical; and one could see it as a survival of the rite in the Apostolic Tradition. However it is precisely that text, attributed to Hippolytus, which, long before the speculations of scholastic theologians and their transcriptions of the rite, seems to offer the explanation of the development which would occur. According to the text of the Apostolic Tradition, in fact, [23] the *cheirotonia* done by the ordinary priests does not signify the imparting of the Holy Spirit, which the priests can only receive and not give; no, it signifies that the same Spirit which they possess is that which is being transmitted to the new priest. The gesture, then, does not have any sacramental value, but they lay their hands on the new priests *propter communem et similem cleri spiritum*, because of the one common spirit which they share. By the gesture of the laying on of hands, the priests show that they are one with the bishop: 'they are not isolated individuals, each one having his own mission; it is a college which shares in the ministry of the bishop'. [24] It is the common spirit of the *Ordo presbyterii*, or the presbyterium, in which the new priests are from now on to have a share.

Now, as we have already said, entrance into the ordo cannot take place except by the gift of the character and of the grace of the priesthood, a sacrament which only the bishop, priest of the first order, the *Ordo Episcoporum,* has the power to administer. It is the following prayer or preface of consecration which will develop the reasons for the divine institution of the priesthood and which will confer the sacerdotal dignity.

• *The* Oratio consecrationis.

The prayer of consecration invoking the Holy Spirit, found in the *Apostolic Tradition,* asked for the spirit of counsel and of power to be given to the chosen one, so that he might participate in the government of the Church. In so doing, it referred to the person of Moses whom the Lord directed to call to himself a group of elders, 'presbyters', filled with the same spirit which God had imparted to him. [25] The reference to Moses helps us to understand that the priests share in the same spirit as the bishop. The prayer ended with a request on behalf of the whole presbyterium in which the new priest was from now on incorporated, a prayer referring to time now and hereafter: that the spirit of grace we have received be preserved in us, and that we might be worthy to serve God in faith *(et dignos effice ut, credentes, tibi ministremus)* and with a sincere heart. [26]

As Gregory Dix writes, 'the presbyter, according to the *Apostolic Tradition,* is certainly not a 'Church Councillor' or even an 'assessor' on behalf of the bishop in the administration of the Church. He is truly part of the *kleros* and enjoys liturgical prerogatives'. [27] However, the text of the prayer does not give any indication of liturgical prerogatives for the presbyter, unlike the rite of episcopal ordination which enumerates them clearly. [28] The liturgical prerogatives of the presbyter are evidently not unknown at this date, but they appear in a dependent way, through their sharing, their association and their subordination to the prerogatives of the one who, in the ancient terminology, (as early as the year 200, as Fr. Pierre-Marie Gy has shown us [29]) was alone given the name of *sacerdos,* in other words the bishop, the hierarch, the primal celebrant of the liturgy. The presbyters are in effect, as Saint Cyprian puts it, 'associated with the bishop in the honour of the priesthood'—*cum episcopo presbyteri sacerdotali honore conjuncti.* [30] The presbyter is the co-consecrating or co-celebrating minister with the bishop. He does not therefore have, as Gregory Dix underlines, 'any particular liturgical function in the presence of the bishop, who is the ordinary sacramental officiant in his particular Church, with the assistance of his deacons. But in his absence, the presbyter can officiate as a delegate of the bishop and carry out, assisted by deacons, episcopal liturgical functions'.[31]

That is what we find in the text of the *Apostolic Tradition,* which is the most ancient of all rites of ordination. Our documentary research must now advance until the seventh century, to the Sacramentary of Verona, and the old Gelasian

Sacramentary. These preserve for us not so much a ritual, but prayers, which go back probably to the fifth century, and are to be read, almost unchanged, in the Pontifical of 1595. These prayers are three in number. We have already discussed the first two: the invitation *Oremus, fratres dilectissimi,* and the prayer *Exaudi nos.* In our Pontifical, these are placed between the laying on of hands in silence and the third of these prayers which is the *Oratio Consecrationis,* the one to which we shall now turn our particular attention.

The mediæval pontificals preferred to use the term *Præfatio* rather than *oratio.* It is introduced with the same dialogue as the Preface of the Mass, and there follow the words *Vere dignum et justum est,* etc., which express with equal solemnity as in the Eucharistic Sacrifice the thanksgiving of the Church at the moment of preparing for the sacramental act.

The bishop sings the preface of consecration, standing, head uncovered, turned towards the ordinands who are all kneeling. He holds his hands outstretched: by this gesture, the *cheirotonoia* appears to be repeated, in close association with the sacramental words. At one and the same time it affirms that God himself is the author and organiser of all hierarchy and of all honour—*honorum auctor et distributor omnium dignitatum,*—and in particular of the priestly hierarchy. At the head of this hierarchy are the bishops, named here *summi pontifices,* charged with governing the people. But God has chosen to call 'men of a lesser order and of a secondary dignity'—*sequenti ordinis viros et secundæ dignitatis*—in order that they might assist the bishops and cooperate with them in the same work. Is this not the same doctrine as in the prayer of the Apostolic Tradition? Just as in the old text attributed to Hippolytus, the *Præfatio* then applies the principle foreshadowed in the Old Testament: Moses surrounded himself with a council of seventy elders, just as Eleazar and Ithamar, the sons of Aaron, had received the abundance of grace given to their father. This same providence is later made manifest, confirmed and elevated in the New Testament by the addition of the disciples to the apostles.

The bishop then humbly begs God to give him the co-workers of whom he has the greatest need. For 'the action of divine grace,' as Dom P. de Puinet writes, 'is greatly preponderant in a priestly ordination: there is nothing which does not come from it, in the preparation of souls called to the priesthood and in the accomplishment of the sacramental work'.[32] This work is what God is about to accomplish, through grace, while the bishop pronounces the essential words of the form which determines the application of the matter, the imposition of hands: 'Father almighty, we pray thee, grant to thy servants here present the dignity of the priesthood *(Presbyteri dignitatem)*; renew in their souls the spirit of holiness, that they might possess—received from thee, O God—that commission of the second rank *(secundi meriti munus),* and that the example of their life might bring about a reform of morals'. These words signify the effects of the sacrament, enunciating what they really effect in conjunction with the laying on of hands: that is to say, firstly the character of the priesthood of

Christ, with the prerogatives which are attached to it, and secondly the renewal and increase of the spirit of sanctification proper to the Sacrament of Order, and necessary in order to carry out well the functions of the priest. The text speaks of a renewal or increase of the spirit of priestly sanctification, for the grace has already been conferred on the candidate by the diaconate, albeit in a lesser degree.

However, you will have noticed that the *Oratio Consecrationis* of the Verona Sacramentary, (which is the same as the Preface of our 1595 Pontifical), is just as silent as the consecratory prayer of the *Apostolic Tradition* on the functions of the priesthood of the second order. In Rome, between the fifth and the fifteenth centuries, the functions of the priest continue to be essentially defined in terms of subordination to the priestly function of the bishop, which the bishop himself clearly expresses when he prays: *Sint providi cooperatores ordinis nostri* —'that they might be worthy cooperators with our order'. We shall see that the complementary rites which come later express new developments, essentially justifiable by the need to articulate the powers received with the character and grace of the sacrament.

THE COMPLEMENTARY RITES

• *The Prayer of Blessing,* Deus, omnium sanctificationum auctor...

In the old Gelasian Sacramentary, compiled only a few decades later than that of Verona, other rites were added: priestly ordination was completed with the *Consummacio presbyteri,* then by the *Benedictio,* both derived from the Gallican liturgy. Of the *Consummacio* there is no trace in the *Ordines Romani,* and even though it passed into the Romano-Germanic Pontifical, it did not find its way into the mediæval Roman pontificals. The *Benedictio* is also unknown in the ordines, but the entire text can be found in the Roman Pontifical of the twelfth century and subsequently in the 1595 Pontifical.

The *Benedictio* of the old Gelasian Sacramentary, which subsequently got into the Gellonense, is, in fact, a prayer of entreaty. In the Gallican liturgy (according to the eighth century *Missale Francorum)* it took the place of the *Oratio Consecrationis* of priests. Inserted into the Roman books, it surely was from the outset (as Monsignor Righetti suggests [33]), no more than a simple, inoperative, but beautiful duplication of the Roman prayer of consecration, adapted to become a blessing suitable for the conclusion of the first part of the rite. Possibly, however, the liturgy of the high Middle Ages adopted this prayer in order to make explicit the priestly prerogatives which derive from the character and grace of the priesthood.

Allow me to quote two passages of this *Benedictio* which seem to me particularly important: 'That meditating thy law, night and day, they might believe what they read, teach what they believe and practise what they teach...

That for the sake of thy people they will carry out by their holy blessing the transformation of bread and wine into the body and blood of thy Son...'. It seems clear to me that the *Benedictio,* as well as most of the other rites which will follow and of which I will only offer a very brief analysis, serve to express the priestly powers, as much over the real Body of Christ, by the consecration of the Eucharist, as over the mystical Body of Christ by the administration of the sacraments, the presiding *(præesse)* over the Christian assembly and the ministry of preaching: *Sacerdotem etenim oportet offerre, benedicere, præesse, prædicare et baptizare.* We have already said that this phrase in the admonition allows us to detect a development with regard to the concept of the priesthood from that of the *Apostolic Tradition* at the beginning of the third century and the strictly Roman *Oratio consecrationis* of the fifth to sixth centuries.

Indeed the *Benedictio* of the old Gelasian Sacramentary provides evidence for this development. What happened was that, from the fourth century on, the increase in the number of the faithful and in consequence of the number of places of worship, the penetration of Christianity into the countryside, and what we might call 'pastoral need' demanded that liturgical functions be delegated by the bishop to members of the presbyterium. Even though at Rome the old understanding was preserved as far as possible, because of the intervention of the great Station ceremonies, which testifies to a new development at the end of the sixth century, everywhere else, little by little 'we begin', writes Gregory Dix, 'to meet the 'parish priest', a presbyter who gives instruction and who administers the sacraments to separate congregations, which the bishop, although he remains nominally the 'high-priest' as in ante-Nicene days, only visits occasionally'. [34] As Fr. Gy remarks, the word *sacerdos* which initially was only used to mean 'bishop', begins to be applied to the role of presbyter around the end of the fourth century. In the Carolingian era it was used most often to mean 'priest', and by the eleventh century it ended up being used more or less exclusively with this meaning. [35] In the Middle Ages the priestly function was perceived essentially as orientated towards the exercise of a ministry or a service, *utilitas* and *caritas*, comprising the sacramental life, the teaching of the faith and the government of the community of the fathful. [36]

Now, *pace* the Anglican Gregory Dix, our Catholic sense of tradition forbids us to class this development as a 'radical modification', or even an alteration. For, as Dom Botte remarked, still referring to the ordination rite in the 1595 Pontifical,

> the liturgical texts which still survive confirm that priests are the co-workers of the order of bishops... What we find in the first four centuries is still, therefore, valid, when it is a question of determining what the priesthood is. The *presbyterium* is still a priestly body which helps the bishop and represents him in his mission of guiding the people of God.[37]

• *Clothing and anointing of the hands.*

After the *Benedictio,* the eighth-century Gelasian Sacramentary then prescribes two other rites: the clothing with priestly vestments and the anointing of the hands.

We find the first trace of a clothing ceremony in the *Ordo Romanus XXXIV,* the old Roman ritual of ordinations contemporary with the *Ordo Romanus I,* and therefore a witness to the period of the pure Roman liturgy. After the litanies and before the *Ordo consecrationis,* outside the choir, in front of the screen, the archdeacon dresses the future deacons in the dalmatic and the future priests in the chasuble, with no texts to recite. [38] Towards the end of the ninth century, in the *Ordo Romanus XXXVI,* and in the *Ordo Romanus XXXV* of c. 925, both of which are Romano-Frankish rituals, the original arrangement is modified: as in the Gelasian Sacramentary of the eighth century, but without introducing its *Benedictio,* it is from now on after the prayer of consecration that the bishop places the vestments on the new priests.

In the Roman ritual, and in the later hybrid ordines, the intention above all was to express a function, while clothing the ordinand with the vestments proper to his ministry. But around 950, in the Romano-Germanic Pontifical, the rite acquired greater solemnity with the adoption of texts with an allegorical flavour. The rite then developed into the Roman Pontifical of the twelfth century, which was when it incorporated the ancient Gallican *Benedictio.* Nevertheless, we now find a change in regard to the directions of the eighth-century Gelasian Sacramentary: although in this the clothing followed the benediction, from now on it preceded it; for the old Gallican formula, as we have seen, no longer performed the function of consecration, it was simply an additional prayer. In the new location, after the rite of clothing, and replacing another formula of blessing, relegated since the Romano-Germanic Sacramentary to the very end of the rite of ordination, it manifests the benediction which comes down to clothe the chosen one with priestly grace, as he is entrusted with the yoke of the Lord. This is how we must understand it in the 1595 Roman Pontifical.

It is again the Gellone Sacramentary, towards the end of the eighth century, which inserts for the first time the Gallican rite of anointing the hands into the Roman ritual. The *Ordo Romanus XXXV* (no. 29) prescribes this rite with a formula identical to that found in the *Missale Francorum.* The Romano-Germanic Pontifical uses it but introduces it with a formula of entreaty: *Consecrare et sanctificare digneris, Domine.* Thence it enters the twelfth-century Roman Pontifical. In the thirteenth-century Pontifical of the Roman Curia, the clothing is immediately followed by the singing of the hymn to the Holy Spirit, *Veni Creator,* with a *Pater noster* and a versicle, then as a collect the *Benedictio* from the Gelasian Sacramentary. Durandus restored the *Benedictio* to its place, and then had the *Veni Creator* sung, without *Pater noster* or versicle. From the beginning of the second verse of the hymn, the bishop, who had been kneeling during the intonation, stands up and proceeds with the anointing of the hands, so that this significant ceremony is enfolded into the invocation of the life-giving Spirit by the whole Church.

While he anoints the hands of the new priest with the sign of the cross, and then spreads the oil of catechumens over the whole surface of the palms, the bishop pronounces these words: 'Vouchsafe, O Lord, to consecrate and sanctify these hands by this anointing and our blessing'. He then makes the sign of the cross with his right hand over the hands of the new priest, and adds, 'That everything they bless might be blessed, and all that they consecrate might be consecrated and sanctified in the name of our Lord Jesus Christ.' The anointing of the hands refers therefore to the powers of the priesthood, specifically the power to offer the Eucharistic Sacrifice and the power to bless. In the Carolingian period, Amalarius of Metz, the official commentator on the Romano-Frankish liturgy, treats of the symbolism of the rite, finding a precedent in the Levitical priesthood: 'it seems that the hands of priests receive the holy anointing, in order to be pure for the offering of the holy sacrifice to God, and to be fit for the exercise of certain ministries of religion. Two things are in effect signified by the oil: the grace of healing, and the love of pure charity'.[39]

• *The* Traditio Instrumentorum.

In the lengthy rubric of the introduction *De Ordinibus Conferendis* of the 1595 Pontifical, we read as follows: 'Let the Bishop be attentive that the ordinands touch the instruments by which the character is received'. In giving the bread and wine to the new priest, the bishop pronounces the following words: *accipe potestatem offerre Sacrificium Deo*, 'Receive the power to offer the sacrifice to God, and to celebrate the Mass for both the living and the dead, in the name of the Lord'.

It is in the tenth century, in the Romano-Germanic Pontifical, that the rite of the *traditio instrumentorum* appears for the first time in priestly ordination. Doubtless, in conjunction with the clothing and the anointing, it was intended to express entrance into the sacerdotal office more clearly by the handing over of the instruments proper to the priestly state. Although the rite was a novelty in the rite of priestly ordination, it was not an innovation in itself. One can find, in fact, traces of the *traditio instrumentorum* in the fifth century, in the minor ordinations of the Gallican *Statuta Ecclesiæ Antiqua,* [40] and even in the *Ordo XXXIV,* a pure Roman ritual, in the course of the ordination of the acolyte. This does not seem to allow the *traditio instrumentorum* to originate in feudalism , as Angelo Lameri proposed in a recent study, even if it is undeniable that the rites of vassaldom have contributed to development of the rite. [41]

According to Angelo Lameri, the introduction in the tenth century of the *traditio instrumentorum* into the giving of the major orders seems to indicate that at this time the gesture of the imposition of hands 'no longer seemed sufficient to express, still less to confer, a sacrament'. [42] In fact, the formula which accompanied the gesture was of such a nature as to make the gesture assume a determining role. 'The imperative *Accipe*', remarks Angelo Lameri,

> does not refer directly to the instruments which are being handed over, but rather to the priestly *potestas* to offer the sacrifice, to celebrate Mass. It was no longer a question therefore of a simple exhortation, taking occasion of the handing over of the instruments, but rather of the handing on of priestly power itself, which is specified as consisting in the celebration of the eucharistic sacrifice...'. [43]

We know that in the Middle Ages, and virtually universally during the entire Baroque period and beyond, it was considered that the *traditio instrumentorum,* being here the handing over to the ordinand of the chalice filled with wine and the paten bearing a host, was a rite essential for imparting sacramental character. [44] However, the study of the sources of the Roman liturgy, linked to a theological reflection, gradually enabled us again to restore the full significance to the gesture of the imposition of hands with the invocation of the Holy Spirit in consecration.[45] It was on this basis that Leo XIII determined the invalidity of Anglican ordinations, [46] before Pius XII made a definitive ruling in the Apostolic Constitution Sacramentum Ordinis. [47]

The action of the *traditio instrumentorum* merits more attentive study, in order to establish the circumstances which led, in the opinion of theologians and liturgists, to the development in understanding from its being the expression of power to the actual conferral of that power. We must be content here to remark, from a simple examination of the rite and of its formula, that the sign introduced by the Romano-Germanic Pontifical expresses the essential and primary power of the Christian priesthood, that is to communicate the benefits and the merits of the Redemption through the celebration of the Eucharistic Sacrifice, which is the sacramental continuation of the saving work of Christ. Such is, we believe, the primary function of the priesthood, by which the Church is constituted, and towards which is orientated the whole of sacramental life and the order of worship. It may be that, from the tenth century onwards (that is to say following the first eucharistic controversy, between Paschasius Radbertus, Abbot of Corbie, and his opponent the monk Ratramnus), as the systematic reflection on the mystery of the Eucharist first commenced, and as the Christian people grew in eucharistic devotion, there was a temptation to see the *traditio* as more than a mere explanation of what had been conferred by the cheirotonoia and the prayer of consecration. Doubtless they had also lost sight of the origins of the rites of ordination. In this perspective, one can understand why St. Thomas Aquinas, following in this the common opinion of scholastic thought, decided in favour of the rite and formula of the *traditio instumentorum* being the matter and the form, which enabled him to specify the moment when the priestly character is impressed on the soul of the candidate. [48]

Pius XII, basing himself on what had been done always and everywhere - because the *traditio instrumentorum* had never existed in any eastern rite -

made an infallible [*sic.*] decision on the matter and form not only of the priest-hood but also of the episcopate and the diaconate. In consequence, the Pope decreed that the sacramental words be printed in bold characters in the new editions of the Roman Pontifical, that they be recited without chant, and that the rubric in the Pontifical which we have quoted with regard to the impression of the character by touching the instruments should disappear. The *traditio instrumentorum,* therefore, now appears only as a ceremonial elaboration of the essential power received to consecrate the Body and Blood of the Lord.

SACRAMENTAL CONCELEBRATION.

After the singing of the gospel and the offering of their candle to the bishop, the new priests exercise this power of consecration immediately through the rite of sacramental concelebration. This is not without its difficulties in our analysis, and we ought to devote to it a treatment completely different from that which our time allows us here. Also I do not wish to do more than mention in passing the problems that arise from the study of the sources of priestly ordination alone.

The text of the *Apostolic Tradition* on the ordination of presbyters does not give us any indication; it finishes with a prayer of consecration invoking the Holy Spirit. The *Ordo Romanus XXXIV* brings the ordination to an end with the kiss which the new priest exchanges with the bishops and priests, and then indicates that he should stand in the order of presbyters and complete the Mass according to his order, *stat in ordine presbiterii... et completur missa ordine suo.* (n. 12) The *Ordo Romanus XXXV* changes nothing of this direction. The twelfth-century Pontifical retains it, then follows it with the offertory. There is thus no trace of sacramental concelebration. I do not mean to deny its exist-ence, but we must observe that there is nothing to indicate it. On the contrary, these texts seem rather to indicate concelebration of a purely ceremonial type, consisting of a celebration carried out by the bishop, surrounded by his clergy hierarchically arranged in 'orders'.

In the thirteenth century, the pontifical of the Roman Curia completely modi-fies the previous directive. The new priests are no longer instructed to stand *in ordine presbiterii* but, after the offertory they go up to the altar, where they stand on either side of the bishop. Following in their missal they say everything in a low voice, in the same way as if they were celebrating—*sicut si celebrarent.* There is a sacramental concelebration. If it is the Pope who officiates at the ordination, the priests and deacons communicate under both species: the Pope administers the Body of Christ with a kiss on the hand before and on the face afterwards, while the deacon of the Gospel gives them the Precious Blood. If it is a bishop who ordains, communion takes place only under one kind.

Sacramental concelebration during the ordination of priests seems then to be an innovation of the Roman Curia. St Thomas Aquinas characterizes it in the

Summa as a 'custom of certain churches'. [49] Durandus leaves it to the choice of the one who has been ordained: *ordinati, si velint, habeant libros coram se dicentes tacite canonem et quæcumque de missa dixerit ordinator.* [50] In the 1595 pontifical, the new priests celebrate with the bishop. However, they do not go up to the altar, but remain on their knees with the book in front of them, and read the prayers of the Mass after the *Suscipe sancte Pater.* The bishop must be careful to say the canon slowly, and in a slightly raised voice *(morose et aliquantulum alte),* since they must say everything with him, especially the words of consecration, which should be said simultaneously *(secum omnia dicere et præsertim verba consecrationis quæ dici debent eodem momento).* It is because they are concelebrating, as Luzzi and Burckhard showed in their edition of the pontifical of Innocent VII in 1497, that the priests do not have to say the *Confiteor* before receiving communion. [51] They do not receive the Precious Blood.

In the Middle Ages and beyond, as Catalani testifies in 1738, in his *Commentary on the Pontifical,* it seems that sacramental concelebration had already become the object of quite heated debate. [52] It seems therefore significant that the post-Tridentine Pontifical should have confined it exclusively to priestly ordination and to episcopal consecration. Why? We have seen from the documentary sources that the rite of sacramental concelebration does not seem to have been included in ordination to the priesthood until the thirteenth century, at a time when, as I have stressed previously, the priesthood was perceived essentially in its eucharistic function, and when it was believed that it was conferred by the *traditio* of the matter of the Sacrifice. Is it perhaps this same understanding which was the origin of the change, despite the lack of support for sacramental concelebration at the time, of which the thirteenth-century pontifical of the Roman Curia is the witness?

In an attempt to see more clearly, independently of documentary research on the antiquity (real or presumed) of the practice of sacramental concelebration in the manner in which it is practised today, to say nothing of the ill-considered popularity which it seems to enjoy, we can draw a conclusion from an examination of the 1595 Roman Pontifical. Sacramental concelebration does not consist in simply assisting the celebrating bishop; it is something quite different. It goes further than a simple expression of the unity of the presbyterium around the bishop. It consists of a true celebration of the Eucharistic Sacrifice on the part of the one who is celebrating with the bishop, in this same celebration of the liturgical rite in which he shares the ministry.

FINAL RITES BEFORE COMMUNION.

We owe entirely to Durandus the arrangement of the secondary and complementary rites which take place after communion. These rites do not derive from the old Roman ritual or from the Gallican. They are probably mediæval usages of dioceses in France or Germany which the bishop of Mende thought suitable to express certain aspects of the priestly ministry.

After the ablutions, the bishop intones on the epistle side the chant *Jam non dicam,* which brings together the very words of the Saviour, to evoke the state of friendship of the newly ordained with their Saviour and the gift of the Holy Spirit. After intoning the chant, the bishop turns towards the new priests who stand in front of the altar and face him, to recite the Apostles' Creed. It is easy to see that what is happening here is their proclamation of the faith which they are going to have to teach.

The bishop then sits at the faldstool, and the new priests approach and kneel in front of him. He lays his hands on each one of them while saying: *Accipe Spiritum Sanctum,* 'Receive the Holy Spirit: the sins that you forgive shall be forgiven, and those that you retain shall be retained'. Here too we can see the meaning of the rite as an expression of another power of the priest, the power to absolve.

However, this rite demands a deeper examination. For Durandus and his contemporaries, the sacramental character had been conferred by the *traditio instrumentorum,* with an essentially eucharistic emphasis. This gesture renewed the commandment of the Saviour by which, during the institution of the Eucharistic Sacrifice, he instituted the priesthood: *Hoc facite in meam commemorationem.* 'Since', says St Thomas Aquinas in the *Summa contra Gentiles,*

> the purpose of the power of order is the consecration of the body of Christ and its distribution to the faithful; this power must also be able to make them worthy and able to receive this sacrament. But, this worthiness, this aptitude, is given by the absence of sin ... therefore the power of order must extend to the forgiveness of sins: it does so by the administration of the sacraments which remit sins, Baptism and Penance. That is why the Lord, having given to his disciples the power to consecrate his body, gave them likewise the power to forgive sins. [53]

It is easy to see what power is given by this second imposition of hands. If one is sensitive to symbolism, it is the setting of this rite after communion which evokes the appearance of our Lord to his apostles after his Passion and Resurrection, on the occasion when he breathed upon them and pronounced the words here repeated by the bishop. [54]

Although the majority of mediæval theologians considered that this power had already been conferred on the new priests during the *traditio instrumentorum,* and that here we have only an expression of it, there are others who base themselves on the unambiguous character of the texts which accompany the *traditio* as well as the second laying on of hands, and find quite another significance in the latter action. Such in the sixteenth century was the position of St Robert Bellarmine, [55] and it is one which a commentator as authoritative as Catalani continued to support in the eighteenth century. The theory is that priestly ordination confers two powers, one over the Eucharistic body of the Lord, by the power to consecrate, the other over the mystical body, by the power to absolve, therefore there should be two ceremonies to perform, the handing over of the instruments, and the imposition of hands with the words, *Accipe Spiritum Sanctum...* To those such as Morin who object to such a theory, because of the first, more primitive, laying on of hands, [56] Catalani replied that the second imposition of hands is quite as necessary as the first. He denies the intermediate opinion of those who see this rite as merely the unfolding of the power received. This gives us the impression that the true imposition of hands is the one after Communion, since it is accompanied by a formula. The Prayer of Consecration is thus demoted to a lesser significance.

It does not seem that Durandus would ever have held this opinion, [57] but it is probable that in his eyes this rite would have been the unfolding of a power which has been received but is still bound, just as the chasuble has been until now bound up on the priest's back, and is now unfolded by the bishop. It is interesting to observe that this rite is inserted between the Profession of Faith and the promise of obedience made to the bishop. After this follows the kiss of peace, which had concluded the rite of ordination ever since the *Ordo Romanus XXXIV,* but was latterly exchanged with the bishop alone, and emphasized with the formula from the Romano-Germanic pontifical. In an original and significant way, these last ceremonies demonstrate once again the subordinate relationship between priest and bishop.

It is to the Bishop of Mende yet again that we owe the last short instruction, telling the new priests to learn the ceremonies of the Mass carefully, especially the rites of consecration, fraction and communion. The rite of ordination finally concludes with a blessing. This comes from the Romano-Germanic pontifical, and is already seen in the Roman pontificals of the twelfth and thirteenth centuries. Durandus places it after the *Ite, missa est,* replacing the blessing in the Common of the Mass. However the 1595 pontifical distinguishes it from the blessing imparted to the whole assembly. The bishop pronounces it at the end of the complementary rites which conclude the rite of ordination; he entreats God that the new priests be blessed *in ordine sacerdotali.*

CONCLUSION

The analysis which I have had the honour of presenting to you permits us in conclusion to distinguish three major stages in the development of the rite of priestly ordination as it appears in the 1595 Roman Pontifical. The first stage is that of the period of pure Roman liturgy in the early Middle Ages, consisting in the prayers from the Verona Sacramentary and the rites described in the *Ordo Romanus XXXIV.* We have seen that there is still a direct link with the *Apostolic Tradition.* The priest, chosen and consecrated by divine grace, participates in the priesthood of the bishop to a lesser degree. He is aggregated into the second order, the *Ordo Presbyterii,* which assists the bishop in his tasks of governing, teaching and sanctifying the community of the faithful. Delegated by the bishop, in whom resides the fullness of priesthood, he exercises the powers of the Christian priesthood, first and foremost of which is the power of celebrating the Eucharistic Sacrifice.

In the second phase, the texts provide a contemporary witness to the development from the ancient concept of corporate priesthood to the more individualistic concepts of the Carolingian period; these texts and rites are found in the hybrid sacramentaries and *ordines,* and in that of the tenth-century Romano-Germanic Pontifical, which 'give legitimate expression to what was implicitly contained in the more simple rituals of antiquity'. [58] By outward rites, such as the clothing, the anointing, and the *traditio instrumentorum,* they shed light on the transmission of the liturgical powers linked to the reception of sacramental character, and stress the orientation of priesthood towards the Eucharist. At the same time, these texts insist on the spiritual and moral obligations inherent in the sacerdotal character.

Finally, in the mediæval Roman pontificals, at the time when sacramental theology developed, we can discern in some manner the organization or early codification of rites and prayers. At the end of the thirteenth century, William Durandus demonstrates a desire for rigorous systemization. He specifies rubrics, he composes admonitions, he enhances and completes. His book did not take long to become that of the Roman Church.

The rite of ordination in the Roman Pontifical of Clement VIII appears at the end of this continuity, the liturgical transcription of a slow historical and doctrinal evolution. For this reason, to know it, and even more to practice it, serves as a bulwark of orthodoxy in the crisis which threatens the identity of the ministerial priesthood. From the traditional or classical perspective which we take, there is no room for any manner of opposition between a so-called golden age supposed to be the primitive liturgy, reputedly Roman, and an era of alterations and accretions attributed to foreign influences, two contrasting eras corresponding with two almost antagonistic conceptions of the Christian priesthood.

In the realm of liturgy, as in that of theology, evolution can never be anything but homogenous, because of the link between the *lex orandi* and the *lex credendi.* That is what Pius XII demonstrated in his constitution *Sacramentum Ordinis,* when although he relegated the *traditio instrumentorum* to a secondary position, he nevertheless did not judge it necessary to suppress the rite or even its formula. It was the same conception that guided the revisers of the old books, the so-called Tridentine rites, when, under the orders of Pius XII and John XXIII on the eve of the council, they were working on a new edition of the Roman Pontifical.

NOTES

1.   P.M. Gy, O.P., 'Remarques sur le vocabulaire antique du sacerdoce chrétien', in *Etudes sur le sacrement de l'Ordre, Lex Orandi* 22 (Paris 1957), pp.125 sq.

2.   Tertullian, *De exhort.* cast. 7, ed. Oehler, I, 747.

3.   *Pontificale Romanum,* anastatic reprint of the first edition of 1595-1596, by M. Sodi and A. M. Traccia, in the series *Monumenta Liturgica Concilii Tridentini* (Vatican City 1997).

4.   See M. Dykmans, S.J., *Le pontifical romain révisé au XVème siècle; Studi e Testi* 311 (Vatican City 1985), pp.149-157.

5.   Mgr. M. Andrieu, *Le pontifical romain au Moyen Age, Vol.. III, Le pontifical de Guillaume Durand; Studi e Testi 88* (Vatican City 1940), pp.364-373.

6.   *La Tradition apostolique:* ed. Dom B. Botte, O.S.B., in the series *Sources chrétiennes* 11 bis (Paris 1968). [English edition *The Apostolic Tradition,* ed. by G. Dix, 1968] See also J. M. Hanssens, S.J., *La liturgie d'Hippolyte* (Rome, 1970).

7.   Such criticisms may be found for example in Bl. Card. I. Schuster, O.S.B. The Sacramentary (Liber Sacramentorum) (London 1924), Vol. I, pp. 126 sq.; Dom P. de Puniet, O.S.B., Le Pontifical Romain, histoire et commentaire (Paris 1930), Vol. I, pp. 234 sq.; Mgr M. Righetti, Manuale di storia liturgica (Milan 1959), Vol. IV, pp. 405 sq. Dom B. Botte, O.S.B. displays a much more subtle approach in 'L'Ordre d'après les prières d'ordination,' in Etudes sur le sacrement de l'Ordre, Lex Orandi 22 (Paris 1957), pp.13-35.

8.   Mohlberg, Eizenhöfer and Siffrin, *Sacramentarium Veronense, in Rer. eccl. documenta,* 1st Series, Fontes I (Rome 1956).

9.   Mohlberg, Eizenhöfer and Siffrin, *Liber sacramentorum Romanæ ecclesiæ ordinis anni circuli (Sacramentorium Gelasianum), in Rer. eccl. documenta,* 1st series, Fontes IV (Rome 1960).

10.   For the 8th-century Gelasian Sacramentary, we cite the evidence of the Gellone Sacramentary, in A. Dumas and J. Deshusses, *Liber sacramentorum Gellonensis,* in *Corpus Christianorum Ser. Lat.* 159-159 A (Turnhout 1981).

11.   Mgr M. Andrieu, *Les ordines romani du haut Moyen Age,* in *Spicilegium sacrum lovaniense* (Louvain). *Ordo Romanus XXXIV,* in *Spicilegium* vol. III, 24 (1974), pp.603-613; *Ordines Romani XXXV* and *XXXVI,* in *Spicilegium* vol. IV, 28 (1965), pp.33-47, pp.195-205.

12.   C. Vogel and R. Elze, *Le Pontifical romano-germanique du Xème siècle; Studi e Testi* 226, 227 and 269 (Vatican City 1963-1972).

13.   Mgr M. Andrieu, *Le pontifical romain au Moyen Age,* op. cit.; esp. Vol. I, *Le pontifical romain du XIIème siècle; Studi e Testi 86* (1938), pp.134-137; Vol. II, *Le pontifical romain de la Curie romaine au XIIIème siècle; Studi e Testi 87* (1940), pp.341-350.

14.   See P. de Puniet, op. cit., p. 235: 'It is quite clear and quite certain that the similarity is intentional - there was once even anointing of deacons - for the effect produced and expressed by the consecration of the deacon is the same as that of the priest. This is what makes the sacrament of Order a single sacrament, for the deacon participates already, though to a lesser degree, in the one priesthood. He already bears in himself the character of holy order, which differs not in essence but only in degree from that of the priest and bishop. Just as the unity of the sacrament of order demands a similarity in the external rites, so this similarity of rite expresses and symbolises that unity of the sacrament'.

15.   St Jerome, *Epist. 146, ad Evangelum, P.L.* XXII, 1194.

16.   This can be found in the 13th-century Roman Pontifical, as well as in some editions of the 12th century. See M. Andrieu, *Le Pontifical Romain au Moyen Age, op. cit.* Vols. II and III.

17.   P. de Puniet, *op. cit.,* Vol. I, pp. 240-241.

18.   See 'L'ancien rituel romain des ordinations du haut Moyen Age', in C. Vogel, *Introduction aux sources de l'histoire du culte Chrétien au Moyen Age* (Spoleto 1981), p.152. Text in M. Andrieu, Les ordines romani, op. cit., nos. 8 et 9.

19   *'Cum autem presbyter ordinatur, imponat manum super caput ejus episcopus, contingentibus etiam præsbyteris, et dicat ... orans et dicens ...';* La Tradition Apostolique, ed. by B. Botte, chap. 7, p.56 [ed. G. Dix, viii, p. 13]

20. *Ordo Romanus XXXV*, ed. by M. Andrieu (1956), Vol.IV, p.38: '... *Nam ceteri episcopi, quando consecrant presbiterum, alii presbiteri astantes duo vel tres cardonales manus super caput ipsius qui consecratur imponunt'.* (n. 38)

21. *'Numerus sacerdotum a rubricis non determinatur; duodecim dicimus, et non plus, est enim antiquum presbyterium in memoriam duodecim apostolorum, quod etiam nunc a Pontificale Romano pro oleorum consecratione præcipitur. Tres tamen semper requiruntur; ait enim rubrica, tres aut plures, duo enim non faciunt capitulum neque presbyterium constituunt'.* Mgr J. Nabuco, *Pontificalis Romani expositio juridico-practica* (Paris 1962), p.104, note 2.

22. Here again we see the liturgical importance of the chapter, which is none other than the survival of the ancient presbyterium. If we read the commentaries on the rubrics, it appears that whereas the chapter assists the bishop in the ordination of priests, there is no requirement for other priests present to lay on hands. *'Si præter canonicos paratos'*, writes Mgr J. Nabuco, *'aderint in choro alii sacerdotes, invitari et ipsi poterunt ad manus imponendas...'* (*op. cit.,* p.104, n. 6).

23. *La Tradition Apostolique*, ed. by B. Botte, chap. 8, p.61 [ed. G. Dix, viii, p. 13-15].

24. B. Botte, 'Caractère collégial du presbyterat et de l'épiscopat,' in *Etudes sur le sacrement de l'Ordre, op. cit.*, p.100.

25. See *Apostolic Tradition*, ed. Botte, chap. 7, p.56 [ed. G. Dix, viii, pp. 13-14]: *'Deus meus, pater domini nostri et salvatoris nostri Jesu Christi, respice super hunc servum tuum et impertire ei spiritum gratiæ et consilium præsbyterii ut sustineat et gubernet plebem tuam in corde mundo, sicut respexisti super populum electum et præcepisti Moysi ut eligeret præsbyteros quos replevisti de spiritu quem donasti famulo tuo et servo tuo Moysi'.*

26. *'Et nunc, Domine, præsta indeficienter conservari in nobis spiritum gratiæ tuæ et dignos effice ut credentes tibi ministremus in simplicitate cordis, laudantes te per puerum tuum Christum Jesum per quem tibi gloria et virtus ...'* *(Ibid.,* p.58 [Dix, p. 14])

27. Gregory Dix, *Le ministère dans l'Eglise ancienne,* (Neuchâtel 1955), p.58. [Ed. I can find no version of this in English]

28. 'That he may pasture your holy flock, and exercise the sovereign priesthood in your sight without reproach, serving you night and day; that he may ceaselessly make your face propitious, and offer the gifts of your holy Church; that he may, by virtue of the spirit of the sovereign priesthood, have the power to remit sins according to your command; that he may impose ecclesiastical censures according to your order, and may release from every bond by virtue of the power which you have given your apostles'. *Tradition apostolique,* ed. Botte, chap. 3, pp.45-47 [ed. Dix, iii, p.5). G. Dix says, 'The bishop represents God before the Church, and the Church before God, or, as Hippolytus more concretely puts it, the bishop exercises the same functions as Our Saviour, those of the Good Shepherd of the holy flock of God, of the high priest in the order of Melchisedech, searching to obtain from God, by the offering of the eucharistic sacrifice of the Church'. (*op. cit.*, pp.32-33)

29. P.M. Gy, O.P., *Remarques sur le vocabulaire antique, op. cit.,* pp. 141-144.

30. Cyprian of Carthage, *Epistolæ* 61,3 (ed. Hartel, Vol. II, pp.696-697).

31. G. Dix, op. cit., p.59. The author adds that he does not at all share in the creative power of the bishop, who distributes the Spirit in his Church. The bishop alone, by the dispensation of the Spirit, creates laymen (that is, members of the laos, the people of God) by Confirmation, creating clergy by Ordination.

32. P. de Puniet, *op. cit.,* Vol. I, p.271.

33. M. Righetti, *pp. cit.,* p.416.

34. G. Dix, *op. cit.,* p.131.

35. P.M. Gy, *op. cit.,* p.141-144.

36. R. Gregoire, 'L'Ordine ed il suo significato: 'utilitas' e 'caritas' in *Segni e riti nella Chiesa altomediævale occidentale,* Settimane di studio del Centro Italiano di Studi sull Alto Medioevo, XXXIII (Spoleto 1987), Vol.. II, pp.639-697. Beginning with the study of Carolingian sources, Fr Gregoire is able to say that the priestly ministry presented 'a vital variety of application, ecclesial and social, spiritual and pastoral, cultural and political'(p.695).

37. B. Botte, *Caractère collégial..., op. cit.,* p.106-107.

38 *Ordo Romanus XXXIV,* ed. M. Andrieu, *Les ordines romani..., op. cit.,* Vol. III: *'Si vero voluerit*

eum consecrare presbyterum, tenens eum archidiaconus ducit foras rugas altaris, exuit eum dalmatica et sic eum induit planeta et ducit iterum ad episcopum'. (p.606, n. 11).

39. See *Amalarii Episcopi opera liturgica omnia,* ed. J.M. Hanssens S.J., Vatican City, *Studi e Testi* 139, Vol.II, Liber Officialis, L.II, c. 13, n. 1, p.227: *'ut mundæ sint hostias Deo ad offerendum, et largæ ad cetera officia pietatis; utrumque designatur per oleum, et gratia curationis, et caritas dilectionis'.*

40. Text of the *Statuta* in *Concilia Galliæ* A. 314 - A. 506, ed. Munier (Tournai 1963), *Corpus Christianorum* 148, pp.163-188.

41. A. Lameri, *La Traditio Instrumentorum e delle insegne nei riti di ordinazione, Bibliotheca Ephemerides Liturgicæ Subsidia,* no. 96, (Rome 1998) pp.171-177.

42. A. Lameri, *op. cit.,* p.167.

43. A. Lameri, *op. cit.,* p.158.

44. This opinion is backed by the Decree for the Armenians of Eugenius IV, promulgated 22 November 1439, during the Council of Florence. For the theological value of this decree, see Mgr A. Piolanti, *I Sacramenti* (Vatican City 1990), pp. 494-495.

45. Writing at the beginning of the twentieth century, Bl. Ildephonso Schuster asserts, 'The imposition of hands and the episcopal epiclesis thus constitute the essential mark of the sacrament of holy orders, which must be retained intact in all rites and in every age.' (*The Sacramentary,* op. cit., Vol. I, p.126)

46. Leo XIII, Apostolic letter *Apostolicæ Curæ,* 13 Sept. 1896, in AAS 29 (1896/97), pp.198 sq.

47. Pius XII, Apostolic Constitution *Sacramentum Ordinis,* 30 Nov. 1947, in AAS 40 (1948), 5-7.

48. St Thomas Aquinas, *IV Sent.,* d. 24, q. 1, a. 2, sol. 2. See also *Suppl.,* q. 37, a. 5. In the *Summa contra Gentiles* Book IV, chap. 74, St Thomas writes, 'Given these two facts, that spiritual power derives from Christ to the ministers of the Church, and that the spiritual effects which come to us from him are made real through the mediation of certain visible signs, we must conclude that the spiritual power in question must also be transmitted by means of visible signs. Among these are certain words, certain actions, like the laying on of hands, the anointing, the handing over of the book, or the chalice or some such object, which is used during the exercise of that spiritual power'.

49. St Thomas Aquinas, *Summa Theologica* IIIa, q. 82, a. 2: '... *secundum consuetudinem quarundam ecclesiarum, sicut Apostoli Christo cenanti concenaverunt, ita novi ordinanti concelebrant'.*

50. *Le pontifical de Guillaume Durand,* ed. M. Andrieu, *Le pontifical romain...,* op. cit., Vol. III, pp. 370-371, n. 20.

51. See M. Dykmans *Le Pontifical Romain révisé...,* op. cit., p.129.

52. I. Catalani, *Pontificale Romanum in tres partes distributum ... et commentariis illustratum,* (Rome 1738), Vol. I: '... *cum ipse ritus, amplissima fuerit Doctoribus Scholasticis innumerarum difficultatum seges; nonnullis afferentibus, hoc fieri posse, aliis negantibus, aliis certos quosdam possibilitatis modos, ac terminos excogitantibus; omnibus deinde, ut se se ab adversariorum telis tuerentur, novas, et involutas reculas cudentibus, et recudentibus'.* (p. 141).

53. St Thomas Aquinas, *Summa contra Gentiles,* Book IV, c. 74.

54. John 20:22-23.

55. St Robert Bellarmine, *De Sacramento Ordinis.* We have followed the debate in I. Catalani, *Pontificale Romanum...,* op. cit., p.131, where Bellarmine is cited among others.

56. J. Morin, *Commentarius de sacris Ecclesiæ ordinationibus,* (Paris 1655).

57. I refer here to what Durandus writes in *Rationale Divinorum Officiorum* II, chap. 10, no. 14, ed. A. Davril and T.M. Thibodeau, *Corpus Christianorum, Continuatio Mediævalis* CXL (Tournai 1995), p. 170. *Sane ei qui in presbyterum ordinatur traduntur sub certis verbis stola et casula, calix cum patena, et etiam inungitur, que res et verba sunt hujus sacramenti substantia, cetera vero precedentia et sequentia de sollempnitate sunt.* The second imposition of hands is therefore not essential to confer the sacrament.

58 B. Botte.

LITURGY AND PERSONALITY IN THE THOUGHT OF DIETRICH VON HILDEBRAND

Wolfgang Waldstein

Professor Waldstein holds a doctorate in Law from the University of Innsbruck, where he subsequently taught and currently is the Rector. He is also President of the Antonio Rosmini International Institute of European Studies at Bolzano; an Honorary Doctor of the University of Miskolc (Hungary); a Lecturer in Roman Law at the University of Salzburg; a Member of the Pontifical Academy Pro Vita since 1994; and Professor at the Lateran Pontifical University since 1996.

I F one wishes to speak of liturgy and personality in the thought of Dietrich von Hildebrand, one must first make clear how he views the human personality. Von Hildebrand says:

> Every man is a person in that his being is essentially conscious: he is a subject who enters into relations with others, who knows, wills, and loves. A person is a being who ... has the power to choose freely. But not every man is a personality. Only persons can be personalities, but in order to be a personality it is not enough just to be a person'.[1]

More precisely:

> The average man, the inoffensive, colourless, ordinary man without a clearly expressed individuality is not a personality. But neither is the abnormal man, the crank who astonishes others because of his peculiarities and who falls out of the common range because of his oddities and eccentricities. Nor can the pathological man be considered a personality. A personality in the true sense of the word is the man who rises above the average only because he fully realized the classical Human attitudes.

And he adds further characteristics of this attitude:

> To confuse the normal man and the average man is an error typical of the narrow-minded Philistine. This error holds that the ordinary, aver-

age: run-of-the-mill type is the normal man, regardless of whether he is above or below the average: or simply outside it. The genius and the insane man are seen as related because both of them stand outside the range of the average man. [2]

His further analysis cannot be given here, but this summarising remark is important:

Every normal man, in our sense of the word, is a personality, but this does not mean that he is a genius. Under the term 'personality' we understand the complete, classical man, in whom are revealed the great fundamental traits of man, undistorted and unbroken. [3]

Von Hildebrand then asks the question: 'is it possible for every man to become a personality'? [4] This question leads him to the decisive point. Within the context of an immanantist philosophy it would be 'absurd to expect a middling man to become a personality, just as it would be absurd to expect a man not musically gifted to become a Mozart.' But he then adds:

...everything now bears the mark of the almost inconceivable exaltation of humanity brought about through the Incarnation of God and through baptism which implants in man a new principle of life, participation in the life of Christ and the Holy Trinity.

And further:

He who is immersed in the life of Christ, he in whom Christ is truly imitated - the saint - becomes a personality no matter what his essential endowments are. [5]

From this it is clear that the significance of the liturgy in the development of the personality must be seen in connection with the general call to holiness, which is given an entire chapter to itself in *Lumen Gentium,* Vatican II's Dogmatic Constitution on the Church. [6] While it is impossible to discuss all of von Hildebrand's points, I wish

1) to discuss briefly the council's teaching concerning the universal call to holiness, then
2) to highlight upon this background what, in agreement with the Church's teaching, von Hildebrand sees as the nature of the liturgy, and
3) to show what the importance of the liturgy is for the formation of personality.

The 1993 edition of *Liturgy and Personality* contains a remark of the editor, which, as it will help to avoid misunderstandings, we reproduce here:

Because *Liturgy and Personality* concerns the essence of the liturgy rather than the details of any particular liturgy, no effort has been made in these pages to document changes in the liturgy (or in the structure and discipline of the Church) that have taken place since these pages were written sixty years ago. Rather, the reader is urged to use von Hildebrand's numerous liturgical examples to discover the gist of his arguments demonstrating the personality-forming power of the liturgy. Once understood, those points can then be related, when appropriate, to comparable elements in today's liturgy'.[7]

THE UNIVERSAL CALL TO HOLINESS

Against the general opinion that holiness is only for a few specially chosen people, the council answered with the words of the Apostle: 'For this is the will of God, your sanctification'(Art. 39). And concerning the universal call to holiness itself the council says:

> The Lord Jesus, divine teacher and model of perfection, preached holiness of life (of which he is the author and maker) to each and every one of his disciples without distinction: 'You, therefore, must be perfect, as your heavenly Father is perfect' (Mt 5: 48)... The followers of Christ, called by God not in virtue of their works but by his design and grace, and justified in the Lord Jesus, have been made sons of God in the baptism of faith and partakers of the divine nature, and so are truly sanctified. They must therefore hold on to and perfect in their lives that sanctification which they have received from God. 'They are told by the Apostle to live 'as is fitting among saints'(Eph 5: 3)'.

The council has here clarified, and dogmatically, what von Hildebrand says about baptism: In baptism the baptized has implanted within him a new principle of life, through which he participates in the life of Christ, indeed, in the Holy Trinity'. The council then states a principle with an opening remark which is more a wish than a fact: 'It is clear to everyone' (*Cunctis proinde perspicuum est*). What, then, should be clear to everyone is that

> ...all Christians in any state or walk of life are called to the fullness of Christian life and to the perfection of love, and by this holiness a more human manner of life is fostered also in earthly society' (Art. 40).

From this it follows that the normal goal of every Christian is perfect love and the holiness which flows from it. The council adds:

> In order to reach this perfection the faithful should use the strength dealt out to them by Christ's gift, so that, following in his footsteps and conformed to his image, doing the will of God in everything, they may wholeheartedly devote themselves to the glory of God and to the service of their neighbour' (Art. 40).

The seriousness of this call is emphatically underlined by Cardinal John Henry Newman in his sermon *Holiness and its Necessity for Future Blessedness:* 'Holiness, without which no one shall see God'.[8]

If one attentively reads this chapter, of which only excerpts can be cited, it becomes clear that no one who does not strive with God's help after this holiness can become as a Christian a 'personality' in the sense of the 'unbending and unbroken' development of the 'great human characteristics'. Thus von Hildebrand can say:

> To die in ourselves so that Christ may live in us is thus the only path leading to full personality in a far truer and higher sense of the word; and it is this path which is open through the grace of God even to those who possess only a humble, natural, essential endowment. This dying to oneself does not, however, mean the giving up of individuality. On the contrary, the more a man becomes another Christ, the more he realises the original unduplicated thought of God which he embodies. [9]

Von Hildebrand can offer many great saints as illustrative of his point: St. Augustine, St Francis of Assisi, St Catherine of Siena, and, to add some additions of my own, St Thomas More and St Thérèse of Lisieux.

What von Hildebrand says at the end of this chapter is very important:

> Nevertheless it should be borne in mind that it would be a great mistake to place before ourselves the specific aim of becoming personalities in this higher sense of the word, or of becoming powerful individuals. High as the value is which inheres in the participation in the breadth and fullness of God, in becoming a true personality, nevertheless, this is not the unum necessarium; it is subject in a special way to the words of Jesus: 'Seek ye first the kingdom of God and his justice, and these things shall be added unto you'. [10]

This leads us already to our second section concerning the essence of the liturgy.

OF THE NATURE OF THE LITURGY

The third chapter of von Hildebrand's book is entitled: 'Characteristics of the Liturgy and the Basis of Personality'. Concerned here are those 'characteristics' which reveal themselves in liturgical participation, particularly in the Mass and the Breviary. Before discussing particulars, I would like to insist upon their essential foundation. In the Dogmatic Constitution on the Church the council taught: 'As often as the sacrifice of the cross by which 'Christ our Pasch is sacrificed' (I Cor 5: 7) is celebrated on the altar, the work of our redemption is carried out' (Art.3). The Constitution on the Sacred Liturgy speaks also to this truth:

> From this it follows that every liturgical celebration, because it is an action of Christ, is a sacred action surpassing all others. No other action of the Church can equal its efficacy by the same title to the same degree (Art. 7).

Thus ;

> ...the liturgy is the summit toward which the activity of the Church is directed; it is also the fount from which all her power flows, (Art. 10, 1)

and

> From the liturgy, therefore, and especially from the Eucharist, grace is poured forth upon us as from a fountain, and the sanctification of men in Christ and the glorification of God to which all other activities of the Church are directed, as toward their end, are achieved with maximum effectiveness. (Art. 10, 2)

To understand better the significance of this and other [11] conciliar statements, one should read *Mysterium Fidei,* the encyclical of Pope Paul VI which was published two years after the liturgy constitution. Here I can only give one excerpt from this exceptionally important encyclical. The Pope writes:

> First of all, we want to recall something that you know very well but that is absolutely necessary if the virus of every kind of rationalism is to be expelled; it is something that many illustrious martyrs have witnessed to with their blood, something that celebrated Fathers and Doctors of the Church have constantly professed and taught. We mean the fact that the Eucharist is a very great mystery—in fact, properly speaking and in the very words of the sacred liturgy, the mystery of faith. 'It contains within it' as Leo XIII, our predecessor of happy memory very wisely remarked, 'all supernatural realities in a remarkable richness and variety of miracles'. [12] And so we must approach this mystery in particular with humility and reverence, not relying on human reasoning, which ought to hold its peace, but rather adhering firmly to divine Revelation. [13]

From this it is clear that the liturgy is an unfathomable gift of God. 'The work of our salvation is accomplished through Christ's sacrifice on the cross, which is celebrated upon the altar.'[14] Both Pope Pius XII in his encyclical *Mediator Dei* and Pope Paul VI in *Mysterium Fidei* have made clear how we are to respond to this unfathomable gift of God. Pope John Paul II expressly refers to the latter encyclical in his letter *On the Mystery and the Veneration of the Most Holy Eucharist.* [15] If one contemplates these documents and all the rest with which the Church has taught over many years, then one understands what Cardinal Ratzinger means when he remarks, in view of widely-diffused ideas and practices;

> ...where liturgy is merely self-made it does not give us any longer what its own particular gift should be: the meeting with the 'mystery', which is no production of our own, but rather the origin and source of our very life.[16]

Von Hildebrand's remarks can only be understood against this background. Hesays at the very beginning of his work:

> Although the present book seeks to stress the exceptional power of the liturgy for the forming of personality, we must at the same time emphasise that this formation is not the primary intention of the liturgy'.[17]

This is as true for the Breviary as it is for the Mass. About the latter von Hildebrand says:

> Glorification of God is also the primary intention of the Mass, along with the bestowal of redeeming grace upon men. But holy Mass must never be offered with the sole intent of participating in its graces. The intention of adoring God and sacrificing to him 'through Christ, with Christ, and in Christ' is the true condition for renewed incorporation in Christ and increase of grace'.[18]

We are here dealing with 'intention' as it is expressed by Pope Pius XII:

> Now the exhortation of the Apostle 'Let this mind be in you which was also in Christ Jesus' requires that all Christians should possess, so far as it is humanly possible, the same dispositions as those which the divine Redeemer had when he offered himself in sacrifice: that is to say, they should, in a humble attitude of mind, pay adoration, honour, praise and thanksgiving to the supreme majesty of God.[19]

Also the

> breviary deserves the first place, because God, the very personification of all holiness and glory, deserves all praise and honour, and not because it works a change in us. It is in no way in the first place a means to our holiness, as though it were merely some sort of ascetic practice. Above all should our intention be primarily that which the words of the *Gloria* in the Mass express: 'We praise thee. We bless thee. We adore thee... We give thee thanks for thy great glory... For thou alone art the Holy One. Thou alone art the Lord'. [20]

THE SIGNIFICANCE OF THE LITURGY FOR THE FORMATION OF THE PERSONALITY

Before I deal with particulars, it must be emphatically repeated that, as von Hildebrand reminds us at the very beginning of his book: 'the forming of personality is not the primary intention of the liturgy'. [21] Rather is it the case that concern for the essential characteristics of the liturgy, mentioned in the last chapter, is essential if the 'exceptional power of the liturgy for the forming of personality' is to have any effect. 'Interpreting the liturgy as some kind of pedagogical means, [22] would not only fully misinterpret the essence of liturgy, but also deprive it of its inherent power of forming the personality. This is even more the case when, as so often today, liturgy is understood as a kind of religious entertainment, which needs to be constantly varied in form. If one has been confronted with the advice of the 'liturgical committee' of a parish, then one understands where it leads when one no longer recognizes the liturgy as both a great mystery and an unfathomable gift of God, nor any longer sees that 'we must approach this mystery with particular humility'. [23] Then Cardinal Ratzinger's words take on their full significance: 'where liturgy is merely self-made it does not give us any longer what its own particular gift should be'. [24]

As far as the 'power of the liturgy for the forming of personality' is concerned, we will once again stress von Hildebrand's insight concerning the prerequisites for the transformation of the personality. He says:

> ...we shall see that one of the special reasons for the strength and depth of the transformation of a personality brought about by the liturgy is that this transformation is not the end in view; ...For the deepest transformation of a personality occurs not when the means for this transformation are deliberately sought, but when it is brought about in an entirely gratuitous manner through an attitude meaningful in itself.

Von Hildebrand illustrates this by taking love as his example, a love which is entirely directed towards its object, 'and which would cease to exist the moment that it became a pedagogical means for one's own improvement.' Only from a love which is fully directed to the beloved 'emanates a liberating, mellowing, value-disclosing action of incomparable strength and intensity'.[25]

Von Hildebrand recognises that

> a distinction must be made between the two fundamental elements in the formation of personality...The first is the purely ontological basis for the development of personal life, which man can in no way bestow upon himself. It is a pure gift from the hand of God, in the giving of which, man's freedom can play no part. [26] This natural basis is the existence of man as a spiritual person,

with all of his physical and spiritual organs, faculties (including the faculty of knowing), and talents, including those which are a matter of heredity.

> The supernatural basis of the imitation of Christ is the divine life implanted by Baptism... In this divine life...bestowed as a pure gift of God, is found the ontological basis for transformation in Christ, the vital principle of all saintliness. [27]

Von Hildebrand adds:

> 'The second, no less indispensable and fundamental element of all natural and supernatural formation of personality, is the intentional contact with the world of values...' [28]

because 'natural moral values do not arise of themselves'.

They can only grow through the apprehension and affirmation of values, through a conscious response to them. The simple faculties of knowing, willing, and loving do not yet imply virtues; these spiritual faculties do not confer humility, purity, or love. Virtues only blossom out of the conscious union [29] of man with the world of values. It is the same in regard to the supernatural life of man.

Von Hildebrand refers in this context to the words of St. Augustine: *Qui fecit te sine te, non te justificat sine te* (He who made you without you, will not justify you without you), and then adds: 'and what is true of justification is also true of sanctification'.[30]

Von Hildebrand decides, then, that

the meaning of the liturgy for the formation of personality will be considered here from the point of view only of the second fundamental element, the conscious root of sanctity.

He goes on:

When we examine the spirit embodied in the liturgy, which informs itself upon the person who participates in the liturgy, it appears that this spirit is revealed in three ways.

These von Hildebrand sets out as follows:

First of all, the spirit of the liturgy is expressed in the liturgical act as such, in the holy Sacrifice of the Mass (the eternal loving sacrifice of Christ), in the sacraments (the communicating love of Christ), and in the Divine Office (the loving adoration and eternal praise which Christ offers to his heavenly Father). In the second place, the spirit of the liturgy expresses itself in the meaning and atmosphere conveyed by single prayers, antiphons, hymns, and the like, in all that the liturgy expressly says, in the thought and spiritual climate which pervades its forms and words. In the third place, the spirit of the liturgy is expressed in its structure and its construction: in the architecture of the Mass, of the rites, of the different sacraments, of the Divine Office, in the successive accentuation of praise, thanksgiving, and prayer found in the structure of the liturgical year, [31]

and generally in the liturgical rules as to the order and ranking of feasts, and such like.

Von Hildebrand continues his book by consecrating a chapter to each of the following eight marks of the true liturgical spirit, each of which is decisive for the formation of the essential elements of the 'personality':

communion in the liturgy, reverence in the liturgy, response-to-value in the liturgy, wakefulness in the liturgy, *discretio* in the liturgy, continuity in the liturgy, the organic element in the liturgy, and the classical spirit in the liturgy.

I can highlight here only some of the many deep insights made under these headings, and the selection is not an easy one. I can only hope that these few hints will move the listener to seek out and to read von Hildebrand's book, which alone can give him the complete picture.

Concerning 'The Spirit of Community' von Hildebrand remarks:

> The liturgy, as the official prayer of the Church, [32] the prayer of the Mystical Body, is, in its very meaning and essence, the prayer of a community. Each man, even when praying the liturgy alone, enters consciously—if he understands this prayer—into the wider stream of prayer; he takes part in the prayer of the Head and through him also of the Mystical Body of Christ. [33]

Here I would like to add what the council has to say on this topic. It names the approved forms of the *Liturgy of the Hours* 'truly the voice of the Bride herself addressed to her Bridegroom. It is the very prayer which Christ himself together with his Body addresses to the Father'. [34] Von Hildebrand saw that the liturgy, precisely because

> in it we touch Christ without any sort of falsification or subjective alteration… awakens us to that true, ultimate consciousness of communion, that ultimate, victorious union in love which is the very opposite also of all human relationships of boisterous good-fellowship…The liturgy alone, because of its supra-national stamp, its all-embracing breadth, never violates man's separate individuality. [35]

Concerning the 'Spirit of Reverence' von Hildebrand says:

> Reverence is the essential basis for such a perception of values and for a true relationship with the whole realm of values, with what is above and with what speaks from above: with the absolute, the supernatural, and the divine. Reverence is the mother of all virtue, of all religion. [36]

After analysing the causes and the types of irreverence and after depicting true reverence, von Hildebrand remarks:

> The liturgy is penetrated more than anything else by the spirit of true reverence and it draws those who live it directly into this spirit. The right fundamental relation to God and to creation lives in all its parts and it leads to the classical attitude toward God through Christ. [37]

From this it also follows that

> the man formed by the liturgy is reverent toward his neighbour, in whom he sees (if this latter is a member of the Mystical Body of Christ) a 'second Christ'. [38]

All of this is then illustrated using many examples from the liturgy itself.

Concerning the 'Spirit of Response-to-value' von Hildebrand begins with one of 'the most elementary truths' which he formulates as follows. '...to every value an adequate response is due on the part of the person because it is a value' [39] and from no other motive. In the liturgy

> the Holy Sacrifice of the Mass as a whole is the supreme fulfilment of adoration and love which gives itself and sacrifices itself completely. The sacrificial love of the God-man, the gift of himself to the heavenly Father, is the primal theocentric attitude. And to the extent that a man is inwardly formed through participation in the Holy Sacrifice of the Mass, all egocentric deviation from response-to-value is bound to disappear. The spirit which breathes in the holy Mass is penetrated with the fundamental fact that the response of adoring and atoning love is due to God's endless majesty and to his holiness. Likewise the various thoughts and words in the Mass are penetrated with this truth. The *Gloria* clearly expresses it: *Gratias agimus tibi propter magnam gloriam tuam.* [40]

The further chapters concerning the spirits of 'wakefulness', *'discretio'*, 'continuity', and also the 'organic element' and the spirit of the 'classical' in the liturgy offer a rich collection of deep insights into both the nature of the liturgy and the influence upon the development of the personality which flows from it. Von Hildebrand can demonstrate, using many examples from the liturgy, how it calls us to that inner watchfulness from which alone the 'response-to-value' to God and all other values is possible. The Lord himself calls us unceasingly to this attitude: 'Watch ye, and pray that ye will not enter into temptation'.[41] Concerning the 'spirit of the classical' he summarizes:

> All the features of the liturgy which we have so far discovered disclose to our spiritual eyes its deeply classical nature: the spirit of true communion and the spirit of reverence; the truth, which is everywhere affirmed, that an adequate response is due to every value, together with the sense for the hierarchy of values which this fact implies; the light of wakefulness which irradiates the liturgy; its spirit of *discretio* and continuity, its deeply organic structure. [42]

I would like to end with a citation which makes clear what is meant by the 'classical nature' of the liturgy. At the end of his book von Hildebrand says (and what he says is also true, *mutatis mutandis,* for the new liturgy):

> Our gratitude should know no boundaries when we hear the priest pronounce 'I will go unto the altar of God (*Introibo ad altare Dei*)' and the holy Sacrifice of the Mass begins; when 'O God come to my assistance (*Deus in adjutorium meum intende*)' solemnly resounds at the beginning of the Divine Office; when we are enveloped in this ultimate, fully genuine world of truth; when we grasp that here, despite our own narrowness, errors, and slumbers, God is adored in Truth and Spirit; that the true, genuine Word is spoken to God because Christ himself sacri-

fices, praises, and glorifies God in our midst; and that we are allowed to sacrifice to God, to adore and to praise him through Christ, with Christ, and in Christ. Then an endless stream of gratitude surges up within us. Then we experience what the Church is, what the Mystical Body of Christ is, and that God loved us first before we loved him. [43]

If one considers all of this sufficiently, then it is clear what it means for the forming of the personality to live in the midst of the liturgy. The liturgy reveals to us 'the great fundamental traits of man, undistorted and unbroken' and thus helps us 'despite our own narrowness, errors, and slumbers' to be transformed into the 'complete, classical man', [44] who, with God's help, can reach his eternal goal.

NOTES

1. *Liturgy and Personality,* Helicon Press, USA, 1993, 19.

2. *op. cit.,* 20.

3. *op. cit.,* 20.

4. *op. cit.,* 24.

5. *op. cit.,* 24f.

6. *Lumen Gentium* Ch. V, Art. 39 - 42.

7. *Liturgy and Personality,* S. XV.

8. Sermon based upon Hebr. 12: 14. 'Pursue peace with everyone, and the holiness without which no one will see the Lord'.

9. *Liturgy,* 26f.

10. *op. cit.,* 27. Compare Mt. 6,33 and Luke 12, 31.

11. Note particularly SC 47: 'At the Last Supper, on the night he was betrayed, our Saviour instituted the Eucharistic Sacrifice of his Body and Blood. This he did in order to perpetuate the sacrifice of the Cross throughout the ages until he should come again, and so to entrust to his beloved Spouse, the Church, a memorial of his death and resurrection: a sacrament of love, a sign of unity, a bond of charity, a paschal banquet in which Christ is consumed, the mind is filled with grace, and a pledge of future glory is given to us'.

12. Pope Leo XIII, Encyclical *Miræ Caritatis*

13. *The Papal Encyclicals 1958-1981,* Claudia Carlen, H.M., A Consortium Book, McGrath Publishing Company, 1981, 167.

14. Compare the text above from *Lumen Gentium,* Art. 3,

15. Letter of 24 February 1980, nr. 13.

16. Joseph Cardinal Ratzinger, *Aus meinem Leben Erinnerungen* (1927 - 1977), Stuttgart 1998, 174. Ratzinger's comments on the problem of the reform of the liturgy, found on pp. 172ff and pp.188-90 are exceptionally important and illuminating. But we cannot go into these questions here. For my own comments on the problem see my paper in CIEL 1995, *La Liturgie Tresor de l'Eglise: Actes du premier colloque d'études historiques, theologiques et canoniques sur le rite catholique romain,* Paris 1996,163 -182.

17. *Liturgy,* 4.

18. *op. cit.,* 5.

19. *Mediator Dei,* 64. Compare there the following text: 'Moreover, it means that they must assume to some extent the character of a victim, that they must deny themselves as the Gospel commands, that freely and of their own accord they do penance and that each detests and satisfies for his sins. It means, in a word, that we must all undergo with Christ a mystical death on the Cross, so that we can apply to

ourselves the words of St. Paul 'with Christ I am nailed to the Cross' (Gal 2,19)'.

20. The rendering of the original text in German is not good and I have used the Schott version.

21. *Liturgy*, 4.

22. *ibid.*, 6.

23. Compare with *ibid* 11.

24. Compare with *ibid* 14.

25. *ibid.*, 6f.

26. *ibid.*, 29

27. *ibid.*, 29f.

28. The editor of the English edition remarks here; 'Here von Hildebrand employs the technical philosophical sense of the term intentional, meaning by intentional contact with values a "conscious awareness of them"'.

29. *Liturgy* 30.

30. *ibid.*, 30f.

31. *ibid.*, 31f

32. *Sacrosanctum Concilium* 98.

33. *Liturgy*, 35.

34. *Sacrosanctum Concilium*, 84. *The Catechism of the Catholic Church* (1993) takes up this comment and says in nr. 1174: 'In this 'public prayer of the Church'(SC. 98) the faithful (clergy, religious and lay people) exercise the royal priesthood of the baptized'.

35. *Liturgy*, 38.

36. *ibid.*, 47.

37. *ibid.*, 53.

38. *ibid.*, 56.

39. *ibid.*, 60.

40. *ibid.*, 65.

41. *ibid.*, 90. see Mt 26:41 Mk 14:38

42. *ibid.*, 147.

43. *ibid.*, 160.

44. compare with *ibid.*, 3.

CONCLUSION: LITURGY AND HOLINESS

Rudolf-Michæl Schmitz

Born in 1957 in the Rhineland, Mgr Schmitz was ordained priest in 1982. He is incardinated in the archdiocese of Cologne and a Member of the Priestly Institute of Christ the King Sovereign Priest. After a Doctorate in Dogmatic Theology at the Gregorian University in Rome in 1988, Mgr Schmitz obtained a Licentiate in Canon Law at the University of Munich and was subsequently academic assistant at the Canonical Institute of the Ludwig Maximilian University in Munich 1993-1995. During his time in Munich, Mgr Schmitz gained pastoral experience in the city parish of St Peter. Having been appointed Attaché to the Apostolic Nunciature in Kirghizistan (in central Asia) and Director of the Kirghiz Catholic Cultural Centre, Mgr Schmitz was given a chair at the Russo-Kirghiz University at Bishkek and became State Professor of the Kirghiz Republic in 1997. In September 1998, Mgr Schmitz was made a Domestic Chaplain to His Holiness. He is also a Chaplain of Magistral Obedience of the Sovereign Military Order of Malta; a Member of the Pontifical Academy for Theology in Rome and academic counsellor to the International Centre for Liturgical Studies (CIEL). Mgr Schmitz has published several works and articles on topics concerned with philosophy, theology, and canon law.

THE universal call to holiness, irrespective of state of life, sex or age, which was propagated by the great bishop of Geneva and Annecy, St Francis de Sales, has been taken up repeatedly by the papal Magisterium during the course of the intervening centuries. It was also vigorously recalled by the Second Vatican Council, which by citing the encyclical *Rerum Omnium* of Pius XI, does, refer to Saint Francis, who was for Pius XI the doctor *par excellence* of this truth of our Faith (LG 40 note 4). In his *Introduction to the Devout Life* and in many other places the 'doctor of hearts', as the venerable Pope Pius XI calls him, underlines the importance of the liturgy and in particular of the holy Sacrifice of the Mass for holiness. In this way the second Vatican Council does not fail to draw attention to the liturgical origins of the gift of personal sanctification. Saint Francis de Sales had shown that true devotion is shown by loving promptness in fulfilling God's will manifested by love towards him and our neighbour. Likewise the Second Vatican Council says the same in the Constitution *Lumen Gentium* (LG 41) regarding priests, but it is certainly applicable to all Christians, that we are called to fulfil our duties *'sancte, alacriter, humiliter et fortiter'*, with holiness, alacrity, humility and courage, in the image of Christ. In this way the accomplishment of our duties will become *'præcelsum sanctificationis medium'*—the principal means of sanctification (LG 41). The primary means to obtain this charity towards God and neighbour, which marks the true disciple of the Lord, are clearly enumerated by the fathers of the last council: we must not only listen to the Word of God, but above all *'sacramentis, præsertim Eucharistiæ, et sacris actionibus frequenter participare'*, often participate in the sacraments, in particular the Eucharist, and in liturgical rites (LG 42). This phrase faithfully echoes No. 2 of *Sacrosanctum Concilium* where the fathers accentuate the liturgy as the prime means of access to the mystery of the Lord and the essential context of our Redemption. Without being able here to go into the history of how these texts came to be formulated, we can still affirm that, in fidelity to tradition, the Second Vatican Council drew a direct connection between participation in the liturgy and the grace of holiness which the Lord himself wished to be universal.

To show the reasons for this connection, now at the close of our colloquium, we can point to three characteristics which sharing in the holy mysteries must develop in every Christian, in order for this participation to be a source of holiness. These three distinct elements seem to have clearly emerged in the various papers. Firstly we see that this participation, like holiness itself, is a gift of grace flowing from the God of Holiness present in liturgical celebration under sacramental and ceremonial signs with their different degrees of efficaciousness. Secondly, the call to holiness through liturgical participation, sustained by grace, is brought about when individual piety is drawn close to the *pietas objectiva,* the objective piety of the Church, which alone is capable of rendering divine reality truly present. Finally, through participation in liturgical rites which are symbolically effective, and through objective forms of the Church's prayer, liturgical participation becomes set within an ecclesial context. In this way such participation will be purified of all pietist, subjectivist or arbitrary elements in order for it to conform that much more closely to the Holiness of the Mystical Body itself *'quod est Ecclesia',* which is the Catholic Church (cf. OE2).

THE ANOINTING OF GRACE

On several occasions the talks, notably those of Fathers Gallet, Deneke and Contat, have shown how the holiness of each Christian must develop according to the respective grace state of the hierarchical priesthood or the common priesthood, freely received in baptism, confirmation and holy orders. Of course, unless we collaborate freely with these gifts, especially by removing whatever for each one of us personally might hinder this effective flowering in our souls, these *gratiæ gratis datæ,* graces freely given, will remain paralyzed, or, in the case of the priesthood, strictly limited to their objective sacramental power. But if one becomes open to the operation of *gratia gratum faciens,* sanctifying grace, and the actual graces which begin, accompany, and complete our sanctification, we will be capable of developing the graces of our state more and more deeply. As far as man is concerned, therefore, it is not a question of some sort of acquisition or production of holiness through personal effort independent of divine activity, but above all of our well-disposed will to accept these free gifts with the alacrity and zeal which are due to the merciful will of our High Priest and Redeemer. So the participation of the hierarchical priesthood or the royal priesthood in the divine work of the holy liturgy, before emerging as a human activity, will always result from an immersion in the mysterious union between the divine and the human which comes about in the sacramental mysteries. Here the divinity deigns to make use of us in accordance with the particular activity or receptivity relevant to our state within the entire mystical body of Christ, head and members. Fathers Edwards and Barreiro have illustrated these truths from the texts of the recent Magisterium, and Fr Nay from Holy Scripture, which also sheds light on other aspects that characterize effective participation.

Saint Cyril of Alexandria in fact makes use of the concept of the anointing to signify how divine grace must penetrate the humanity of Christ to be able to use it as the intrinsic instrument of our Redemption. Thus we could say that grace must penetrate each one of us that we might become effective instruments of the divine action: the only action really efficacious for our holiness and our salvation. Now, this heavenly anointing unfolds in the first place through immersion in the actions which grace itself has prepared as the place and the means for it to be communicated, in other words in the liturgical ceremonies.

OBJECTIVITY: A SENSE OF THE REALITY

That sacred rites can make a particularly effective and intense bestowal of grace possible, is what makes comprehensible the need for a greater objectivity in these rites, where sinful man encounters divine majesty. Up until the most recent times the historical development of liturgical ceremonies has shown a concern to guarantee this sense of objectivity which, by its very symbolism, guarantees the immersion of man in grace. Sacred language, chant, historical forms of participation of the faithful, have all contributed to safeguard this sense of objectivity, as Fr Finnegan, Dom Emmanuel de Butler, Professor Pérès and Dr Gribbin have shown us. Without a doubt the Church's Magisterium, even after the changes effected under Pope Paul VI, has constantly reiterated the obligation of the priest and congregation to adhere strictly to the rubrics indicated by the supreme authority; this supreme authority however does not always seem to appreciate that there is a mounting pastoral subjectivism that often arises from the very choices made possible by these same rubrics. Despite this last problem, the repeated attempts of the legislators to combat the 'abuses of the liturgical reform' as they are called, does at least demonstrate a determination on the part of all the recent Popes not to allow the liturgy to become a prey to the whim of the individual.

This determination derives from the awareness the Church has of her duty to administer the mysteries of the faith in such a way that they remain an objective source of the sanctifying presence of God, who wishes to give himself to us in order to draw us towards him. For the same reason, not only has the personal piety of Catholics always been a piety principally centred on the liturgical mysteries, but this focus of piety has been encouraged time and time again by the Magisterium both past and present. Such piety will never be limited only to participation in the Holy Sacrifice of the Mass, but will always embrace the full wealth of the liturgical life of the Church. Even the most popular forms of devotion, for example, Marian devotions in May, private family devotions, pilgrimages without priests, where these still exist, reflect the concern of the faithful to stay close to the sacred forms of the Church's worship. It was in this sense that Pope Leo XIII said that the best way to recite the rosary was during a *sacrum,* that is to say during Mass or adoration of the Blessed Sacrament. This of course did not mean that the best way to assist at adoration or at the Mass would be to do so whilst reciting the rosary! Pope John XXIII in promoting the veneration of the Precious Blood chose to emphasize the need for every Christian to conform his individual piety to the *pietas* of the Church, the Bride of the Lord, so as not to fall into the trap of 'pietism'.

It is fair to say that the subjectivism which has managed to penetrate the heart of the sanctuary has not only given rise to the Charybdis of a banal rationalism, but also, often amongst the most devout, the Scylla of a sugary bigotry or apparition mentality which are opposed to the Magisterium. Each weakening of the objectivity of the rites, which is the final guarantee for the reservation of a healthy piety on the part of the People of God, can only impede the fulfilment of the universal call to holiness. This is so because instead of approaching the divine sources of salvation in order to drink of the fullness of grace, people are trying to find their own private entrances whether they be rationalistic or fideistic. In the long run these can only lead to a Protestant individualism in the unacceptable sense either in clandestine or public forms.

SENTIRE CUM ECCLESIA - OF ONE MIND WITH THE CHURCH

Now, the sanctification of the soul must not and cannot be achieved in this purely subjective way. It is always the fruit of objective participation in the divine life present in the Church, our mother. As outside the Church, and deprived of her sacred mysteries, no salvation is possible, holiness is a gift dispensed throughout the Mystical Body of the Lord, visible on this earth as the Catholic Church. We are not here to discuss all the invisible ways in which the

Lord deigns to effect salvation with the aid of his bride, the Church, because our subject is the liturgy which actually renders the treasures of the Kingdom of God visible amongst us. But we can be very sure that the moment when people voluntarily and definitively cut their links with the true Church of Christ, they are no longer able to participate fully in the liturgy or the abundance of grace which it confers.

Furthermore, one must clearly state that 'liturgy', giving the word its full ecclesiastical import, would not take place in a situation where the authority of the Church to guarantee the objectivity of such transmission of salvation were denied in a formal manner. Even if through the objective power of sanctification the sacramental signs were still ordered in a valid manner, the celebrations of such communities would cease to reflect the whole of hierarchical dimension required. With such celebrations one would be bordering on an extreme situation, individualist or even objectivist, for they would be unable to receive the real and necessary mediation of the representative of Christ, the Roman Pontiff. So such pseudo-liturgical forms will either dissolve into subjectivism originating from individualism, or petrify in an objectivist formalism. Both these forms are destined to destroy the basis of *sentire cum Ecclesia* and consequently of a true holiness willed by Christ.

This ecclesiastical dimension of the rites was illustrated by Fr Quoex, and, regarding preaching during liturgical celebration, by Mgr Brandmüller. The fundamental recognition of the mediation of the Church, concentrated in the primacy of Peter - also exercised in the dimension of liturgy - is denied by these two extremes which, as always, meet; yet this recognition remains the distinctive sign of all true liturgy and all true holiness. Through this Roman principle, this very 'Roman-ness' as one could express it, we may avoid equally pedagogical and æsthetic excesses in liturgical celebration and Jansenist and Quietist excesses in the moral sphere. The profession of faith in the hierarchical presence of Christ the Head in the Liturgy will be, therefore, for all time, the key to the gifts of grace which the Lord has entrusted to the faithful rulers of his Church.

CONCLUSION

From these brief considerations, it seems clear that each liturgical participation must have the three characteristics elaborated by the speakers at this conference:

• such participation must be informed by grace; it must be related as closely as possible to objective liturgical reality, and it must profess fully the sense of ecclesiastical communion, regardless of the state of life of the participant and irrespective of whether his role in the holy mysteries be active or passive. It is only under these conditions that such participation may effectively contribute to the sanctification of the faithful participant through his priesthood, royal or hierarchical.

The philosopher Dietrich von Hildebrand in his book *Liturgy and Personality* draws a link between participation in the liturgy and the development of the truly Christian personality. His conclusion, highlighted in our proceedings by Count Wolfgang Waldstein, leads him to identify the 'man of liturgy', in the complete sense of the term, with the saint.

In fact, it is true to say that those who here on earth participate fully in the liturgy of the Church while respecting the above characteristics, far from indulging merely in a liturgical activism, will gradually transform their whole lives into an act of praise and adoration offered to God. It will be their ultimate joy to be able to participate in this heavenly adoration where the grace of holiness, the objective reality of the mystery and Christ himself will be visible and present in the unique light radiating from the Lamb, illuminating forever the cathedral of the eternal liturgy. If our colloquium has contributed to bringing us a little closer to this final aim of all liturgy, the organizers and speakers may expect a far greater reward for their work than our gratitude, which I express now as your humble spokesman.

HOMILY
AT THE THIRD SOLEMN MASS

9th October 1998

Fr Seán Finnegan

'The blood of the martyrs is the seed of the Church'

In the name of the Father, and of the Son, and of the Holy Spirit. Amen.

THE analogy that is often made between the Christian life and the arduous journey is one not exclusively confined to the circles where what passes for popular spirituality is practised. In fact, it has a most ancient pedigree and indeed lies deeply at the heart of both our theology and our liturgy. The Christian going through life is seen as the citizen of the kingdom of God enduring a long and arduous journey through a land that is not his own: indeed, to which, he has died in baptism, in order to reach his own promised homeland. I was struck, on the very first day of the colloquium, how Fr Deneke compared the role of the priest to that of the mother. How true it is that in that sacrament of baptism the neophyte is like a child being sent to school on a dark morning by its mother, first cleansed, clothed in white for the road, given a light to show the way and blessed at the door, to be sent out into a hostile world. The important difference is that Holy Mother Church continues to nourish her children throughout the journey, and that the destination is not a foreign land but one for which the neophyte was destined all along, since the moment of his baptism. Paradoxically, although we leave the familiar, we journey to where we truly belong, where we will be most truly ourselves, to that place we call 'home'.

The Church has long seen in the exodus of the children of Israel from Egypt a paradigm of the same, Christian, life. Those Israelites were freed from slavery to Pharaoh in the kingdom of Egypt by passing through the waters of the Dead Sea, the point of no return. We, on the other hand, were freed from slavery to sin in the kingdom of this world by passing through the waters of baptism. Journeying through the desert, the Israelites sinned repeatedly, losing faith and courage, and even turning to idols. Similarly, we, too, lose courage sometimes. The road seems too hard, the task too strenuous, the allure of the kingdom of this world too strong, and we, like the Israelites, fall. They had Moses and Aaron to intercede for them and bring God's forgiveness. We have the priests of the

Church to do the same. The Israelites were fed with manna, bread from heaven: *'panem de cælo præstitisti eis'*. We, too, have the much more wonderful bread from heaven that is the very presence of God himself under the form of bread. They were led by the pillar of fire, we by the Easter light of the paschal candle, lit symbolically at our baptism and standing around our coffins when we die; on the day when we finally reach that longed-for home in the heavenly fatherland, that true home-country of which we became citizens on the day of our baptism. But like the United States of America (at least until recently), the kingdom of God will brook no dual nationality: to become its citizens we have to depart from, die to, the kingdom of this world. The world in which we have lived must pass away, and we live as pilgrims and strangers in it until, like the Israelites, we pass over the River Jordan into the promised land.

The possibility of a new, better, and eternal home was brought about by the death of a lamb. For the Israelites, it was the little innocent passover lamb whose life was sacrificed that God's chosen might be spared the vengeance which he took on their oppressors, and whose flesh nourished those same chosen for their long journey. In our case, the lamb is the very Lamb of God who takes away the sins of the world, whose blood saves us from sin, and whose flesh we eat as our bread from heaven on our spiritual journey to the kingdom of God. That lamb is Christ himself who gives us his body, blood, soul and divinity to incorporate us into his mystical body, as St Augustine reminds us. And the Mass is that very sacrifice that won for us our freedom, and our citizenship of the kingdom of God. Concerning that death of Christ on the cross; is it not true that, since we, the Church, together make up his Mystical Body, which actual body suffered the torments of crucifixion, that we, too, in a sense hang on the cross with him? 'With Christ I am crucified', says St Paul, and this crucifixion will endure until the day we die; this daily crucifixion to the world and the world to us. We await the goal of our journey: our own death, accepted with perfect resignation in union with the death of Christ, offered to the Father for the salvation of the world, and in expectation of that glorious resurrection that awaits those that have died with him.

Given, then, that the holy Sacrifice of the Mass *is* the death of Christ, mystically re-presented in an unbloody form, how can the Christian *not* be most profoundly involved in it, since it intimately concerns his very salvation won for us by the passion, death and resurrection of our blessed Lord? The Mass touches us all most intimately at all levels. It is not necessary to jump around, or busy ourselves externally in order to participate at Mass: the Mass is the life we now live, it is the death that we will die, and even foreshadows the eternal life which, God willing, we shall one day lead. It is everything we have and are.

In today's epistle we read of St Paul's appearance before the Athenian Areopagus. This must have been a great symbolic moment for St Paul. He had, inspired by the Holy Spirit, decided to take the Gospel to the gentiles, and here he was before one of the beating hearts of the pagan gentile world; in the very city where Socrates and Plato had taught. And he delivered to the Areopagus a homily that would have found great favour in the seminary where I studied: he proceeded from something that was well known (the altar to the unknown God) and proceeded to tell of the resurrection of Christ, without going through any of the unpleasant bits that might put people off: no passion, no crucifixion, no sin: and this to a people who understood well how the death of Socrates had given strength to his teachings. And, commented the famous American preacher, Archbishop Fulton Sheen, so it seemed that his great opportunity before the Areopagus was a failure. Perhaps, Sheen went on, it is not too fanciful to suppose that it was this failure that inspired those words written in his first letter to the Corinthians: 'I am resolved henceforth to preach nothing but Christ, and him crucified'. For that death signifies our utter turning away from, and our despite for, the standards of this world. It lies at the very heart of the Christian kerygma; in that death is our passing from death to life, in that sacrifice is all that we have and are, as I have said. Once more we come back to the Mass.

And yet that sermon before the Areopagus was not a total failure. Some were clearly inspired to return to St Paul and hear more. We are told of one Damaris and a handful of others; but above all today we remember Dionysius, known as the Areopagite. He, like many other biblical characters, took up the Christian challenge to leave his old life behind, and literally move to another land to take up a new life. Legend identifies him with St Denis of Paris, whose feast we celebrate today. Legend or not—and we can always learn something from a moral story or a pious parable—he followed his pillar of fire and came at last, like us on this colloquium, to Paris, there to treat of the holy things of God. Here it was that he lived out the implications of that baptism which he received at the hands of St Paul; here he celebrated with those first Parisian Christians those mysteries of the passion, death and resurrection of the Lord which we celebrate here today, and it was here that he found the consummation of all his love for the Lord whom he discovered in the Areopagus, by giving his very life in love for the true God: the God who in Athens was worshipped unknown, but who in his death in Paris he had come to know as fully as he, Dionysius, was known. And so, as his blood poured out upon Parisian soil, he watered that seedbed in which he had planted his own life, in order that countless millions of Parisians might have that eternal life won for them by that very sacrifice of Christ in which we all, priests and faithful, participate actually and fully today.

St Dionysius, pray for us.

In the name of the Father, and of the Son, and of the Holy Spirit. Amen.

ACKNOWLEDGEMENTS

W E would like to express our thanks to our benefactors, to those who helped CIEL UK to develop during the year and to all those who have given their time, effort and expertise freely. Without the considerable effort, dedication and forbearance of such people the publication of this book would not be possible.

We are once more indebted to Mgr Canon Frederick Miles and Fr Andrew Wadsworth for the magnificent Pontifical High Mass at St James' Spanish Place in May. Again we thank Fr Martin Edwards and the priests of the Association of St John Fisher, the Oratorians and all our priests and lay translators. Our special thanks also to Eleanor Murphy, Anthony Ozimic, and Anthony Dickinson.

Editor:

Rev. Seán Finnegan M.A. B.Th.

Translators:

Dr Mary Berry M.A., PhD. (Mus), B. Hon. F.R.A.M.
Rev. Jerome Bertram Cong Orat., M.A., F.S.A.
Ailsa Burois B.A.
Anthony Delarue K.C.V.V. M.A. R.I.B.A.
Rev. Mark Drew M.A.
Rev. John Emerson B.A. B.Phil.
The Count of Évora R.I.A. pp
Nicole Hall
Rev. Nicholas Kearney, M.A., Mag. Theol, Lic.Phil.
Rev. David McCready M Theol., Lic. Theol. Cath.
Ferdi McDermott M.A.
Hugh Scott M.A., Dip Ed.
Peter Spurgeon MIL, MITI,

Apology:

We would like to apologize profusely to Fr Mark Drew for inadvertently leaving his name off this list last year, despite the fact that he translated two main texts.

Second Translator Readers:

Rev. Jerome Bertram Cong Orat M.A. F.S.A.
Olivier Burois M.Sc D.E.A.

G. K.Connelly M.A.(Cantab)
Michæl Real
Ruth Real B.A.

Translation Editor

Rev. Nicholas Kearney

Translation Co-ordinating Team:

Rosa Gillibrand B.A., M.A.
Christopher Gillibrand,
Nicole Hall,
Ruth Real B.A. (Hon Sec CIEL UK)

Final Readers:

Monica Flynn,
Anthony Dickinson,
John and June Wood,
Terence McAuliffe.

Final Manuscript Readers:

Monica Flynn,
Dr Joseph Gribbin B.A. (Hons), M. Phil. (Cantab), Ph.D (Cantab).

ALL ABOUT C.I.E.L.

Loïc Mérian, president of C.I.E.L., explains the raisons d'être of this association of lay Catholics.

• *What is CIEL?*

C.I.E.L. (*Centre International d'Etudes Liturgiques* in French) was founded in 1994 by a group of French lay Catholics. Its aim is to make known and to increase the understanding of the traditional liturgy of the Latin Church (that is to say the liturgical forms used in the Latin Church up until 1969) in a spirit of total fidelity to the Holy See.

• *Why this objective?*

Since the last liturgical reforms, a number of liturgical experts have drawn frequent attention to major theological and pastoral problems to be seen today. In this context, the traditional Latin liturgy is a very important point of reference, too often today considered the concern of merely a few nostalgics. This is illustrated by the fact that for the last twenty years the traditional Latin liturgy has not been considered an interesting and living subject for researchers and university students. Since the 70s, it has been, as it were, excluded from Church life and from the fields of interest of theological experts.

Consequently, the aim of those in charge of C.I.E.L. has been to put the traditional liturgy back in the place it deserves, in particular by re-introducing it into the intellectual world in order to 're-include' it and to point out its unique riches and dynamism.

• *How do you hope to achieve this aim?*

By organizing an academic colloquium each year, bringing together international specialists from various ecclesiastical disciplines. Through the quality of their work, they provide a demonstration of the spiritual and doctrinal riches of the traditional Roman rite and thus supply the basis for future work to be undertaken in the years to come.

The aims of these colloquia are thus threefold:

• to bring together experts who rarely have the occasion to meet one another due to geographic distance, allowing them to exchange their opinions;
• to allow clergy and laity interested in these subjects to benefit from these activities;
• finally, to ensure publication of these studies in French, English, Italian and German, and widespread distribution of the Proceedings of these colloquia to the faithful and to universities and seminaries.

Thus the liturgy will be shown to have a living character and the promotion of the traditional liturgy can therefore be assured by a truly intellectual and academic work.

• *Are these conferences reserved for experts?*

Not at all! Our colloquia are open to all. Is the liturgy not public worship? It is therefore the concern of both clergy and laity alike. There are, of course, eminent personalities amongst our participants; prelates (cardinals, bishops, abbots), superiors of religious communities, university professors, and leaders of lay associations and movements. But many of the participants, from more than ten countries of the world, are also parish priests, religious and a large number of simple layfolk wanting to learn more about the traditional liturgy.

• *Are there not already a number of church institutions officially in charge of liturgical questions?*

Of course. But there are also, as in all spheres, a number of local initiatives fostering a deeper understanding of the meaning of the Catholic liturgy for priests and faithful. The special contribution of our enterprise is to offer a place to meet and to reflect on liturgical questions relatively openly and in a way that shows that the traditional Roman liturgy is not an archaism.

Furthermore, we do not wish this colloquium to be confined to studies which appear far from reality and accessible only to experts. We would like the pastoral dimension to remain important, so as to produce tangible fruits from these works.

• *What are your links with ecclesiastical authorities?*

Although run by laypeople who look after the organization of the colloquia and the publication of the Proceedings, our Centre wishes to maintain a close link with Church authorities, both through our invited speakers, and through contacts at Rome as well as in the dioceses. Our activities are carried out in the service of the Church, and we undertake our work respectful of the Church authorities.

• *Are lectures the only activity during the conferences?*

Of course the colloquium is not only made up of lectures. We would wish to emphasize also the magnificent ceremonies celebrated according to the liturgical texts of 1962 which allow each and all to unite at the foot of the altar or to join in the singing at evening Compline. There again it is not simply an exercise in intellectual speculation. Furthermore, the allotted free time—meals, aperitifs, meetings—provides occasion for contact and exchange of views.

• *Does your activity have an international character?*

It is certain that the universality of the Church encourages us to make our colloquia international meeting-places. Our guest speakers and our participants come from the five continents, and year after year, new local correspondents relay the work of CIEL in their countries. We would indeed like the colloquia Proceedings to be available throughout the world. The publication of the Proceedings in French, German, English and Italian allows them to be sent free of charge to all bishops, seminaries, ecclesiastical libraries, and Roman congregations that use those languages. It is a great task, but which, alone, can help to advance thought on these liturgical questions.

• *What have been the fruits of the conferences?*

The colloquia have shown that the faithful attached to the traditional liturgy represent a dynamic movement in the Church. The youthfulness of a number of the participants and even of some of the speakers was particularly remarked. Here is a dynamism which must be reckoned with. Many contacts have been made, and the Proceedings have been sent to a number of bishops, seminaries and religious superiors. It is an encouraging enterprise as a number of meetings have stemmed from it.

• *What future for the traditional Roman liturgy?*

As our disoriented contemporaries turn finally to sects or seek certainties in other religions, is it not time to show them the inestimable benefits of the Catholic liturgy?

It is the treasury of divine omnipotence, which is offered to us in a redeeming sacrifice. God is there, truly present amongst us, at the heart of our Masses. Each gesture, each symbol of the liturgy is an affirmation of faith. The traditional liturgy, by its sacred character, its theological solidity, carries with it certainties, hope and joy. The proof is in the multiplication of parish communities or religious communities which use it.

PROCEEDINGS OF THE FIRST COLLOQUIUM OF THE

INTERNATIONAL CENTRE FOR LITURGICAL STUDIES

9th-12th October 1995

The Liturgy - Treasure of the Church

The aims of C.I.E.L.
  Loïc Merian (France)

The need for a better knowledge of the liturgy
  H.E. Cardinal Alfons Stickler SDB (Austria)

The birth of the liturgy and its guiding principles
  Dom Daniel Field OSB (France)

The reforming decrees of the Council of Trent
  Rev. Reinhard Knittel (Austria)

Episcopal jurisdiction and sacramental practice
  Rev. Pierre Blet S J (France)

Moral implications for a priest of celebrating Mass
  Rev. Dario Composte SDB

The inestimable blessings of the liturgy
  Rt Rev. Dom Gerard Calvet OSB (France)

The problem of concelebration
  Very Rev. Mgr Rudolf Michæl Schmitz (Germany)

Devotion in the Church following the Council of Trent
  Professor Dieter Weiss (Germany)

The liturgical movement from Dom Guéranger to the eve of Vatican II
  Professor Wolfgang Waldstein (Austria)

Reflections on the orientation of the altar
  Rev. Louis Bouyer (France)

The orientation of the altar ; history and theology
  Rev. Martin Reinecke (Germany)

Ecclesiology through liturgical books
  Rt Rev. Mgr Gilles Wach (France)

Sermon at the closing Mass
  Rt Rev. Georges Lagrange, Bishop of Gap (France)

These Proceedings are available in French only *from C.I.E.L., 84 avenue Aristide Briand, 92120 Montrouge, France. The volume contains 266 pages with photographs and costs FF160.*

PROCEEDINGS OF THE SECOND COLLOQUIUM OF THE

INTERNATIONAL CENTRE FOR LITURGICAL STUDIES

9th-11th October 1996

The Veneration and Administration of the Eucharist

Introduction to the activities of CIEL
Loïc Mérian (France)

Eucharistic devotion in the teaching of John Paul II
Rt Rev. Georges Lagrange, Bishop of Gap (France)

The Church's theological response to the principal heresies relating to the Eucharist.
Rev. François Clément (Switzerland)

Veneration of the Eucharist in the 16th century Anglican Reformation
Michæl Davies (England)

The history of the Rite of distributing communion
Rev. Martin Lugmayr (Germany)

Homily delivered at the opening Mass 9th October 1996
Rt Rev. Georges Lagrange, Bishop of Gap (France)

Gestures accompanying the words of consecration in the history of the Ordo Missæ
Dom Cassian Folsom OSB (United States)

Concerning Exposition of the Blessed Sacrament
Rev'd Fr Christian-Philippe Chanut (France)

The Encyclical Mediator Dei *and eucharistic doctrine*
Dr Wolfgang Graf (Germany)

Theological and pastoral reflections on the history of frequent communion
Rev. Bertrand de Margerie SJ (France)

Homily delivered at the High Mass on 10th October 1996
Dom Hervé Courau OSB (France)

Eucharistic rites from papal ceremonial to the Roman Missal
Rev. Franck Quoëx (France)

Gregorian chant as a sign and witness to faith and its relation to the Most Blessed Sacrament of the altar
Professor Jan Boogarts (Netherlands)

Homily delivered at the closing Mass on 11th October 1996
Rt Rev. Bernard Jacqueline former apostolic nuncio to Morocco (France)

Communion under two kinds : theological and pastoral aspects
Rev. Wladimir-Marie de Saint-Jean OM (France)

'Homo Adorans'. Some concluding remarks at the end of the Second Collo-quium
Very Rev. Mgr Rudolf Michæl Schmitz (Germany)

These Proceedings are available in French, English and German. The English volume runs to 255 pages with photographs and is available, price £12.95 incl p&p, from Damian Riddle Esq. 26a Great College Street, London SW1P 3RT.

Please make cheques payable to CIEL UK

PROCEEDINGS OF THE THIRD COLLOQUIUM OF THE

INTERNATIONAL CENTRE FOR LITURGICAL STUDIES

1st-3rd October 1997

Altar and Sacrifice

Opening remarks
Loïc Mérian (France)

Can there be a Christianity without Sacrifice?
Professor Robert Spaemann (Germany)

The Altar: place of sacrifice and sacred space in the religious building
Rev. Ephræm Chifley OP (Australia)

The notion of sacrifice according to the Summa Theologica *of St Thomas Aquinas*
Rev. Bernard Lucien (France)

The meaning of the Altar in sacred liturgy
Rev. Jerome Bertram of the Oratory (Great Britain)

Sermon given at the solemn opening Mass 1st October 1997
Rev. Wladimir- Marie of Saint John

The liturgical rites of meal and sacrifice
Rev. François Clément (Switzerland)

The celebrant at the altar before and after Vatican II
Dom Emmanuel de Butler OSB (France)

The doctrine of sacrifice in the theology of Martin Luther
Mgr Bruno Gherardini, Vice-Pres. Pontifical Academy of Theology, (Italy)

The rite of consecration of the altar
Rev. Hervé Courau OSB (France)

Sermon given at the second solemn Mass 2nd October 1997
Rev. Ignatius Harrison of the Oratory

Meal and sacrifice in the Magisterium of the Church
Rev. Denis Le Pivain FSSP

From table to altar of stone: an historical analysis
Mgr Antony Conlon (UK)

Conclusion : The Sacred Heart: altar of redemption
Very Rev. Mgr Rudolf Michæl Schmitz

These Proceedings are available in French, English and German. The English edition runs to 192 pages with photographs and is available, price £12.95 incl p&p, from Damian Riddle Esq. 26a Great College Street London SW1P 3RT. *Please make cheques payable to CIEL UK*

LAUNCH IN ROME OF
ALTAR AND SACRIFICE

ON Monday 23rd March 1998, the Presidents of the *Centre International d'Etudes Liturgiques,* (C.I.E.L.) , Loïc Mérian, Ulrich Bork,
Martin Kristen and Mrs Nicole Hall met at the office of Cardinal
Poupard, French President of the Administration for Culture. For two days we
visited various Roman commissions and congregations, totalling fourteen interviews, at which we explained the work of C.I.E.L. and left a copy of *Altar
and Sacrifice* in each language. Much interest was shown in C.I.E.L., and considerable appreciation for the work involved in producing the *Proceedings* in
three languages.

Amongst the Cardinals who granted us interviews were: Cardinal Antonetti,
who is in charge of the patrimony of the Holy See, Cardinal Medina Estevez,
Prefect of the Congregation for Divine Worship, Cardinal Stickler, former Vatican Archivist and *peritus* of the Second Vatican Council, one of C.I.E.L.'s two
Cardinal patrons, Cardinal Felici of the *Ecclesia Dei* Commission, and Cardinal Thiandoum. We received special blessings from Cardinals Stickler, Estevez,
and Thiandoum and Felici. We also had a most interesting lunch with Mgr

Perl, from the *Ecclesia Dei* Commission, and later also with Mgr Arthur Calkins.

On Tuesday 24th at 6p.m. the launch of *Altar and Sacrifice* took place at the Hotel Columbus in the *Via Conciliazione*. Cardinal Stickler presided and Mgr Rudolf Michæl Schmitz addressed a full hall, which held about 120 people from various Roman Congregations and universities, including:

His Excellency Mgr de Magistris, Regent of the *Penitenziera Apostolica*
His Excellency Mgr Pereira, Archbishop, member of the Chapter of St Peter
His Excellency Mgr Tricarico, Nuncio, member of the Secretary of State
Mgr Coquetti, Pontifical Master of Ceremony to Popes Pius XII and Paul VI
Mgr Wladimir-Marie de Saint Jean, Abbot, Canons Regular of the Mother of God
Mgr Gilles Wach, Superior of the Institute of Christ the King and High Priest
Mgr Camille Perl from the *Ecclesia Dei* Commission
Mgr Arthur Calkins from the *Ecclesia Dei* Commission
Mgr Rolf Thomas from the Prelature of Opus Dei
Rev'd Fr Pierre Blet from the Gregorian University
Professor Wolfgang Waldstein from the Lateran University

The main importance of this visit to Rome was twofold: Firstly, the universality of the Church was demonstrated by the Colloquium *Proceedings* being available in three languages. Secondly, the timing (just before Easter) and conspicuous situation of this launch gave far greater publicity and prominence to our work than initiatives taking place in any particular country would have received.

THE FIFTH COLLOQUIUM OF THE

INTERNATIONAL CENTRE FOR LITURGICAL STUDIES

November 1999

The History and Theology of the Roman Missal

C .I.E.L. will be holding its fifth Colloquium of historical, theological and canonical studies of the Catholic Roman Rite in November 1999. Speakers of many nationalities, liturgists, historians, theologians and canon lawyers will be addressing different themes which promote a better understanding of the liturgy of the Roman Church and in particular the close link between the Eucharistic Sacrifice and the sacred altar.

The Colloquium is open to all, priests, religious and lay who seek to deepen their understanding of the mind of the Church. The speakers will consider the following subjects:

- The origin of the Roman Missal in the reform of St Pius V.

- History of the Canon.

- History of the Offertory prayers.

- History and spirituality of the Missal of the faithful.

- Dom Guéranger and the restoration of the Roman Missal.

- Ecclesiology in the Roman Missal.

- Christology in the Roman Missal.

- The influence of the doctrine of St Thomas on the Roman Missal.

- The preservation and propagation of the Faith in the Roman Missal.

The talks will be given in the language of the speakers. Translations in several languages will be available to participants. Bookings may be made through the CIEL office. Further information can be supplied on request.

Please apply to :
CIEL UK
PO Box 587A
Kingston & Surbiton
KT5 8YD
FAX 44 (0) 181 715 2316

C.I.E.L. WORLDWIDE

The International Centre for Liturgical Studies (C.I.E.L.) is proud to announce the foundation of two new official delegations that will be able to make our studies known in their countries to the relevant authorities. For any information in one of those countries, it is advised to contact, in the first instance, the official national delegate.

Loïc MERIAN, president of C.I.E.L.

C.I.E.L.   Canada

Shawn Tribe / Adam DeVille
352 Somerset St. W. #303
Ottawa, Ontario, Canada.
K2P 0J9

Fax: (613)593-8863

Email: stribe@execulink.com (Shawn Tribe)

bx057@freenet.carleton.ca (Adam DeVille)

website :   http://freeweb.digiweb.com/education/ciel/main.htm

C.I.E.L.   Philippines

William Llorenzo
1763 Dumas Street
1204 Makati City
Philippines

Email: scherzo@mnl.sequel.net